Social Work and Social Policy

An understanding of social policy is vital for engaging practically with social work values, dealing with political and ethical questions about responsibility, rights and our understanding of 'the good society'. This textbook provides a comprehensive introduction to social policy, tailored to the needs of a social work audience.

Jonathan Dickens analyses current policies and policy themes relevant to social work and locates them in the context of fundamental social policy principles and debates. He discusses the nature of social policy and its relationship to social work, and covers essential themes such as:

- Service user participation and involvement

- The balance between individual, societal and state responsibility for people's well-being

- The proper roles of the state, the private sector, voluntary organisations and the family

- The relationships between needs, rights and choices

- The purposes and challenges of professional social work

- The meanings of 'inclusion' and 'personalisation'.

Each chapter ends with activities for reflection and analysis, and suggestions for further reading.

This text develops a dynamic and compelling framework for critical analysis of contemporary social policy and social work. It will be invaluable for students undertaking social work qualifying courses, all of whom are required to demonstrate an understanding of the social policy contexts of practice.

Jonathan Dickens is Senior Lecturer in Social Work and Course Director for the MA in Social Work at the University of East Anglia, UK.

Student Social Work

This exciting new textbook series is ideal for all students studying to be qualified social workers, whether at undergraduate or masters level. Covering key elements of the social work curriculum, the books are accessible, interactive and thought-provoking.

New titles

Human Growth and Development
An introduction for social workers
John Sudbery

Mental Health Social Work in Context
Nick Gould

Social Work and Social Policy
An introduction
Jonathan Dickens

Social Work Placements
Mark Doel

Forthcoming titles

Integrating Social Work Theory and Practice
Pam Green Lister

Social Work
A reader
Vivienne E. Cree

Building Relationships and Communicating with Young Children
A practical guide
Karen Winter

Social Work and Social Policy

An Introduction

Jonathan Dickens

Routledge
Taylor & Francis Group

LONDON AND NEW YORK

First published 2010
by Routledge
2 Park Square, Milton Park, Abingdon, Oxon, OX14 4RN

Simultaneously published in the USA and Canada
by Routledge
711 Third Avenue, New York, NY 10017 (8th Floor)

Routledge is an imprint of the Taylor & Francis Group, an informa business
© 2010 Jonathan Dickens

Designed and typeset in Rotis by
Keystroke, Tettenhall, Wolverhampton
Printed and bound in Great Britain by
TJ International Ltd, Padstow, Cornwall

British Library Cataloguing in Publication Data
A catalogue record for this book is available from the British Library

Library of Congress Cataloging-in-Publication Data
Dickens, Jonathan, 1961–
  Social work and social policy : an introduction / Jonathan Dickens.
      p. cm.
  1. Social service. 2. Social policy. I. Title.
  HV40.35.D53 2010
  361–dc22   2009024401

ISBN10: 0–415–45412–3 (hbk)
ISBN10: 0–415–45413–1 (pbk)
ISBN10: 0–203–86326–7 (ebk)

ISBN13: 978–0–415–45412–4 (hbk)
ISBN13: 978–0–415–45413–1 (pbk)
ISBN13: 978–0–203–86326–8 (ebk)

Contents

Illustrations

Boxes

Figures

Tables

Acknowledgements

I would like to thank my colleagues in the School of Social Work and Psychology at the University of East Anglia, for covering for me for a semester's study leave to write this book. I am especially grateful to Ann McDonald and Clive Sellick, for that and all their support and encouragement over the years. Thanks to all at Routledge, especially Grace McInnes and Khanam Virjee, for their help and advice with the book. Special thanks and love to Julia and Caitlin for putting up with me while I wrote it.

Introduction

The roles and tasks of social work are always up for grabs, always the subject of discussion, debate and disagreement. Different people have very different views about what social workers are doing and should be doing, and how these responsibilities and functions fit into the broader range of social policies and welfare services – for example, how they link with health and education, 'welfare to work', 'joined-up' inter-agency and inter-professional working, all the systems and procedures that are meant to ensure high-quality services and 'value for money'. Social work practitioners, managers, local authority councillors, central government ministers, civil servants, journalists, academics, service users, people who have been refused a service, people who provide care for relatives or friends – all will have a view about what social work is or should be, and probably several views. Their own expectations may not always be consistent, and then there will be tensions and sometimes outright conflict with what others think.

In this complex and hotly contested context, the central questions are 'What is social work for?' and 'Who is social work for?', and these are the guiding questions that shape this book. My interest is to set social work in its wider context of social policies, social values and other welfare services. The focus is social work in England, but I also refer to developments in the other countries of the United Kingdom (Wales, Scotland and Northern Ireland). Social care and social work are devolved to the different countries of the UK, although other crucial policy areas, notably taxation and welfare benefits, are not. There are organisational and policy differences between the four countries, but the underlying issues are recognisably similar, as they will be for readers in other Western, democratic and industrialised countries. My approach is to use a variety of 'models', or frameworks, to try to capture the main ideas. I say more about this approach in Chapter 1, but also offer a few thoughts here.

Chapter 1

There are three main challenges for writing a book about social work and social policy. First is to strike a balance between comprehensiveness and focus; second to ensure that it is relevant to practice; and third that it will have some relevance over time. It is not possible to describe everything about current

1

social policy – which is a huge, expanding and fast-changing aspect of government – and there would be no benefit in trying to do so because, inevitably, policies and organisational details will change. So I have picked a selection of aspects that seem most relevant to social work, and try to give up-to-date examples and pull out the underlying issues. Some of the contemporary detail will be overtaken by events but should still be useful for following the later developments, and the underlying issues will not change – for example, the need to balance individual freedoms with the safety of others, or the dilemmas of respecting people's choices but providing services within limited resources. Such key challenges last over time. As Martin Rein (1976: 24) put it, social policy has

> a general tendency . . . to develop in a cyclic rather than a linear manner. Since the problems are in essence intractable, and can rarely be resolved without sacrificing some strongly held values, the issues tend to be recurrent. Each generation takes up the same issues again and seeks to re-define them in the light of its own political, economic and social reality.

One lesson from this quotation is to be wary about political or professional claims to have 'solved' social problems, or to have found the perfect way to organise and deliver welfare services. I do not mean this in a jaundiced or defeatist way: on the contrary, it is to stress that the underlying issues are far more important and difficult than organisational and procedural changes alone can ever solve. By focusing on the central ideas and the enduring challenges, I hope that the book will be useful for making sense of policies and organisational structures now and in the future.

There is a further dimension to relevance to social work practice. Sometimes, the bigger picture can seem too daunting, and it is more satisfying to stick to the interpersonal aspects of practice; or the routines and procedures of everyday work can seem too much, and it is easier to concentrate on just getting them done. Certainly, relationships with service users and organisational competence are both crucial, and social workers will fail in their duties to service users if they are not skilled in these. But understanding the policy context is also crucial, in three ways. First, because major features of social work epitomise some of the major themes in social policy, notably about the importance of responsive, preventive services, about listening to and empowering service users, about flexible inter-professional working, about standards, accountability and budgets. Second, because an awareness of the policy picture is vital if social work is not just to be on the receiving end of these policies, responding all the time to an agenda set by others, implementing plans drawn up by people far removed from the realities of front-line practice. Social workers, and other social professionals (Banks, 1999), can influence policy, but to do so they need to ensure that they are aware of what is going on, and are thinking beyond, or behind, their casework – an often-used image is that they should be looking 'upstream'. The third reason is that what social workers do *is* the reality of social policy for the people they work with. For service users, all the policies in the world are of little use unless they are put into practice by social workers and other front-line public service workers (Lipsky, 1980, who uses the term 'street-level bureaucrats'). And, as Lipsky points out, things are more dynamic and subtle than simply 'putting policy into practice', because the reality of policy is *made* by everyday practice – by the way laws and procedures are interpreted and applied, through routines and shortcuts, rule-bending and rule-breaking, strict action sometimes and leniency at others, doing extra work in some cases and not in others. In other words, social workers do not just implement policy; in a sense they create it as they go.

The books aims to be an introduction to the main ideas about social work and social policy, and also an argument about the role that social work can and should play in making social policy – in the sense mentioned above, that social policy is made in and through everyday practice. In some ways, social work is at the heart of current social policy, because the reality of themes such as personalisation and prevention depends to a large extent on the practice of social workers. In other ways it is strangely marginal and isolated, left out of new policy initiatives. My argument is that social work could make a significant contribution by bringing a better-informed, more subtle and more human perspective to social policy, but we need to prove that we can.

The challenges for social policy and social work are especially great at the present time. Writing this book in spring 2009, the global economy is in crisis and the UK is facing a lengthy recession and beyond that a long period of limited spending on public services. This will increase the number of people in need, as they lose their jobs, their savings and perhaps their homes. It will reduce the resources available across all social welfare agencies, as government spending is cut back, donations to voluntary organisations drop, and families and individuals have less to spend on the services they need. Prominent policy themes for all public services in the UK, not just social work, are to ensure that they get better at preventing problems arising or worsening, and to personalise them, to make them more responsive to service users' needs and choices. These goals are likely to be severely tested by the new economic situation. The risk is that lower-level preventive services will be cut back as funding dries up and eligibility thresholds are raised ever higher, and that personalisation will be distorted by cost-cutting priorities and end up shifting responsibilities from the state to the individual in ways that are burdensome rather than empowering (CSCI, 2008a). Social work stands in the middle of these predicaments, in between the state and the individual.

To explore these themes, the book is structured in three parts. The first part sets out three overarching models – of social work (Chapter 1), social policy (Chapter 2) and the role of the state (Chapter 3). The second part focuses on a selection of key issues in social policy that are especially relevant for social work. It offers a further variety of models to highlight the complexities and tensions, hopefully to clarify the questions and bring out the implications for social work. The themes are needs and rights (Chapter 4), inequality and poverty (Chapter 5), and participation and choice (Chapter 6). The third part of the book looks at three current topics that are central to the delivery of welfare services, and where the debates are especially sharp for social work. These are the themes of professionalism and inter-

professional working (Chapter 7), organisational and regulatory structures (Chapter 8), and money (Chapter 9). The conclusion pulls together the arguments of the book and suggests how we might revitalise the professional standing of social work – not in any self-serving sense of professionalism, but in a way that raises the challenge to ourselves by reasserting the intellectual, political and ethical dimensions of the everyday job.

Chapters 1–9

Part 1
Core models

The chapters in this part of the book introduce three core models for making sense of social work in its broader context of social policies, other social services and social values.

Chapter 1 opens with a brief summary of major trends in current social policy, showing the great relevance of contemporary priorities and dilemmas to social work. This policy context is complex, ambiguous and demanding, and the chapter describes the use of models to pull out the key features of a situation or policy. It then outlines the first model, the social work diamond, which locates social

Chapter 1

work in the middle of competing responsibilities to the state, service users, professional values and organisational imperatives. The chapter shows that the key policy themes and the tensions of social work's multiple obligations can be seen in the history of social work (the Seebohm report of 1968 and the Barclay report of 1982), and in recent debates about its roles and tasks.

Chapter 2 takes a look at the broader social policy context. It introduces the second model, the social policy triangle, to illustrate the three interweaving objectives of social policy in Western countries – to secure people's wellbeing, to promote individual responsibility and to facilitate the smooth working of

Chapter 2

the market economy. It gives an overview of the range of social services that social policy covers, highlighting their links with social work. The final section of the chapter reviews current policies about social exclusion, which exemplify important issues and debates about prevention, inter-agency working and personalisation, and about the place of social work in the bigger social policy picture.

Chapter 3 gives the third model, four perspectives on the role of the state in ensuring people's welfare in capitalist societies. The chapter describes the main features of the minimalist, integrationist, social democratic and radical approaches, and draws out their implications for social work. It discusses the contribution of radical social work. The chapter emphasises that there are complex mixtures of all four approaches in welfare policies and individuals' beliefs. It illustrates this ambiguity with reference to three important policies for social work – community care, social inclusion and personalisation.

Chapter 3

1 What is social work for?

What is social work for? And who is social work for? Different people will give different answers to these questions, but it is impossible to answer them fully without referring to social work's broader context of social values, social policies and other welfare services. Discussions about the role, or roles, of social work are not new, of course, and are reflected in government policy documents, professional literature, the views of service user groups, and the policies of organisations that employ social workers – to mention just four major sources of ideas. They are also reflected in media coverage about social work, and in debates with other professionals about who should be doing what and how. They are at the root of disagreements with people who receive social work services, perhaps without wanting to; or those who wish to receive them, but do not.

The aim of this book is to highlight some of the fundamental debates about social work and social policy, exploring the links between them and the implications that they have for one another. The focus is on social work in the UK, and more specifically England. There are differences between the four countries of the UK, but the underlying issues and dilemmas are similar, as they are for all Western countries with democratic political systems and developed economies. Therefore, even where the detail is specifically English, it should still spark ideas about parallels, or contrasts, in readers' own countries.

Looking at social work in England, it can sometimes seem as though it is being reduced to an ever more mechanistic, semi-skilled activity – a matter of following the voluminous, highly prescriptive guidance from central government, complying with procedures manuals, performing predetermined tasks, ticking check-boxes on forms. Yet social workers are often called upon to deal with the most complex and demanding situations, which cannot be solved by applying simple formulae. What sort of people are fit to look after children? What duties do adult children owe to their aged parents? If they cannot, or will not, fulfil them, what responsibility does the state have? Who should pay? What rights do individuals have to live their lives as they see fit, if that jeopardises the health or wellbeing of others? What about their own health and wellbeing? These are questions that philosophers and politicians have debated for centuries, and social workers make decisions about them every day (Reamer, 1993; Dingwall *et al.*, 1995). These decisions are often extremely difficult, and the difficulty reflects the tensions between important social values – between choice and safety; liberty and equality; individual responsibility and society's responsibilities; state help and state control.

Social workers make these difficult decisions in a context shaped by legislation, government guidelines, organisational priorities and resource availability. In their daily practice, social workers are more likely to be mindful of meeting legal requirements, following procedures, hitting deadlines, returning telephone calls and e-mails, and balancing budgets, rather than overarching principles like 'liberty' or 'equality'. Yet behind the tasks of practice, and behind policy initiatives such as personalisation and joined-up working, at the centre of social work lie those fundamental social principles, with all the tensions, ambiguities and dilemmas that they generate. That is why this book emphasises the importance of understanding social work practice and decision-making in terms of long-standing social values as well as current social policy trends.

Current social policy trends

Before going any further, it may be helpful to provide a quick overview of major themes in current UK social policy that are especially relevant to social work. Ten stand out – five Ps and five Rs. Of course, this is a great simplification, but it shows how social work stands in the middle of so many important social policy developments. It highlights the main priorities and principles, and begins to expose some of the crossovers and contradictions. It is meant as a checklist, a sort of ready-reckoner for the rest of the book.

The five Ps

Personalisation has become the mantra for all public services, not just social work. The term covers a number of requirements, notably to make services more flexible, responding to service users' choices as well as their needs, to promote their independence and social integration, and to give them more control over the services they receive (PMSU, 2007). It has been criticised, though, for shifting unreasonable risks and responsibilities to service users (e.g. Ferguson, 2007; Scourfield, 2007). It is a crucial theme for social work at present, and I shall explore its implications and challenges throughout the book.

Participation is a central aspect of personalisation, bringing greater involvement of people who use public services in deciding what services they receive, when and how. More generally, it also refers to the full involvement of all citizens in social, economic and political life, an end to social exclusion. However, critics argue that participation can be used as a cloak to disguise existing power relations, to give a democratic veneer to decisions that have already been made. Participation is discussed further in Chapter 6.

Prevention encapsulates a new policy emphasis on 'wellbeing' rather than just 'welfare'. The former is seen as a wider and more positive concept, incorporating a sense of social worth, rather than the stigmatising and limiting effects of being 'on welfare'. The key is to improve universal services (notably education and health care) to prevent problems emerging, and to target early intervention services to prevent them escalating. These goals are challenged by limited resources and the priority of dealing with the riskiest cases. These aspects are examined in more detail in Chapter 4.

Partnership working is the vital means to achieving prevention, and a crucial part of personalisation and participation. There is an emphasis on partnerships between service users, their carers and professionals, to 'co-produce' plans and services to meet people's needs and choices. There is also an emphasis on partnerships between the different agencies involved, in the public, voluntary and private sectors. The aim is to break down barriers, promote joint planning and working and ensure 'joined-up solutions to joined-up problems'. However, there are many challenges to effective inter-professional and inter-agency working, discussed further in Chapters 7 and 8.

Privatisation captures the growing role of the private sector in providing welfare services: for example, private businesses that provide home care and residential care for older people. More than that, private sector principles have shaped the way that public services are organised and run (e.g. 'business units' and commissioning), and there is a bigger influence, a philosophy, that people should make private provision for their needs rather than rely on public services. We look more closely at these themes in Chapters 8 and 9.

The five Rs

Rights are central to the new approaches to social policy and social services. They underpin ideas of personalisation and partnership, but can also generate new challenges. In one sense, they give people a powerful language to demand services; in another, they limit the state's powers, giving people a basis on which to resist intervention they do not want. In both senses, rights challenge social workers to justify their decisions and actions. This is proper and to be welcomed, but it is certainly not straightforward because social workers often have to deal with complex situations where there are competing rights (e.g. the right to freedom from harm versus the right to private life). Rights are discussed in Chapter 4.

Responsibility is a many-edged sword at the heart of social policy. One aspect is that the government, on behalf of society, has a responsibility to help those who have fallen into difficulties, but it must also protect individuals and society from harm. Meanwhile, individuals, families and communities are expected to behave responsibly, and are held responsible for their own wellbeing. They are expected to respond positively to any help that is offered (the government's catchphrase is that 'rights bring responsibilities'). Those who do not take advantage of the supportive approach are likely to be on the receiving end of more coercive measures. This state of affairs is thoroughly familiar to social workers, who attempt to work in cooperative and voluntary ways with individuals and families, but always have to bear in mind their legal, professional and organisational responsibilities to protect the vulnerable and others in society. And experience shows that social work organisations, and social workers as individuals, can be held responsible for shortcomings here, in very public and painful ways.

Risk, then, is another central notion to social workers, who are used to assessing and managing it. This involves working out (as far as possible, in partnership with service users) what the risks are, what sort of support could reduce them and what level of risk is tolerable. There is no such thing as an entirely risk-free option, but political, public and media reactions can make it very risky to live with risk (Parton, 1998).

Resources are crucial, too, and again there are two sides to the coin. All welfare organisations have to make the best use of finite resources, the well-known catchphrase being to ensure that services are

'economic, efficient and effective'. But resources in welfare agencies are often very tightly restricted and demands very high, so social workers may well have to make hard decisions about whether people meet eligibility criteria, acting as 'gate-keepers' to funding and services. The challenge is to assess risks accurately to make the best use of the available resources. The financial aspects are the focus of Chapter 9.

Regulation is a dominant theme for public services (and private and voluntary agencies that provide welfare services). There is a vast and complex range of regulatory agencies and requirements – legislation, procedures, registration, inspection, audit, performance indicators, league tables. Control of funding is another way that central government can regulate what local agencies do. There are challenging questions about who should be doing the regulating, according to what principles, what room there is for flexibility, and how much time, energy and money are used in meeting (or appearing to meet) the targets.

This overview of current policy trends has already begun to show how social work stands at the hub of many of the most thorny issues, faced with the challenge of putting complex, ambiguous and often incompatible requirements into practice.

The use of models: the social work diamond

The use of models is one way of helping to make sense of complex situations like this. Other terms that could be used for 'model' are 'framework', 'approach', 'construct' or 'theory'. Models work by simplifying matters, pulling out the key themes in a situation, highlighting the central features or ideas. In that sense, they are not descriptive, but analytic. It is better to think of them as a caricature rather than a photograph. So there is a danger of oversimplification, but one can recognise people from a good cartoon just as much as from a good photograph; and a good cartoon can deepen understanding by conveying the character of the person depicted, not just their physical appearance. As Richard Titmuss (1974: 30), one of the leading figures for social policy in the UK, put it: 'The purpose of model-building is not to admire the architecture of the building, but to help us see some order in all the disorder and confusion of facts, systems and choices concerning certain areas of our economic and social life.'

It may help to think of this book as an exhibition or gallery of different models (O'Brien and Penna, 1998: 1). This analogy helps to clarify the role of models in social policy and social work. Readers are likely to prefer some models to others, just as gallery-goers are likely to have their favourite exhibits. Different models may appear more striking than others, some will have greater relevance and explanatory value, depending on the circumstances and interests of the reader. A model is a starting point for reflection, analysis and application. If it helps you to understand things, use it; if not, look for another that works better, or another to complement it (life is complicated, so you are likely to need more than one model at a time), or adapt it – but above all, use it, test it. Apply the model to your circumstances, in order to shed light on them; but apply your circumstances to the model too, to shed light on it.

The key model of social work in this book sees it as poised between the four points of a diamond – its duties to the state, its obligations to service users, its responsibilities to its own professional standards, and its accountability to organisational imperatives. Figure 1.1 introduces the model and shows some of the main features for each point, but the ideas are discussed in more detail throughout the book. Although this book is about social work, the model is also useful for thinking about the work of other social professions (e.g. health professionals, teachers, lawyers, community workers). The dilemmas are not exclusive to social work – other professionals face similar tensions between following law and government policy, responding to consumers, upholding their own values and skills, and complying with organisational procedures and budgets.

Walter Lorenz proposes a model of social work that uses the first three of these points in his book *Social Work in a Changing Europe* (1994). He uses it to great effect, showing the dangers that can arise if social work becomes too closely aligned with any one point. If social work becomes too strongly an agency of state policy, it risks losing its critical voice and becoming oppressive (Lorenz gives the chilling example of social work in Nazi Germany). Alternatively, if it is too closely aligned with particular user groups, it risks becoming the tool of those who are more vociferous or socially powerful, and losing sight of the wider picture, of justice between different groups. And if it becomes too focused on its own professional expertise and status, it risks becoming self-serving and once again oppressive. Lorenz argues that the challenge for social work is to stay balanced between the three points, holding them in creative tension.

It is a powerful model, and like all good models opens up new lines of thought. This leads me to add a fourth point – the organisational dimension of social work policy and practice. Organisational goals,

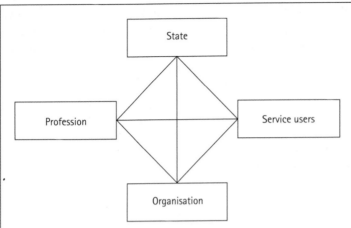

Figure 1.1
The social work diamond

State

Social policy, social work and other social professions as parts of the machinery of state support and control.

Key factors: Roles of central government and local authorities. National policies, legislation, taxation and government spending. Roles of Parliament, courts, regulatory bodies. Overlaps and tensions between these different parts of the state. Political conflict about the proper role of the state.

Profession

Social policy, social work and other social professions as 'top-down', expert-led activities.

Key factors: Professional attributes such as training and expertise, standards and skills, service ethic, self-regulation. But there are criticisms of elitism, self-interest and status, and the disabling effects of professionals.

Service users

Social policy, social work and other social professions as 'bottom-up', user-led activities.

Key factors: Roles of individuals, families and neighbourhoods; campaign groups and self-help groups. Concepts of participation, inclusion, empowerment, control. But there are tensions between different service users, and questions about how much power and choice they really have, or should have.

Organisation

Social policy, social work and other social professions as activities that are shaped by their organisational setting.

Key factors: Type of organisation – statutory (e.g. local authority), voluntary or business. Inter-agency working. Processes for user involvement. Bureaucracy, regulation and managerialism. Budgets and profits.

structures and dynamics shape the expectations that social workers and other welfare professionals have about their jobs, and the work that they do, at least as much as formal government policy, disciplinary knowledge and users' views. This applies whether workers are employed by governmental or non-governmental agencies. The substantial majority of social workers in the UK work for local government (Northern Ireland is the exception, where the main employers are Health and Social Care Trusts), but others work for charities and other voluntary organisations, some for private welfare businesses (e.g. private foster care agencies, private children's homes), and some work independently, as agency workers or accepting commissions for particular pieces of work. Whatever the setting, the four points of the diamond come into play. For example, the state is still important for voluntary and private sector organisations, through legislation, national policies and funding; and even the work of an independent social worker is shaped by organisational matters, namely the budget and policies of the commissioning agency. Financial imperatives are a crucial part of this organisational dimension. Workers in all welfare organisations have to show that they are achieving value for money, may well be involved in lengthy work to secure funding for their plans, and often have to make tough decisions about the allocation of limited resources between needy causes.

Thinking more about the organisational and financial dimension, a major trend in current UK social policy is the restructuring of public services in order to get them to achieve the goals of greater economy, efficiency and effectiveness, and closer links between the public sector and other providers of welfare. This 'mixed economy of welfare' includes statutory agencies; private, profit-making businesses; charities and voluntary organisations (sometimes referred to as the 'third sector'); and informal sources of help and support (families, friends, neighbours). There have always been these different components, but the balance between them is changing as more and more services are provided by the private and voluntary sectors. The role of the state has moved from simply purchasing services from other suppliers to one of more active collaboration, or commissioning, working with private, voluntary and community partners to plan services, and to support a variety of provision.

An important feature of the diamond is that there are tensions *within* each of the four points as well as *between* them. So, within the state there may sometimes be conflict between political priorities and court decisions, and there is often tension between central and local government. There may be tensions between different service users (e.g. a child and parent), and between service user groups, particularly in a world of limited resources. Organisations are torn between being lean and efficient, or flexible and open. Professionals have to reconcile their responsibilities to the state, service users and the organisation. The four points are continually interacting with one another, adapting themselves and bringing about change in the others in a dynamic, ongoing manner. For example, notions of professionalism have changed to accommodate the greater emphasis now placed on involving service users – listening to their views and empowering them to make their own choices are now seen as professional things to do. The increasing profile of service users and carers is also challenging notions about the proper roles of the state and welfare organisations, pressing them to become more responsive and enabling. But pressure is never all in one direction. Legal responsibilities about protecting people from harm, and organisational requirements such as compliance with tight procedures and timescales, can restrict the influence of service users and limit the extent of professional discretion. In terms of the state's powers, government policy has dramatically changed the organisational

requirements and context of social work practice in recent years. A particular issue has been New Labour's emphasis on targets, performance indicators and inspections, and the creation of a whole new range of regulatory agencies (see Chapter 8). And yet the flow is not all one-way, government-down. Welfare organisations may resist externally imposed requirements, reinterpret them or modify them; and state policies take effect, become

Chapter 8

'real', only through the activities of street-level bureaucrats such as social workers (Lipsky, 1980; Evans and Harris, 2004; Ellis, 2007). For service users, the practices and decisions of front-line workers have more direct impact than the formal policies of government.

Who is social work for?

One of the debates about 'who social work is for' is whether it should focus on the most vulnerable people in society, or rather should play a greater role with a wider group of people, where need is less urgent and earlier intervention might prevent later problems. This may mean preventive work with individuals and families, or with groups and communities. But there is a further dimension to it, which is that social work also serves a wider function for society as a whole – for the many, not just for the few who receive (or might receive) services. There are two angles to this further dimension: one that sees it as beneficent (everyone benefits from an orderly society in which social problems are minimised and dealt with early on), and the other that sees it as controlling (social work as a subtle way of monitoring people who might cause problems, keeping them in order, so that the rest of us can have a trouble-free life).

So, referring back to the diamond, the questions are: 'Who are the service users?' and 'What sort of role does social work have beyond helping those in direct receipt of a service?' These questions apply as much to social policy generally as to social work in particular, and we shall return to them

Chapters 2, 3 and 4

throughout the book: whether the focus should be on the very needy or the not-quite-so-needy, and the wider impact on society as a whole. The issues come up especially when we look more closely at social policy (Chapter 2), the role of the state (Chapter 3) and models of need (Chapter 4). For now, we explore the significance of these questions by looking at debates about the roles and tasks of social work.

For the background, Boxes 1.1 and 1.2 summarise two important historical documents for social work in England: the Seebohm report of 1968 and the Barclay report of 1982. Scotland was ahead of the game with the Kilbrandon report (1964), which led eventually to the creation of social work departments under the Social Work (Scotland) Act 1968. Even if some of the language has changed, the older reports are shaped by the same issues of personalisation, participation, prevention and partnership, and the challenges of rights and responsibilities, risks, resources and regulation. The private sector has become much more significant since then. But we can see the tensions, even in those days, between statutory functions, organisational dynamics, service users' interests and professional values. More recently, all four countries of the UK have undertaken reviews of the roles and tasks of social work, and we look at these in the following section.

The Seebohm and Barclay reports' visions of a preventive, community-based service did not come to pass. By the mid-1980s the dominant political mood was anti-local authorities and anti-welfare, and a succession of child abuse scandals dragged local authority child care social work in a very different

Box 1.1 The Seebohm report (1968)

The 1960s was a period of rapid social change, and in many ways an optimistic time for social work and social policy. The Report of the Committee on Local Authority and Allied Personal Social Services in 1968 is a high point of this era. Known as the Seebohm report, after Frederic Seebohm who chaired the committee, it called for local authority children's, health and welfare services to be brought together into unified social services departments. It led to the Local Authority Social Services Act 1970, and the creation of social services departments in England and Wales in 1971.

Seebohm argued that the fragmented structure of local authority services meant that each department tended to focus on its own responsibilities, failing to recognise the full needs of the people using them – an analysis that is still echoed today in calls for organisational reforms to ensure better inter-agency and inter-disciplinary working. The report's recommendation about unified departments is expressed in inspiring, universalist terms, looking to the wider benefits for society as a whole, not just the most needy:

> We recommend a new local authority department, providing a community based and family oriented service, which will be available to all. This new department will, we believe, reach far beyond the discovery and rescue of social casualties; it will enable the greatest number of individuals to act reciprocally, giving and receiving service for the well-being of the whole community.

> (Seebohm, 1968: para. 2)

To achieve this goal, the report called for field-level social workers to be skilled in working with a wide range of needs, not narrow specialists (paras 516–20). It called for a greater emphasis on supporting families and individuals to prevent problems emerging or escalating, although it noted that this might be hard to achieve given the levels of casualty work which absorb so many resources (paras 427–54). It also called for social workers to work with voluntary organisations and local people to promote community involvement. It noted the potential for conflict between local authorities and voluntary groups, but regarded this tension as essential 'if the needs of consumers are to be met more effectively and they are to be protected from the misuse of bureaucratic and professional power in either kind of organisation' (para. 496).

The report called for the 'maximum participation of individuals and groups in the community in the planning, organisation and provision of the social services', on the grounds that everyone 'consumes' social services, directly or indirectly (paras 491–2). It proposed a national advisory council to regulate social work education, a national inspectorate (whose role would be 'not so much regulatory as promotional, educational and consultative': para. 649), and the establishment of local advisory committees, which would include service users (paras 506, 628). It stressed that the new service would not succeed without adequate resources (paras 88, 147–51).

Box 1.2 The Barclay report (1982)

In 1980, almost ten years after the creation of social services departments and in a very different political context, the Conservative government of the time commissioned the National Institute of Social Work to undertake a review of the role and tasks of social workers. It was chaired by Peter Barclay, and the report was published in 1982. It identified two key roles for social work (Barclay, 1982: 33–4).

The report called the first of these 'social care planning' ('to plan, establish, maintain and evaluate the provision of social care') and the second 'counselling' ('face to face communication' with service users). It noted that in practice these two were 'inextricably intertwined' (p. 41), but the planning role is not limited to casework, and could be used to tackle wider needs in the community. The report called for a new emphasis on community social work, with social workers working in partnership with local people to support and build on community strengths. It acknowledged that this recommendation echoed the aspirations of the Seebohm committee, but thought that the time might now be right because of a greater belief, in society generally, in the capacity of 'ordinary people'. It considered that the constrained finances of the time made a new approach essential, but warned that it would succeed only if adequately resourced.

As for regulation and standards, the report debated and rejected the idea of a general social work council, but did call for a probationary year for newly qualified social workers. It also called for local welfare advisory committees (pp. 177–97).

Two minority reports were published as appendices, revealing the ongoing tensions about the role of social work. One of them, Brown *et al.* (1982), argued more strongly than the main report for a clear shift to proactive neighbourhood- or 'patch'-based work. The other, by Robert Pinker, resisted the calls for community-based work, arguing that social work would do better to be 'explicitly selective rather than universalist in focus, reactive rather than preventative in approach and modest in its objectives' (Pinker, 1982: 237).

---

direction, becoming much more formalised and investigative, with the focus on risk and statutory responsibilities. In this context, social work was often in conflict with local communities rather than working with them.

The ideas of more preventive ways of working and partnership were never abandoned, though. They are reflected in the two major pieces of legislation that shaped social work in England and Wales throughout the 1990s. The Children Act 1989 reflected the importance of working in partnership with parents and children, promoting the upbringing of children by their families as far as possible. For adult social services, the NHS and Community Care Act 1990 was intended to ensure that assessments were led by people's needs, not dictated by the available services. The aim was to ensure greater responsiveness to individuals' circumstances and wishes. While this did enable some creative care plans to be put in place, financial restrictions came into play and assessments soon came to be dominated by the need to ration services (Means *et al.*, 2008: esp. ch. 3).

The wider social consequences: reciprocity or control?

But what about the wider dimension, the functions and impact of social work on the rest of society, not just those who receive services? The Seebohm report and the majority Barclay report emphasised the positive side, seeing the value of local authority social services as a mechanism through which citizens could work together and demonstrate care for one another. But there is another way of seeing the wider functions of social work and social policy, in terms of the way that they control populations as a whole, not just individuals (Foucault, 1977; Donzelot, 1980; Parton, 1991; for a useful commentary, Hudson and Lowe, 2009: 111–28). This perspective sees the social professions and welfare services in terms of the influence and power that they assert, not just over those who are subject to the more coercive forms of intervention (children removed from families under court orders, people detained in hospital against their will under mental health legislation), or even over those who are receiving voluntary services, but over the people who are not receiving a service, 'everyone else'. The point is that social work, and other welfare services such as education, health, pensions and unemployment benefits, create and enforce wider social expectations and norms. One does not have to receive the services oneself to be aware of what the consequences would be of, say, not caring for one's children properly, or not saving for one's old age. In this way, social work and other welfare agencies serve a role for the state, creating a commonsense way of seeing things, maintaining social order in quiet but very powerful ways.

Ostensibly benign and supportive approaches are far more effective forms of social control than overt repression and punishment of people who break the law or behave antisocially. The idea is that it is far better if people are disciplined from the beginning, in as unobtrusive a way as possible, through training and care, to obey the law and behave in socially acceptable ways. This welfare approach will not succeed all the time, of course, and then the more coercive aspects of state services and the law will have to be employed; but welfare agencies and social policy are crucial mechanisms through which modern, liberal democratic states seek to ensure the wellbeing *and* regulation of their populations.

The roles and tasks of social work today

Much has changed since 1968 and 1982, of course, bringing new opportunities and new challenges. There is demographic change, notably the increased numbers of older people, many in good health and with resources to enjoy their later years, but also more frail older people with high levels of need. There are increased numbers of people with physical and learning disabilities living in the community. We live in a much more ethnically diverse society, and there are new patterns of family life, with more lone and single parents, and changed expectations about the roles of men and women in the home and in paid employment. There is a greater awareness of the abuse that children and vulnerable adults can suffer, from family members, people in the community and professionals working with them. There are new problems, such as the greater use of illegal drugs, but also new opportunities for people to obtain services, gain knowledge and exchange ideas through information and communication technology. Questions about the roles and tasks of social work are as pertinent as ever in these new circumstances; and the underlying debates and demands come up again.

The questions have been revived as part of New Labour's reforms of public services generally, and social care services in particular. The government published a white paper, *Modernising Social Services*, in 1998, with the goals of 'promoting independence, improving protection and raising standards' (DH, 1998). Like the Seebohm and Barclay reports, it stressed that social services are not just about supporting a small number of social casualties, but are 'an important part of the fabric of a caring society' (para. 1.3) because 'we all benefit if social services are providing good, effective services to those who need them' (para. 1.2). Despite that positive tone, the white paper highlighted a wide range of shortcomings, portraying local authority social services as failing and in need of radical reform. For adult services, it stressed the need to promote people's independence while safeguarding them from harm, for greater consistency across the country, and for the system to be centred on service users and their families, with more flexible, accessible and individualised services. For children's services, the priorities were more effective protection from abuse and neglect, better provision and support for children in care, and improving the life chances of children in need, especially through better education and health services.

The white paper proposed a range of organisational changes to achieve these goals, including new regulation and inspection systems, and called for greater partnership working between the various statutory agencies involved, and between the statutory sector and the private and voluntary sectors. It also proposed a range of measures to raise standards in the workforce, including the creation of the General Social Care Council (GSCC) to maintain a professional register, regulate social work education and training, and set a code of practice for social care workers and employers. The other countries of the UK have parallel bodies – the Scottish Social Services Council, the Care Council for Wales and the Northern Ireland Social Care Council (see Chapter 8). All four countries have undertaken reviews of the roles and tasks of social workers in the first decade of the twenty-first century.

Chapter 8

Wales

The review of social work in Wales was led by the Association of Directors of Social Services in Wales, and was part of a programme to address difficulties with the recruitment and retention of social workers. It was undertaken in 2004–5, and produced a report entitled *Social Work in Wales: A Profession to Value* (ADSS (Cymru), 2005). It focuses on the roles of social workers in local authorities, emphasising the statutory responsibilities. It identifies six major roles (p. 56): assessing needs; assessing and balancing risks to promote independence; deciding about the allocation of scarce resources; promoting social inclusion; collaborating with other agencies; and ensuring accountability through effective, accurate recording of decisions.

Scotland

The Scottish review was commissioned by the Scottish Executive in 2004 and produced its final report, *Changing Lives: Report of the 21st Century Social Work Review*, in February 2006 (Scottish Executive, 2006). The review aimed to clarify the role and purpose of social work, to make recommendations about improving the regulatory regime, and to strengthen leadership and management. It commissioned a large number of research reports (e.g. Asquith *et al.*, 2005, a literature review on the role of the social worker; and Leadbetter and Lownsborough, 2005, on the implications of personalisation and participation), and a series of consultation events. The report identifies six core roles for social workers (pp. 28–9):

- Case worker, working with individuals to help them address personal issues;

- Advocate on behalf of the poor and socially excluded;

- Partner, working together with disadvantaged or disempowered individuals and groups;

- Assessor of risk or need for a number of client groups;

- Care manager who arranges services for users, but may have little direct client contact;

- Agent of social control who helps maintain the social system against the demands of individuals whose behaviour is problematic.

It is a comprehensive and positive report, holding that social workers have important skills and a valuable role to play in modern public services. It argues that social workers have the lead role in working with people with the highest needs and risks, in the most complex and unpredictable situations, but also have important roles in earlier intervention, and a significant contribution to make to lower-level, universal services (p. 31). For a helpful commentary on the report and social work in Scotland, see Brodie *et al.* (2008).

England

In England, the government established a review of the social care workforce in 2005, known as *Options for Excellence* (DfES and DH, 2006). This looked at social care as a whole, but as part of it the government commissioned a detailed review of research into the role and tasks of social work. This was published in March 2006 (Statham *et al.*, 2006). In September 2006 the government commissioned the GSCC to produce a statement defining the roles and tasks of social work in England.

The GSCC published a 'literature informed discussion paper' in January 2007 (Blewett *et al.*, 2007), and held a series of meetings over winter 2006–7 with service users, practitioners, managers, academics and other stakeholders. This led to the publication of a consultation paper in March 2007 (GSCC, 2007a), which duly led to further debate (see, for example, Beresford, 2007a, a response that emphasises service users' perspectives) and a 'final draft' in October 2007 (GSCC, 2007b). There was some criticism of this (e.g. Beresford, 2007b), and the GSCC undertook to consider the responses and produce a final statement in November 2007. However, there was a considerable delay involving further discussions with the government departments responsible for social care. The final version was published in March 2008, entitled *Social Work at its Best: A Statement of Social Work Roles and Tasks for the 21st Century* (GSCC, 2008). The main points of the statement are summarised in Box 1.3.

Box 1.3 Key points from *Social Work at its Best* (GSCC, 2008)

- 'Social work is an established professional discipline with a distinctive part to play in promoting and securing the wellbeing of children, adults, families and communities.'

- 'Social work is committed to enabling every child and adult to fulfil their potential, achieve and maintain independence and self-direction, make choices, take control of their own lives and support arrangements, and exercise their civil and human rights.'

- 'Social work is practised, whenever possible, in partnership with the children, adults, families and communities using its services.'

- 'Social work makes a particular contribution in situations where there are high levels of complexity, uncertainty, stress, conflicts of interest, and risk, particularly to children and vulnerable adults.'

- 'Employers must provide social workers with good quality supervision, realistic workloads, access to learning support and continuing development, enabling IT and management systems, and a suitable working environment.'

- 'Social work operates within a constantly developing framework of policies and legislation ... Government policy stresses the need to get away from "one size fits all" provision, and personalise services and responses to the circumstances, strengths and aspirations of particular children, adults and families. The emphasis is on making sure all children are supported to achieve their full potential, and on adults having as much control, independence and choice as possible whatever their age or level of disability.'

- 'Not all the tasks arising in the course of working with a child, adult or family require the full expertise of a social worker ... it is possible for others to undertake and perhaps specialise in tasks which have traditionally been parts of the social work role.'

- 'Social work works closely with other professional disciplines ... It is sometimes necessary to be flexible about boundaries ... Social work has a tradition of not sticking rigidly to professional or agency boundaries where greater flexibility serves people's best interests.'

- 'Social work should be clear and confident about the expertise it has developed, the distinctive contribution it makes and the features of its work particularly valued by people who use its services.'

After all the work that had gone into it, the final document was published without any fanfare and in a rather uninspiring format, nothing like the high-quality product of the Scottish review. It is also quite hard to find the statement and the earlier documents on the GSCC website. (In contrast, the Scottish review has a dedicated website which continues to be updated.) There was no ministerial backing, and concern was expressed that this low-key launch reflected government ambivalence about social work (Brindle, 2008; Samuel, 2008). Analysing the GSCC statement with reference to the current themes of social policy and the social work diamond helps to identify two other points.

First, it is unfortunate that the GSCC statement makes no mention of resource constraints, and the difficulties for social workers faced with ever-increasing demand and limited resources. Turning down someone's request for a service because there is not enough money may not always feel like 'social work at its best', but it is certainly social work in reality. Gate-keeping has to happen, because it is important that limited resources are used on those who need them most, but it can be distressing to individuals and carers, and demoralising for workers, when eligibility criteria are so high that even people with very considerable needs do not receive a service (CSCI, 2008a). The GSCC statement is helpfully clear on the challenges of balancing partnership with risks and legal responsibilities. It is much less clear about the challenges that resource restraints raise for partnership, prevention, participation and personalisation.

That leads to the second observation. The GSCC statement makes close reference to what were, at the time, the most recent government policy documents for children's services and adult social care. Both were published in late 2007, after the final draft, but they were incorporated in the final statement. One is *The Children's Plan* (DCSF, 2007), the government's objectives and strategy for improving services for children and parents. The other is *Putting People First* (HM Government, 2007), a protocol between a number of government departments, regulatory agencies and non-governmental bodies, which sets out the goal of developing personalised services to support independent living. While social work is inevitably shaped by its particular context, it is regrettable that the GSCC statement was so closely tied to current government policy. Social work has not held its position as an independent profession. There is no mention of the wider responsibilities of social work, as described in the British Association of Social Workers' code of ethics, which stresses its duties to service users and as a profession to 'Bring to the attention of those in power and the general public, and where appropriate challenge ways in which the policies or activities of government, organisations or society create or contribute to structural disadvantage, hardship and suffering, or militate against their relief' (BASW, 2002: para. 3.2.2a).

The danger is that social work's capacity and duty to be independent of the state, to be critical, has been compromised.

Northern Ireland

The Northern Ireland Social Services Council undertook a review of the roles and tasks of social work in 2008–9. It was able to draw on the experience of the other reviews and the documents produced by them, as well as commissioning its own research. It had not produced its final report at the time of writing, but a report on the consultation process made the following observation:

> Social work needs to own and profile the conflicts, ethical and moral challenges and paradoxes inherent in the role and tasks ... Working with the most vulnerable and staying with the most distressing and apparently intractable situations is a key feature of social work regardless of setting or job role. This involves working with complexities with no obvious solutions and often working with those whom society would rather pretend do not exist – *social work lifts the rock and looks underneath.*
>
> (Bogues, 2008: 35–6; emphasis in original)

Conclusion

This chapter started by summarising ten key themes in current social policy that most affect social work in the UK. Social workers play a pivotal role in the way that these principles are put into practice, the ways that they actually affect people's lives. It then introduced the first of the core models, the social work diamond, as a way of helping to make sense of the challenges of putting policies into practice. Social workers have to pay attention to four sets of responsibilities, to help them judge whether they are doing the right thing – their responsibilities to the state, to the organisation, to professional standards and to service users. The greatest challenge is that these different requirements do not always pull in the same direction, and social workers have to think clearly, in demanding situations, to make fine judgments on difficult issues. Underneath the pressures and busy nature of day-to-day practice, the same essential dilemmas come up year after year: how are professional standards, state policies, organisational requirements and service users' interests to be balanced? Who are the service users? And how are the supportive and controlling aspects of social work to be reconciled?

The attempts of the different UK countries to formulate their own statements of the roles and tasks of social work demonstrate that these questions have no easy answers. The important thing is to be clear about the questions, rather than trying to settle the debate. It is impossible for any one statement to satisfy all the different interests involved fully. It may be possible to find some points on which service users, family carers, social workers, managers, academics, civil servants, local politicians and national politicians will all agree, but such matters are likely to be very bland. As things become more specific, and in the realities of practice, disagreements are bound to occur. A statement of social work roles, tasks or values that satisfies everyone on paper is bound to be disappointing in reality, sooner or later, to all of them. The challenge of social work, and for social workers, is being in the middle of these competing demands.

Questions for reflection

- Who do you think social work is for?

- Look back to the major themes in current social policy. Think about (or find out about) current policies and programmes for a particular group of social work service users, and consider how they reflect these themes (e.g. policies for older people, or for children and young people in care). What are the main issues for your chosen group?

- Look back to the social work diamond. Think about a social welfare agency where you have worked or been on placement. What were the competing demands on you?

- Do you agree with the BASW code of ethics, that social workers have a duty to bring inadequate or harmful policies 'to the attention of those in power and the general public'? What are the potential benefits and risks?

Useful websites and further reading

The documents for the various reviews of the roles and tasks of social work are a good place to start. These are (mostly) easily available on the internet. The Scottish report, *Changing Lives*, is especially good, available on the Social Work Scotland website: www.socialworkscotland.org.uk.

The British Association of Social Workers' code of ethics (2002) is worth reading for another view on the roles, tasks and values of social work: www.basw.co.uk.

The weekly magazine *Community Care* is a good way to follow the news and debates about social work. It has a very good website, and you can register for a weekly e-mail to help you keep up to date: www.community care.co.uk.

Core models

For an introduction to social work, four recommended books are:

Horner (2009) *What is Social Work? Context and Perspectives*, 3rd edn.

Payne (2006) *What is Professional Social Work?*, 2nd edn.

Cree and Davis (2007) *Social Work: Voices from the Inside*.

Cree and Myers (2008) *Social Work: Making a Difference*.

2 What is social policy about?

Chapter 1

The first chapter made the point that social work exists and is practised within a wider social policy context; indeed, more than that, it is at the heart of many social policy themes and dilemmas. This chapter adds to the picture by exploring in more depth what we mean by 'social policy', and what it is for. It highlights the links and overlaps with social work, and sets the scene for further exploration of the themes in later chapters.

Chapter 1 identified major themes in current policy (the five Ps and the five Rs), which has already given a sense of the breadth and intricacy of the subject. This chapter proposes a model, the social policy triangle, as a way of making sense of the underlying issues and purposes of social policy in Western, capitalist countries. The first section of the chapter considers the outcomes and objectives of social policy, the things it is meant to achieve, and describes the triangle. The second section looks more specifically at the range of services and organisations that deliver welfare services, drawing out the relevance for social work and the importance of an integrated, joined-up approach. The third section looks at current approaches to tackling social exclusion, as these exemplify many of the key themes, notably prevention, inter-agency working and responsibility. They also raise intriguing questions about the place of social work and the meaning of personalisation.

A point to stress at the start is that social policy is political, in two senses of the word: in a party politics sense, different political parties promote policies which they believe will benefit the nation as a whole but which they also calculate will help them to win elections; and in a wider sense, to do with power and control – who decides, or should decide, what people's welfare needs are, whose needs should be met, and how those needs are best met? Politicians, judges, government advisers (the state)? Doctors, teachers, social workers (the welfare professionals)? Managers, directors, accountants (the organisational aspect)? Or service users, carers, consumers, citizens themselves? Asking these questions shows that the tensions social workers face in having to balance the demands of state, profession, organisation and service users (the social work diamond) are not at all unique to social work – they are typical of social policy more generally.

Another point worth noting is the way that the term 'social services' is used in social policy literature. For many social workers in England, 'social services' refers to local authority social services departments. Although these have recently been restructured into separate children's and adults' departments, social services departments were, for over thirty years, the major employers of social workers in England, and the major provider of 'personal social services'. (There are still social services departments in Wales. Scotland has mainly social work departments.) However, in social policy texts, 'social services' often carries a wider meaning, referring to the whole range of services that is intended to meet people's welfare needs. This includes, among others, education, health and income maintenance, as well as social care. So, when reading social work and social policy texts, it is important to be aware of the way that the term 'social services' is being used.

Outcomes and objectives: the social policy triangle

In England, the government has specified five outcomes for children and seven for adults that social services, in the broad sense of the term, are meant to help them achieve. These are shown in Box 2.1. On the surface they seem uncontroversial – who could disagree with children being healthy or staying safe? – but they become rather more interesting when we push hard at the questions 'What are they for?' and 'Who are they for?' From the government's point of view, the stated reason for specifying outcomes is to get away from a narrow focus on 'inputs and outputs' – that is to say, to shift attention away from systems, procedures and organisational boundaries, to the results, the difference that they make to people's lives (DCSF, 2008a). This might seem a bit rich coming from a government that has been obsessed with organisational structures and performance measurement, so we ought not to take the goals entirely at face value.

What might lie behind the stated outcomes? To answer this question, we need to step back from the current detail to look at the bigger purposes of social policy. We can say that the overriding objective of social policy in Western, democratic nations with capitalist economic systems, and its overriding challenge, is to balance three demands – to ensure the welfare of citizens, to promote the values of individual responsibility and family autonomy, and to uphold economic freedom and prosperity. I call this the 'social policy triangle'. Obviously it is a simplification, but it helps to draw attention to the tensions, contradictions and difficult balances that have to be struck. It shows the links between economic policy and social policy, something that became very apparent in 2008–9, as governments invested staggering sums of money in propping up the world economy, to try to save people's jobs,

Box 2.1 Outcomes

Five outcomes for children

- *Be healthy*: includes physical and mental health, sexual health, healthy lifestyles.

- *Stay safe*: includes safety from maltreatment and neglect, from accidents, from bullying, from crime and antisocial behaviour.

- *Enjoy and achieve*: includes attending and enjoying school, meeting educational standards.

- *Make a positive contribution*: includes engaging in decision-making, law-abiding behaviour, choosing not to bully or discriminate.

- *Achieve economic wellbeing*: includes being ready for employment, living in decent homes and households free from low income.

Introduced by the government green paper *Every Child Matters* (HM Treasury, 2003: 14), subsequently developed in *Every Child Matters: Change for Children* (HM Government, 2004) and adopted in the Children Act 2004, s. 10(2).

Seven outcomes for adults

- *Improved health*: includes physical and mental health, freedom from abuse and exploitation.

- *Improved quality of life*: includes access to social activities, lifelong learning and transport.

- *Making a positive contribution*: includes participation in community life through employment or voluntary work.

- *Exercise choice and control*: includes maximum independence and managing risk.

- *Freedom from discrimination*: includes equal access to services and freedom from abuse.

- *Economic wellbeing*: includes sufficient income for a good diet, accommodation and participation in family and community life.

- *Personal dignity*: includes keeping clean and comfortable and appropriate personal care.

Introduced by the government green paper *Independence, Well-being and Choice: Our Vision of the Future of Social Care for Adults in England* (DH, 2005: 26). Subsequently adopted in the white paper *Our Health, Our Care, Our Say* (DH, 2006: 42), and as the framework for measuring performance of local authority adult social care services (CSCI, 2008a, 2009).

savings and homes. Figure 2.1 shows some of the questions the triangle generates, and the links between them.

The tension between welfare and the economy is that high-quality social services are expensive. If the services are provided by the state, then that will mean a high tax bill – but individuals and businesses, on the whole, do not like to pay high taxes. The fear of politicians and policy-makers is that if taxation is too high, businesses will move their factories and offices to other countries, where wages and taxes are lower. In our globalised world, this seems easier than ever. On the other hand, defenders of public services such as health, education and pensions argue that they support the economy by producing a skilled and healthy workforce. More than that, they give people a sense of social and financial security, which builds a general sense of wellbeing in society.

The main tension between welfare and responsibility is that some say overly generous provision from the state undermines individual responsibility – it discourages people from saving for their old age, it weakens family ties because people no longer feel an obligation to help their relatives ('someone else will do it'), and it saps people's dynamism by removing the need to 'get on', making life too soft and too dull. On the other hand, defenders of social services argue that most people who need help do so not because they are lazy or irresponsible, but because their needs – financial, emotional, intellectual, physical and social – are so great. Maybe they do not have families to help, or their needs are so demanding that their families cannot cope. A bit of timely help will enable some to resume self-responsibility. Others will need longer-term support, and it should be accepted as society's responsibility to provide that.

The relationship between responsibility and the economy is that, for most people, the primary way of being responsible for oneself and one's family is to work, to earn money. Welfare sceptics argue that social services make life too easy and too expensive, undermining responsibility and the economy. Supporters argue that they give the vital help people need in times of trouble, and more than that have a positive role in building up a skilled, responsible workforce and a thriving market for goods and services.

Questions about the relationships between welfare, responsibility and the economy recur throughout social policy and throughout social work. We focus on them again in Chapter 3, but Box 2.2 gives a historical picture, by looking at the way they have interacted over the centuries in the Poor Law.

Chapter 3

The legacy of the Poor Law is still with us today, in various ways. For some, it is in the shame of having to accept help from the state. For many, it is reflected in suspicious attitudes towards people who rely on state welfare, especially unemployment benefits – that they are 'welfare scroungers', not deserving of help but rather of a tough, no-nonsense regime that obliges them to go to work. The strict eligibility criteria for state assistance, notably for financial help for people out of work but also for social care, reflect the old concerns to ensure that people use their own resources first and rely on the state only in extreme circumstances. The notion that people should return to their own parish for assistance may no longer exist, but in our globalised world it is echoed in the idea that foreign citizens should have

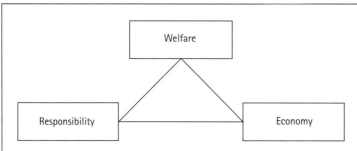

Figure 2.1
The social policy triangle

Welfare

- What sort of things make up 'welfare'? Income, health, education, employment, 'social inclusion'?
- What level of welfare? Should public services aim to provide the highest possible standards or a basic minimum?
- Whose welfare? Are public services for only the extremely vulnerable or a wider population?
- Who deserves help? What happens to people who are judged not to deserve it?
- How should the welfare and freedoms of individuals be balanced with the welfare and freedoms of others?
- Who decides what needs are met, and how? Politicians, experts, consumers?
- Why do people need welfare services? Individual failings, policy shortcomings, wider social and economic forces?
- When should welfare services be provided? Early on (preventive services) or not until later, when need is clearly established?
- Who provides? State, businesses, charities, families?
- Who pays, and how? Taxation, donors, user charges?
- What about people who are not state citizens? Immigrants, refugees, asylum seekers?

Responsibility

- How to help individuals take responsibility for their own welfare and that of their families (e.g. to work, save, bring up children, care for older relatives)?
- What responsibilities does society have when people cannot do these things?
- What to do if people refuse to comply? In other words, how to balance responsibility and individual freedom?
- When to intervene compulsorily?
- How best to help people who need assistance – state intervention, or through voluntary organisations, or private agencies?
- How to balance responsibilities and rights of different individuals or groups (e.g. children or parents, women or men, employed or unemployed)?
- What allowance to make for cultural, religious and ethnic differences?

Economy

- How to protect people from the unfairnesses of the capitalist economy (e.g. redundancy, low pay, high prices for essential goods), but in ways that do not unduly restrict business freedom and incentives?
- How to pay for welfare services without raising taxes too high?
- How to run services efficiently, economically and effectively?
- How to help (or oblige?) people to work, rather than rely on welfare benefits?
- How to ensure that there is a suitably skilled and plentiful workforce?
- How to involve businesses and voluntary organisations in providing welfare services?
- Should there be more private saving or voluntary giving? If so, how should the state change people's financial behaviour?
- Is redistribution of wealth an objective (i.e. through taxation), or is it better to allow the better-off to keep more of their money?

Box 2.2 The Poor Law

The tensions between welfare, economy and responsibility go right back to the beginnings of the modern state and its role in welfare, the Poor Law. There were numerous versions of the Poor Law, but three key dates are 1601, the Elizabethan Poor Law; 1834, the Poor Law Amendment Act (the Victorian or New Poor Law); and 1948, the final end of the Poor Law, with the passing of the National Assistance Act that year.

The Poor Law emphasised that the first responsibility of those who could work was to work; for those who could not work, the first people to have responsibility for them were members of their family; and if there were none, or if they could not meet those responsibilities, then the local community, the parish, was to help. People who came from outside the parish were not entitled to receive help, and would be sent back to their own areas. There was also a distinction between those who deserved help, called the 'impotent poor' (young children, older people, people who were sick or disabled), and those who did not, the 'able-bodied'. Most who got help received it in the forms of food and small sums of money (a 'dole') to support them in their own homes. This was called outdoor relief, but there was also indoor relief, the poorhouse for the deserving poor and the workhouse for those considered able to work. Even so, and especially in times of economic hardship, most would receive outdoor relief.

By the beginning of the nineteenth century, there was growing concern about the cost and effects of the Poor Law, and a Royal Commission was set up in 1832 to investigate what could be done – in our terminology, how the system could be modernised. The 1834 Act aimed to end outdoor relief for able-bodied men and their families, and sharpened the distinction between the deserving and undeserving poor (in terms we might use, it raised the eligibility criteria). The expectation was that all but the extremely needy would work. If they could not support themselves on the outside, they would have to go into the workhouse, where the old and sick would receive care but others would be made to work for their keep. The 1834 Act introduced the notion of 'less eligibility', which meant that conditions in the workhouse were designed to be so undesirable that no one would choose to go unless they absolutely could not avoid it. In this way, it was thought, only the most desperate would claim relief. In reality, there was considerable opposition to the Act and it was implemented differently across the country. In some places it was enforced rigidly, but outdoor relief was never ended. It continued to be used for the majority of people who needed help (including the able-bodied, who were made to work for it).

The state, via the Poor Law, was not the only source of help (and control). There was a growing number of charities in the Victorian era, and also the growth of working-class self-help organisations. Help from charities involved home visiting by charitable visitors, often upper- and middle-class women, to assess need and monitor behaviour. Supplies and money were given in return for living a responsible life (e.g. not drinking, caring for the children, working). The practice and underlying principles here, of visiting, assessment and material assistance in return for responsible behaviour, were characteristic of the nineteenth-century middle-class phil-anthropy movement, and mark the beginnings of casework techniques and professional social work. But help was not only 'top-down': there were also self-help organisations such as friendly societies (to encourage saving and give money to their members in times of trouble), the Cooperative movement, trade unions and the beginnings of the Labour Party. (For the historical background, see Powell, 2001; Fraser, 2003; Harris, 2004; Cree and Myers, 2008; Harris, 2008.)

The fearful image of the workhouse and the shame associated with having to go 'on the parish' were deeply scarred into the consciousness of working people, as was the shame of receiving charity, and resentment at the intrusive and patronising conditions that went with it. The National Assistance Act of 1948 finally ended the Poor Law by transferring responsibility for financial assistance to central government, and separating it from accommodation and residential care (which were local authority responsibilities). Given that it ended only in 1948, it is sobering to realise that even now there are many people alive for whom the Poor Law is not distant history, but living memory.

limited entitlements to state assistance, and that (except for exceptional circumstances) asylum seekers should be made to return to their own countries rather than stay in the UK.

In this context, then, we can look again at the government's outcomes for children and for adults. It is easy to see the importance of responsibility and the economy. For children and young people, there is a strong theme of being prepared for work, and to behave responsibly (Williams, 2004: 412, calls it 'a rather dreary vision of childhood'). For adults, the emphasis on independence can sound like 'you *must* take more responsibility', and there is a priority on getting more people into paid employment. This is not to say that the goals are always wrong, but it is to point out that they are not straightforward, and they are not just about people's welfare.

A good example of the ambiguities of welfare, responsibility and the economy is the 'Be healthy' outcome for children, which includes reducing the rates of childhood obesity (emphasised in *The Children's Plan*: DCSF, 2007). Of course, this is important for children's health, and parents have a responsibility in that. But it is also important not to see it all as a matter of individual and family responsibility. In wealthy countries, rates of obesity are closely linked with social class, with people

Chapter 5

from lower socio-economic groups much more likely to be overweight (Wilkinson and Pickett, 2009). Obesity is a condition of poverty and inequality, themes that we discuss in more detail in Chapter 5. This suggests it is not simply a matter of individual choice, but that there are wider social forces at play (and in some cases, there will be specific medical causes). So, we should not underestimate the difficulties that some children and adults have in keeping to a healthy diet, including affording it, or the limited opportunities that some families have for more active lifestyles (lack of suitable, nearby facilities, lack of encouragement and support, lack of money for equipment and fees). We also have to consider the persuasive marketing of unhealthy options – but that gets into the economic sphere. Businesses may oppose restrictions and governments might be unwilling to enforce them. It is easier for governments to tell poor individuals how to behave than to confront big business. And while it is in children's interests to be healthy, it is also in the state's, by keeping future medical costs down – so we are reminded that social policy is not only for the recipients of the services, but for society more generally.

Services and organisations

So, with which social services is social policy concerned? Traditionally, it has been the 'big five' that made up the core of the British welfare state after the Second World War: health, education, housing, income maintenance (also called 'social security' – pensions, unemployment and disability benefits, child benefit), and the personal social services. The key elements of the post-war welfare state are summarised in Box 2.3. Newer approaches to social policy add other services, such as criminal justice, transport, leisure and the environment, and emphasise the importance of a coordinated approach to tackle disadvantage and social exclusion. Although the focus of social policy is often the role of the state, modern approaches also combine this with a wider look at the roles of international bodies, voluntary organisations and even businesses. The following discussion looks at the primary themes and debates about the main social services, highlighting their relevance for contemporary social work.

Box 2.3 The Beveridge report (1942)

The principles of the post-war welfare state were laid out in the Report of the Inter-Departmental Committee on Social Insurance and the Allied Services, published in 1942. Known as the Beveridge report, after William Beveridge, who chaired the committee and wrote the report, it aimed to tackle the five 'giants' of want (poverty), ignorance, idleness, disease and squalor. The report was undoubtedly important, but not completely revolutionary: it built on existing services and developments, especially the reforms of the Liberal government before the First World War (including the first state old age pension and national insurance for ill health and unemployment). In the context of its own era, it aimed to strike a balance between the three imperatives of welfare, responsibility and the economy.

To tackle want, the national insurance system would be improved, and there would be a safety net of national assistance, the income support of its day, funded out of general taxation – but

---

benefits were to be paid at subsistence levels, to make sure that there was an incentive for those who could work to do so (see Box 3.1 for more on the difference between insurance and assistance approaches). To tackle idleness and help people exercise proper responsibility for themselves and their family, labour exchanges (which Beveridge had helped create in 1909) would help them find work. This service was aimed at men: Beveridge's vision assumed full male employment, with women staying at home to look after the family. To tackle ignorance, there would be an expanded state education system; to tackle disease, a national health service; and to tackle squalor, good-quality housing to be rented from local authorities. The personal social services did not feature in this model, but came to have a role as a residual service for those whose needs were not adequately

met by the main services. Their work expanded greatly in the twenty years after the Second World War, but was under-resourced and spread across many local authority departments. When the Seebohm committee was set up in 1965, its task was to review this situation (see Box 1.1).

Health

Looking at health, the traditional focus in the UK has been the working of the National Health Service (NHS). All the major political parties in the UK claim to be the best defenders of the NHS, committed to it but also resolved to reform and improve it. They all claim that they will preserve the principle that health care should be (largely) free at the point of need, paid for out of general taxation rather than individuals having to pay directly to get a service. Despite the political and public popularity of the NHS, there are often complaints about its inefficiency, high costs, long waiting lists for treatment, and poor hygiene in hospitals. Such criticisms have led to frequent organisational changes and restructurings in the drive to deliver services more effectively and economically.

Yet, for all the political, professional and public attention paid to the NHS, it has had relatively little impact on the health of the nation or on average life expectancy. The major impact on these is from clean water and good sanitation, adequate diet, decent housing and healthy lifestyles. And despite sixty years of the NHS, with free access for all, striking health inequalities continue. The greatest determinant

of a person's health and longevity continues to be their wealth (or lack of it). People in the lower socio-economic groups are more likely than those in the higher groups to die sooner, and to spend longer in poor health. Health inequalities are discussed further in Chapter 5.

There are two important links with social work. The first concerns inter-professional working. Social workers regularly work with such health professionals as health visitors, community nurses, general practitioners and hospital consultants. Sometimes this may be relatively distant contact, simply making a referral or obtaining information, but sometimes it can involve close collaboration (working together on a case where children are at risk, or where a mental health patient is discharged into the community). The opportunities and challenges of inter-professional working are discussed in more depth in Chapter 7.

The second area of overlap concerns community care services and brings major challenges for relations between social work and health organisations. There are often tensions about which service should be responsible for meeting a particular person's needs, whether they should be considered primarily health needs or social care needs. The decision on this issue has implications for the workload of the different services, and profound consequences for the individual and his/her family. This is because health care services are free at the point of need, whereas social care is usually charged to the service user, subject to means-testing. The term 'social care', in this context, includes aspects of personal care, such as bathing, going to the toilet, dressing and eating (DH, 2000). The distinction between health needs and

social care needs can be hard to draw and often appears arbitrary, but the consequences of falling one side rather than the other can be financially devastating. In contrast to England and Wales, personal care for older people in Scotland is not subject to means-testing. The funding of social care is considered further in Chapter 9.

Education

The second of the traditional social services is education. Here, policies and debates have often focused on the standards of work produced by school pupils (are they getting better or worse? Which groups are doing better or worse?); how best to ensure improvements; and on the best ways to organise and fund schools (e.g. how much control should come from central government, local government? How

much autonomy should schools have?). Yet, despite all the attention and money spent on state education, there is still a striking pattern that children from higher socio-economic groups achieve markedly better grades than those from the lower groups (discussed further in Chapter 5).

In England, the *Every Child Matters* programme (see Box 2.1) has brought closer organisational links between education and children's social work. They have been combined into 'children's services departments' at local government level, and into a new central government department of Children, Schools and Families (DCSF).

Whatever the organisational arrangements, there are still significant challenges for practice. Social workers will need to liaise closely with teachers to ensure the wellbeing of children who are in need or at risk of significant harm. They may be working with children who are 'looked after' by the local authority (usually in foster or residential care), and there is a specific legal duty to ensure the educational progress of these children (Children Act 1989, s. 22(3A)). The poor educational achievement of looked after children has long been a cause of political and professional concern (DfES, 2007; House of Commons CSFC, 2009), although most would have had considerable needs before they entered care.

Chapter 7

Some of the children will present very great challenges to the teachers and support staff, or not be able to cope in a mainstream school. Effective inter-professional practice in such circumstances can be very demanding (see Chapter 7).

Housing

The balance between public and private provision is very different in housing compared to education and health. Whereas the majority of the population relies on the NHS and state schools, only a minority of households in England (under 20 per cent) lives in 'social housing' (that is, rented from local authorities or housing associations). The majority of the population meet (or attempt to meet) their housing needs through the market, by buying or privately renting their own home (about 70 per cent of households are owner-occupied, and another 13 per cent rent privately: NCSR, 2008: 11).

Major issues at the moment are the need to increase the supply of affordable homes and access to finance (mortgages) for people to buy them, and to ensure that there is sufficient housing that is suitable for an ageing population. The current strategy on this is called *Lifetime Homes, Lifetime Neighbourhoods* (CLG, 2008d), which makes the point that people's housing needs are not just about the buildings they live in, but require good local services and safe, supportive communities (CLG, 2008c).

Housing has important implications for social work policy and practice. Families may be living in poor-quality accommodation – damp, cold, insecure, noisy – affecting their physical and mental health. Social workers in adult services are likely to be involved in assessing whether people who have become frail or disabled are able to remain in, or return to, their own homes. They may recommend services and adaptations, and good links between housing, health and social services are essential if people are to be helped to stay at home safely and comfortably. Children's services social workers are likely to come across families who are in housing need because they have left their home to escape domestic violence. Social workers will also be working with other groups of people with particular housing needs, such as care leavers, ex-prisoners, vulnerable young mothers, and people with mental health problems. Services may be delivered via a government programme for housing-related support, called Supporting People, established in 2003 (www.spkweb.org.uk; CLG, 2007).

Social workers may also come across service users who complain about others getting preferential treatment for social housing – young single mothers or refugee families are often the objects of such resentment. Community care plans for people with mental health problems or learning disabilities may sometimes provoke opposition from local residents. The typical line that people use is that they are happy to support community care in general, but just not these people here, a phenomenon sometimes referred to as 'nimby-ism' – 'not in my back yard'.

Income maintenance and employment

The general expectation in capitalist societies is that most people maintain their own incomes, through working and saving. However, some people have low-paid jobs that do not cover all their needs, especially if they have children; others are retired, and may never have earned enough money to have a significant pension or savings; some may be ill or disabled, and unable to work; others may be caring for children or other relatives, and not able to work. Some may live in areas where there are not enough jobs. So individual responsibility and marketplace provision are not always enough, and the state has taken on a role in income maintenance.

Current government policy stresses the importance of reducing people's reliance on state benefits, and getting claimants back into work. A good indication of this is that in 2001 the Department of Social Security, responsible for welfare payments, was merged with the Department for Employment, becoming the Department for Work and Pensions. The clear message is that the two aspects go hand-in-hand. Another example is the change of incapacity benefit to employment and support allowance in October 2008, with an expectation that most of those who receive the new allowance will be required 'to take steps to prepare for work'. The only exceptions will be those with severe illness or disability. The government promises a new approach that looks at what people can do rather than what they cannot, with 'personalised support' to help people find and take up work. The main themes are summarised in Box 2.4.

Box 2.4 Welfare reform and personalisation

The government published a white paper on welfare reform in December 2008, entitled *Raising Expectations and Increasing Support: Reforming Welfare for the Future* (DWP, 2008). It makes much of a personalised approach to helping and requiring people to get back into work, using the phrases 'personalised conditionality' and 'personalised support'. It speaks of 'more support matched by higher expectations . . . a decisive step towards a personalised welfare state, where a simpler benefits system underpins the expectation that nearly everyone on benefits is preparing or looking for work' (para. 45).

It has always been the case that receipt of benefits has been dependent on people fulfilling certain conditions, which for those considered able to work (our equivalent of the 'able-bodied') means being ready to start a job, and taking active steps to find one. The new approach seeks to extend the nature of this conditionality, to require many more people to prepare for employment by having a 'back-to-work plan' to improve skills and tackle problems such as debt and drugs (para. 26). The government is considering this for lone parents with children as young as three (para. 29).

> The white paper talks of 'a clear bargain that almost everyone on benefits would be expected to take active steps towards work, but where those expectations are based on an individual's needs and circumstances' (para. 26). It promises 'encouragement and support' from personal advisers but it is clear that the support entails monitoring and enforcement – the white paper threatens 'sanction escalation' for those who do not comply (para. 27).

Linked with this welfare to work approach are other strategies to make work pay, such as the national minimum wage, introduced in 1999, and financial support for low-income families through tax credits, administered by the Inland Revenue. From 1997 to 2008, the booming economy made welfare to work a feasible policy direction for New Labour, because there were jobs to be had. The difficult economic situation since 2008 makes this objective harder to achieve.

Like other aspects of social policy, income maintenance policies and payments raise challenging practical questions and, behind them, profound moral dilemmas. Practical questions include how to avoid unemployment and poverty traps. These arise because benefits are withdrawn as people move into work or better-paid jobs; but the risk is that the loss of benefits can be too rapid, making it not worthwhile financially for people to take a job or increase their pay. This is more than an issue of fine-tuning. Underneath it, there are deeper questions about the purposes of cash benefits and tax credits: are they primarily intended just to alleviate immediate poverty, or do they have a bigger purpose, a more significant redistribution of wealth from the richer to the poorer? Is it better if payments are pitched rather low, in order to 'encourage' people to look for work (an echo of the old Poor Law)? But if so, how is this to be balanced against the welfare of those people and their families – for example, why should their children suffer from living in poverty? Are claimants properly seen as citizens with choices and entitlements, or potential scroungers who need to be carefully monitored and disciplined, if necessary forced back into employment and a more responsible lifestyle?

Social workers encounter people living in poverty all the time – it is the most common factor affecting the service users with whom they work. Despite this, social workers in the UK have traditionally been reluctant to take on tasks associated with income maintenance, such as assessing people for welfare benefits. However, the financial aspects of social work practice have become increasingly important since the 1990s. Adult care social workers are regularly required to assess people's income and savings when arranging domiciliary, day or residential care. The growth of direct payments and individual budgets for service users and carers makes the financial aspects of social work even more prominent, no longer just in terms of complying with the organisation's budgets and financial procedures, but now in working with service users, helping and supporting them in their decisions about how to spend their money. These issues are discussed further in Chapters 6 and 9.

Chapters 6 and 9

Broader approaches

So far we have discussed the traditional social services, but what about the many other issues that affect people's physical, intellectual and emotional wellbeing, and the services that deal with them? Law and order is an obvious example – what about crime rates and ways of reducing offending? The roles of the police, courts and prisons? Modern approaches to social policy will include these too, because of their importance for social life and people's wellbeing. The law and order field has itself been widened over the last decade, with the government focusing on tackling antisocial behaviour as well as criminal offending. The boundary between the two is porous, however, because although an antisocial behaviour order (ASBO) is made in the civil courts, a breach of the order is a criminal matter.

Immigration is another important aspect of social policy today, given widespread media coverage and political concern about the numbers of people coming into the UK. Some welcome the incomers as a boost to the labour force, or stress our moral duties to offer safety to refugees; others voice concerns about the effects on employment and wages, and the extra demands on public services such as education, health, housing and social services. Services for unaccompanied asylum-seeking children and young people are now a significant responsibility for local authority children's services departments.

Transport policies are important too, for individuals, families and businesses. Public transport can be expensive and unreliable, but a car is beyond the means of the poorest families, who are therefore at risk of becoming further excluded from mainstream society. Poor public transport is a particular problem for those who live in remote rural areas, with implications for social care, such as the cost of providing home care services (Manthorpe and Stevens, 2008).

Environmental policy is another new social policy issue, as public and political awareness has risen about global warming, pollution and the degradation of the world's natural resources. This is a good example of the wider perspective on welfare – that it is not just about the neediest individuals and families, but about communities and even the world's population as a whole.

Chapters 8 and 4

Another new element is to look at the role of other organisations, above and below the state. Above the state, there are international bodies such as the European Union, discussed in Chapter 8; and the United Nations, with its international human rights treaties, discussed further in Chapter 4. Below the state, there are all the specialist groups and charities that provide services and campaign on behalf of particular service user groups.

As well as the wider range of issues, newer approaches to social policy emphasise a new style of policy-making, less top-down, in which service users and/or their representatives have a larger say in how services are designed and delivered, and in which service users' rights and abilities are to the fore, not just their needs. Patients, parents, pupils, tenants and social care service users are encouraged to give their views about the services they receive, and to sit on committees to review and plan services. The situation for people who receive unemployment benefits reveals some of the ambiguities about participation and personalisation. Although there are organisations such as claimants unions which press for their voice to be heard at policy as well as individual level, on the whole their position is weak. They are supposed to receive personalised support, taking account of their abilities as well as their needs, but ultimately they are expected to comply with what is required of them (see Chapter 6 for more about participation).

Social exclusion

All the themes discussed so far, about the multiple objectives of social policy, coordination of the wide range of services, the focus on the wellbeing of society as well as individuals and families, and the involvement of service users and communities, come together in the policy drive to reduce social exclusion. The government has defined social exclusion as 'a short-hand label for what can happen when individuals or areas suffer from a combination of linked problems such as unemployment, poor skills, low incomes, poor housing, high crime environments, bad health and family breakdown' (DSS, 1999: 23).

The government established the Social Exclusion Unit (SEU) in England 1997 to raise the profile of the issue and coordinate policy between central government departments, and between central government, local authorities, the third sector and private organisations. It was relaunched as the Social Exclusion Task Force (SETF) in 2006. Over the years it has commissioned research and published numerous reports and policy proposals. A sample of topics are teenage pregnancy (SEU, 1999), education for children in care (SEU, 2003), mental health (SEU, 2004) and older people (SEU, 2006). With the launch of the SETF in 2006, the government published *Reaching Out: An Action Plan on Social Exclusion*, which claimed general success for the earlier programmes but now aimed to tackle the 'persistent and deep seated exclusion' of the 'small minority' whose needs had not been met by the existing strategies (HM Government, 2006: para. 1.3). In March 2007 it launched a review of the needs of 'families at risk', which published its final report in January 2008, entitled *Think Family: Improving the Life Chances of Families at Risk* (SETF, 2008).

The report defines 'families at risk' as 'a shorthand term for families with multiple and complex problems such as worklessness, poor mental health and substance abuse' (p. 4). It is intriguing that it does not include the word 'poverty'; but that aside, this sounds like the sorts of families that social workers are used to working with. The report emphasises four key characteristics of a system that 'thinks family', which strongly echo the themes of the Seebohm report, of preventive work, integrated services and a holistic view of families' situations – yet the term 'social work' is not used at all, and 'social worker' only once. This reflects the way that social work has been marginalised in

many current social policy programmes, at the same time as its key principles and skills are more valued than for many years – principles of personal support, encouraging independence, relationship-based work, inter-professional cooperation (Jordan with Jordan, 2000; Jordan, 2004; McLaughlin, 2008; Parton, 2009). This paradox is a theme I explore throughout the book, especially in Chapters 7 and 8.

The main points of *Reaching Out* and *Think Family* are summarised in Box 2.5. They exemplify the themes of prevention and partnership working, and the ambiguities of personalisation, with its mixture of encouragement and enforcement, support and sanctions.

Box 2.5 Tackling social exclusion

Five 'guiding principles' in *Reaching Out: An Action Plan on Social Exclusion* (HM Government, 2006)

- Better identification of those at risk and earlier intervention.

- Systematically identifying 'what works' and disseminating the results.

- Promoting multi-agency working under local area agreements, and improved information sharing.

- Personalisation, rights and responsibilities – 'tailored programmes of support built around strong and persistent relationships with those at risk'.

- Supporting achievement and managing underperformance – greater freedoms for effective providers and stronger intervention for weak authorities.

Four 'key characteristics' in *Think Family: Improving the Life Chances of Families at Risk* (SETF, 2008)

Chapter 2 of the report says that a system that 'thinks family' will:

- *Have no wrong door*: that is, staff will always be open to identify needs and risks early, to see the wide range of factors, and refer people to other agencies as appropriate.

- *Look at the whole family*: that is, adult services will recognise the needs of their service users as parents, and seek to support them in that role. Services will give consistent messages and work towards the same outcomes.

- *Build on family strengths*: that is, work in partnership with families, empowering them, supporting them to take responsibility for their own lives.

- *Provide support tailored to need*. It gives two examples of what it means by this:

    - Family Nurse Partnerships are preventive programmes aimed at the most at-risk families. A dedicated family nurse works with the family from early pregnancy until the child is two years old, building up the parents' confidence and skills.

- Family Intervention Projects are aimed at families whose antisocial behaviour is causing serious problems in the community and placing them at risk of eviction. There is a dedicated key worker whose role is to 'get a grip' on the whole situation – the family, the problems and the various agencies involved. The projects combine intensive support with 'focused challenge'. There are clear expectations about the required changes, including sanctions for non-compliance. Workers need to show 'persistence and assertiveness' in order to engage these very challenging families and help them turn around their behaviour.

Conclusion

This chapter has approached the question 'What is social policy about?' by looking at outcomes and objectives and the range of services involved. I hope the discussion has sharpened the dilemmas of what, and who, social policy is for. How much is it about welfare, or making people responsible, or the economy? How much about empowerment, and how much about control? How much for individuals, and how much for society as a whole? And especially, what are we to make of the new language of 'personalisation'? In the context of welfare reforms and social exclusion, it seems an exceptionally ambiguous term, offering not just help but very tight control – control on a personalised basis.

One of the key points about social policy is that there are no simple answers to such questions. The answers are usually 'both/and', rather than 'either/or'. There are too many contradictory imperatives, interweaving arguments, potential drawbacks to every initiative, unanticipated consequences, for any simple answer to be convincing. One has to think in terms of tensions and balances, and ongoing, fluid dynamics rather than any static state of affairs.

Questions for reflection

- Identify some of the problems to do with health, education, housing, income and employment that people receiving a social work service may have. To what extent are their difficulties the result of wider circumstances beyond their control, the attitudes of others, the shortcomings of service provision, or their own choices? What could a social worker do?

- Review the material about personalisation in welfare reform and social exclusion. What do you think the lessons might be for social work and social care?

- Think about services and programmes for a service user group you are especially interested in. Use the social policy triangle to identify the balances between welfare, responsibility and the economy.

Useful website and further reading

The websites of the major government departments and regulatory agencies that cover social services (in the broad sense) are the best places to look for current policy documents and reports: see Chapter 8, Boxes 8.1, 8.2 and 8.3 for details. Most reports have an executive summary which gives the main findings and recommendations in an easily digestible form, but to pursue the topics in detail you will need to go into the body of the reports, and read more widely – other research, textbooks and academic journals.

For independent research and comment on social policies in the UK, the leading organisation is probably the Joseph Rowntree Foundation (JRF). It has special interests in income maintenance, social exclusion and housing. Its website is an unbeatable source of information and ideas: www.jrf.org.uk.

The King's Fund is a very good source of information about health policy, including links with social care: www.kingsfund.org.uk.

Paul Spicker's Introduction to Social Policy website has clear explanations of the main issues and concepts: www2.rgu.ac.uk/publicpolicy/introduction.

There is a large number of general textbooks on social policy. Often they have separate chapters on topics directly relevant to social work, but even chapters that are less obviously relevant can offer useful insights and spark off ideas for understanding social work in its broader social policy context. Recommended books are:

Baldock *et al.* (2007) *Social Policy*, 3rd edn.

Blakemore and Griggs (2007) *Social Policy: An Introduction*, 3rd edn.

P. Alcock *et al.* (2008) *The Student's Companion to Social Policy*, 3rd edn.

C. Alcock *et al.* (2008) *Introducing Social Policy*, 2nd edn.

Bochel *et al.* (2009) *Social Policy*, 2nd edn.

Hill and Irving (2009) *Understanding Social Policy*, 8th edn.

Also, the issues come up all the time in the news and in political debates. Get used to following them – the *Today* programme on Radio 4 and the *Guardian* newspaper are great places to start.

3 The role of the state

This chapter looks more closely at different views about the role of the state in providing welfare in capitalist societies, and pulls out the implications for social work. The key questions are: 'What can the state do?' and 'What should the state do?' The chapter outlines a model with four broad approaches to these fundamental questions. Another term that is often used for these categories is 'welfare regimes' (Esping-Andersen, 1990). They are models in their own right, but parts of a bigger model about the role of the state. Each of the four models encapsulates different ideas about the proper powers and responsibilities of the state in balancing the three points of the social policy triangle – the meeting of people's welfare needs, the smooth working of the capitalist economy and the helping, or obliging, of people to take responsibility for their own and their family's wellbeing. Each of the four positions has deep-rooted historical antecedents and the key themes tend to come round repeatedly in social policy writing, with different terminology and labels.

The first three approaches all seek to maintain the capitalist economy, although with different levels and forms of state intervention. I have called these the minimalist, integrationist and social democratic models (drawing on Titmuss, 1974; Esping-Andersen, 1990; Hardiker et al., 1991; Levitas, 1998). The fourth position is rather different in that it seeks the overthrow of the capitalist economy and capitalist-based social welfare systems; I call this the radical perspective.

Of course, these are models and so should be considered caricatures or exaggerations, not descriptions. They do not exist anywhere in their pure form, although some countries are nearer to one model than the others. The United States of America is often seen as the epitome of the minimalist approach; Germany and France as examples of the integrationist model; and the Scandinavian countries as typical of the social democratic approach. However, within each country there are different political, professional and public views about how services should be run, and in any country the reality is an amalgam of competing trends and priorities. Indeed, the beliefs of individuals are likely to be a mixture of the ideas. The overlaps and ambiguities between the approaches are just as important as the differences, if we are to understand how some social policies come to be popular.

Four welfare approaches

Chapters 1 and 2

Table 3.1 summarises the characteristics of each approach. As we explore them in more detail, the ideas will link back with themes that we have discussed in Chapters 1 and 2. Later in the chapter, we shall focus on the implications for the roles and tasks of social work, and consider policy blurring and equivocation.

The minimalist state

The minimalist approach has its roots in the political philosophy of libertarianism, from the eighteenth and nineteenth centuries, which held that the greatest social value was individual freedom. The state should intervene in social and economic life only when absolutely necessary to safeguard the liberties of individuals – for example, to protect private property, to uphold law and order, to defend the nation from attack. Otherwise, it is for individuals to decide how to live their lives, how to spend their money, and for businesses to supply the right sorts of services and goods to meet their needs. People can then choose what services and goods to buy according to their own resources and preferences. Businesses that meet those needs and wishes at the right price will flourish; those that do not will lose money and eventually go out of business. The state's approach is non-interventionist, *laissez faire*, 'let it be'. A key point about this approach is that while the state takes a non-interventionist approach most of the time, when laws are broken it tends to take a hard-line, punitive approach. In order to protect the liberties of the law-abiding majority, and to enforce socially responsible behaviour, it stamps down hard on transgressors. The catchphrase is 'small state, strong state'.

Welfare needs are best met in exactly the same way, not by the state but by individuals and families, who are responsible for their own welfare, and by businesses (e.g. private health care, private schools, private pensions). The main way of obtaining welfare services is to buy them, and the state will have very minimal, basic services for those who cannot afford to do so. Esping-Andersen (1990) calls this a 'liberal' or 'neo-liberal' approach. Titmuss (1974) and Hardiker *et al.* (1991) use the term 'residual'. It is certainly true that the minimalist welfare state tends to offer very poor services to those in need, but it is also necessary to remember that some important principles lie behind the approach. A prime

Chapter 4

example is the idea that the state should not be allowed to intervene in people's private and family lives without good cause (European Convention on Human Rights, Article 8: see Chapter 4), a concept that many would agree with, even if they do not accept the extremes of the minimalist approach.

Table 3.1
The state and welfare

	Minimalist	Integrationist	Social democratic	Radical
Core value	Liberty	Stability	Equality	Transformation
State and society	Laissez faire – belief in individual freedom and the 'market place'. 'Small state, strong state'.	State's role to uphold the status quo but mitigate worst effects of capitalism. 'Social stability'.	Active role for state in ensuring welfare of all citizens. 'Democratic socialism'.	A critical view – state serves the interests of capitalism, but can also challenge it.
State's role in welfare	Minimal – individuals and families should provide and/or purchase.	Significant but limited – collaborates with private and voluntary sectors.	Positive role in planning and providing services, for high quality and equality.	Even greater role for state, to create equality; but state is part of the problem, too.
Approach to social problems	Failings of individuals, families or communities.	Failings of individuals or families, or welfare system failings.	Problems caused by inequalities of power and resources.	Structural causes such as class, race and gender; but state welfare is also seen to mask these differences.
Welfare benefits	'Safety net', means-testing.	Insurance-based, preserving differentials.	Taxation-based, redistributive.	Greater redistribution, current system a con.
Role and functions of social work	Rescue and control.	Treatment and reintegration.	Partnership and empowerment.	Advocacy, adversarial, consciousness-raising.

Charities and other voluntary organisations are also important in this model, to supply or subsidise services for those who cannot afford to purchase them at the market price from private suppliers. However, the state does not take a particularly active role in supporting charities. It welcomes them, but it is for individuals to give their money direct to the charities they support, not for the state to take money away from people through taxation and then redistribute it to charities. The state may give tax allowances on donations to charities (to encourage private giving), but would avoid getting involved in deciding what charities do or how – that's for them.

Although families, businesses and charities are the main sources of welfare support and services, there is recognition that there will be some people for whom this is not enough – those with very great needs, few personal and financial resources, no family or friends. For these people, the state provides a safety net – very basic services, the minimum to meet essential needs, but not so generous or comfortable that they undermine individual responsibility or mean that taxes have to rise too high. So, for example, there might be state hospitals, but they would not be as well equipped as private hospitals, and patients might have to wait longer for their treatment. There might be some basic financial welfare benefits, but they will be only a very modest amount of money, and will involve stringent eligibility criteria to distinguish between the genuinely needy and the 'undeserving'. People of working age who are healthy and able to work would be required to do so rather than receive benefits (an echo of the Poor Law). Decisions about entitlement would also involve means-testing to assess the level of income and savings held by a claimant. They would be required to use them up first, before they are eligible for state assistance.

Under this minimalist approach, social problems (for example, drug misuse, crime, poverty) are attributed to moral weaknesses in the individuals, families or communities that have them – so there are problem individuals, problem families, problem neighbourhoods. The wider social and economic system is not to blame, because capitalism and individual liberty are prized social values. On the whole there is a mistrust and dislike of the poor, who are seen as a 'moral underclass' (Murray, 1990). Levitas (1998) identifies three different approaches to social inclusion, and one of them, the 'moral underclass discourse' (MUD) fits here, in this minimalist model. The socially excluded are excluded, in a sense, by themselves, because they cut themselves off from mainstream society by their own behaviour and their refusal to accept mainstream social values of employment, saving, marriage. The state's primary role is to protect mainstream society from them. It does also have a role to bring them back into mainstream life, but it does so through a punitive approach – sending offenders to prison to teach them to obey the law, withholding unemployment benefits to make people go to work. Of course, some people are the deserving poor – for example, people who are victims of unforeseeable accidents – but even they should be encouraged to 'stand on their own two feet', to 'pull themselves up by their bootstraps'.

In terms of the social policy triangle, the emphasis falls on individual and family responsibility. If only individuals can be made responsible, they will work hard, which will contribute to economic prosperity, and they will provide for their own and their family's welfare.

46

The integrationist state

The second approach sees a greater role for the state in social and economic life. The primary value now is not liberty, but rather social stability and cohesion. There is an emphasis on working actively with the private and voluntary sectors to meet people's needs, but within the limits of current social norms – there is no question of radical social change, it is more a matter of mitigating the worst effects of capitalism. This approach has its roots in the philosophical tradition of utilitarianism – the greatest happiness for the greatest number. The overall objective is the smooth running of society as a whole ('the greatest number'); if that means that some individuals lose out in certain ways, so be it. An example is that individuals might lose out financially, by having limited welfare benefits, if that is what the economy and social stability are deemed to require.

Esping-Andersen (1990) calls this approach 'conservative corporatist', which conveys the sense of the state working with businesses and charities (corporatism) to maintain current social and economic structures (conservatism). Titmuss (1974: 31) labels it the 'industrial achievement-performance' model, and sees it as 'the handmaiden of the economy'. By this he focuses attention on the way that it prioritises the working of the economy (industrial achievement) and the way that, while seeking to assist individuals in need, it also aims to preserve the differentials between those who perform well in the economy and those who do not. Hardiker *et al.* (1991) use the term 'institutional' for this model, capturing the way that welfare is bedded into the structures and functioning of society, through state, private and voluntary agencies, and through legislation, policies and established practices. It also captures the close links between different institutions (state, private and voluntary) in the provision of services. Levitas (1998) refers to a 'social integrationist discourse' (SID) – the aim is for integrated services to integrate people back into mainstream social and economic life, but not to change society. Integrationist approaches lie behind other terms, such as 'the social market economy' (the characteristic approach in Germany since the Second World War) and 'the social investment state' (Giddens, 1998; Lister, 2003).

In this model, the state has a significant but limited role in the delivery of welfare services. It cooperates with the private and voluntary sectors, and tends to take a planning, coordinating and funding role rather than the direct provision of services. The mixed economy of welfare is characteristic of the integrationist model. Social problems such as poverty, child neglect and poor educational attainment may be seen as the result of individual failings, as in the minimalist model, but may also be understood as failings of the welfare system. That is not the whole social and economic system, which this approach seeks to preserve, but specifically the ways that the welfare system works. So, when social problems like poverty, poor health or educational drop-out are identified, they may be analysed as the results of services not being delivered effectively to the neediest people. Accordingly, there is an emphasis on targeting services more accurately, on performance monitoring, on reorganising agencies to deliver services more efficiently.

Under the integrationist model, welfare benefits would be insurance based, so that those who have better-paid jobs would pay in more, but then receive higher benefits when they need them (see Box 3.1). This system therefore preserves differentials between the better-off and the poorer sections of society, and its supporters see the advantage of this being that it secures the support of the middle classes (because they benefit by it). Middle-class support is crucial for the stability of welfare systems, if they are to become firmly established, institutionalised, at the heart of society.

Box 3.1 Welfare benefits: insurance, assistance, universalism

There are three basic approaches to the state's role in organising welfare benefits. A social insurance approach is likely to appeal most to integrationists, and universalism to the social democrats. The minimalists do not really want much of a state welfare system at all, so they would back a minimal version of social assistance. In reality, a national system is likely to contain elements of all three, but the balances between them give a clue to which approach is dominant.

In the social insurance approach, people pay a percentage of their income when they are working, as a contribution to a state-run fund. Their employers pay in a percentage of the employee's salary as well. Then, when the person meets the relevant criteria, such as old age, unemployment or sickness, they will be *entitled* to a payment if they have paid enough contributions. The payment is not based on how badly they need the money, but on their entitlement. State pensions in the UK are a prime example. Integrationists like it because it preserves social differentials and rewards those who have worked hard. Minimalists tolerate it, but would prefer people to take private insurance and pensions rather than have such a large state machinery. Social democrats like the entitlement aspect, but point out that many will not qualify for insurance-related benefits through no fault of their own. Some will not have paid enough contributions (say, they have not worked long enough), or the level of payment to which they are entitled is insufficient to meet their needs (perhaps because they have a large family or special health requirements).

The second basic approach is called social assistance. Here, people in difficulties may be able to get a payment from the state, but this will be based on an *assessment of need* rather than entitlement; and the assessment is likely to include a *means-test*, that is to say an assessment of their financial circumstances. The person's income and savings (and often the income and savings of family members) will be taken into account, and they will be expected to use these first, before receiving a payment from the state. People who do not qualify for insurance-based benefits will have to turn to assistance. Income support is the prime example in the UK. Social assistance is funded out of general taxation. Strict rules about eligibility and low-level payments are characteristic of a minimalist state. The other approaches would have assistance-based schemes too, but with less harsh conditions.

A social democratic approach, though, would try to avoid means-testing because of its stigma and perverse effects (e.g. poverty traps as benefits are withdrawn when people's income increases). Instead, its preference is for universal benefits, to be paid out of general taxation to everyone who has the need, regardless of contributions or means. In the UK, child benefit and attendance allowance are examples. Universal benefits are expensive, but the money is recouped from the better-off by higher rates of income tax.

The insurance/assistance/universalism distinction is a model and the picture can be rather murky in reality because of the mixture of elements in a national system. Still, it is a handy framework for making sense of the range of payments and the underlying principles; and, of course, means and needs tests are very familiar to social workers, who are often required to use these when assessing a person's eligibility for social care services.

In terms of the social policy triangle, the emphasis in the integrationist model falls on the economy. The state cooperates with businesses to provide opportunities for them to supply welfare services, and make a profit out of it. Public–private partnerships and private finance initiatives are emblematic of this approach. If the capitalist economy does run into difficulties, say people are made redundant, the integrationist state would see its role to help people get back into work, through retraining and support, although private and voluntary organisations might be commissioned to provide these services. It aims to integrate people back into the world of work, because that is the best way to ensure that they can provide for their own and their family's welfare. (The minimalist state values work too, of course, but the difference is that the integrationist state plays a more active role in trying to help people into employment.) By preserving differentials in the payment of welfare benefits, it further confirms the benefits of employment and economic success.

The social democratic state

The key value for the social democratic welfare state is equality, with its roots in the philosophical traditions of egalitarianism and moderate forms of socialism. It sees an active role for the state in ensuring that all citizens receive high-quality welfare services. Welfare is at the heart of the state's role in society, and the objective is to raise the quality of life for all citizens, not just the obviously needy. There is a positive view about what the state can do and should do, and the state plays a major role in planning and providing services. State-run services are not seen as a residual, safety net provision for inadequate people, but as services for all, promoting equality and offering high standards. The state's role is not just to prevent difficulties arising (e.g. through targeted services), but to create opportunities and wellbeing for everyone, through universal services. When social problems do arise, these are understood not primarily as personal failings or welfare system failings, but resulting from wider inequalities of power and resources. So, the state will use taxation to redistribute wealth and create opportunities, by funding high-quality welfare services and fully sufficient benefits. There would be greater expenditure on state social services such as education, health and income maintenance, and a positive view about personal social services for those who need extra help.

Titmuss (1974) refers to this approach as the 'institutional redistributive' model, Esping-Andersen (1990) calls it 'social democratic', and Hardiker *et al.* (1991) use the term 'developmental'. Levitas (1998) describes a 'redistributionist discourse' (RED), which captures the features of this model.

In terms of the social policy triangle, the emphasis now is on welfare. The state provides welfare services not just for the needy few but for all citizens. The state can play a positive role in ensuring welfare – and by providing high-quality services for all, it creates employment and ensures a healthy and well-educated workforce. This enables people to take responsibility for themselves, but they also share a sense of social responsibility for the wellbeing of their fellow citizens.

Box 3.2 The state, parents, childcare and work

An effective illustration of how the three models would work differently in practice is to consider how they would each approach the issue of helping (or not) the parents of young children into work. The main focus here is mothers, who usually face the major challenges of balancing childcare and work, but it does not only concern women. Also, this example pushes the models to their extremes, and reality is always more mixed and ambiguous.

In a minimalist state, the answer is fairly simple, although predictably harsh: it is your responsibility; it is your child, and the state certainly is not going to pay you to stay at home and look after him/her (apart, perhaps, for a relatively short period after the child is born). Equally, we are not going to help you go to work: if you want to go, great, but you need to find a job that fits with your childcare arrangements. If you are lucky, you might have relatives who are willing to help look after your child while you are at work. If not, you will have to pay for a nursery or a childminder. If you have highly marketable skills then an employer might pay you well enough that you can purchase good-quality childcare. If not, you will have to decide what you can afford. Different providers will charge different amounts for different levels of service, and different quality of care: you have to decide. Alternatively, if a company needs more workers, then it might decide to increase wages, offer childcare vouchers, or provide a day nursery for the children of staff. The state would not interfere with these decisions. It may inspect childcare facilities and impose some basic requirements, such as health and safety aspects, but these would be at a minimal level. The belief is that the most effective regulation comes from the market – desirable, good-value providers will flourish, while poor-quality and overpriced ones will go bust.

The integrationist state gives a different range of answers, with intriguing variations according to the needs of the economy. There is a tension between its conservatism, which leads it to support traditional family structures, and its corporatism, which leads it to support businesses. So, if the economy has no current need of extra workers, it may give allowances to mothers to encourage them to stay at home to look after their children. It may also do this if low fertility rates suggest that the population is likely to fall, and it needs to boost the number of children who are born to ensure a sufficient number of workers in the future. On the other hand, if the economy requires more workers now, an integrationist state would intervene to encourage more mothers to take jobs. It could do this by reducing state benefits for parents who stay at home, and/or by increasing support to help them go to work – for example, raising tax allowances for working parents, or giving special grants. It would also work with the private and voluntary sectors to ensure that more childcare facilities were provided. It could do this by tax breaks to encourage businesses to run nurseries, or grants to charities to set up nurseries in areas where there is a shortage. An integrationist state would register and inspect nurseries and childminders, and is likely to impose higher requirements than the minimalist state. It is also likely to offer assistance and incentives to childcare providers to improve their standards, through training or financial assistance.

The social democratic state approaches the issue in further different ways. First, as matter of equality it wants parents, particularly women, to have the opportunity to continue working and pursuing their careers when they have children. But also, the high-quality welfare services provided by the social democratic state are expensive, so it needs to have a high employment rate to generate enough taxes to pay for them: therefore, it needs to get women as well as men into work. So it has to provide more childcare, which itself creates new jobs. These would mainly be jobs for women, given that childcare work is predominantly a female occupation (although the commitment to sex equality means there is less occupational stereotyping in a social democratic regime). It would raise the status and pay of childcare work by having high standards and highly valued qualifications for staff (its approach to public service jobs in general). If more childcare is simply tacked on to an integrationist or minimalist approach, the chances are that status and pay will remain low.

The radical perspective

The fourth perspective is rather different in that it takes a critical view of the state and capitalism. It looks, ultimately, for the ending of capitalism and the transformation of society, with power and resources in the hands of working people, an end to privilege and individualism. In the meantime, on the road to that objective, it looks for a new form of state welfare. This approach has its roots in Marxism.

It is mistrustful of the state, arguing that even the social democratic model serves the interests of capitalism more than the interests of workers. The social democratic state might do it more subtly than the minimalist or integrationist states, but the end result is not so different: people are forced to conform to the *status quo*, to work (or not) according to the demands of the economy. It mistrusts social democratic rhetoric about social justice and equality, seeing it as superficial change, and is critical of its tendency towards authoritarianism. The social democratic state requires a high level of social conformity, because citizens are expected to go to work to pay taxes to fund the services. There is not much leeway for alternative lifestyles. So, the minimalist state starts with a belief in individual freedom but ends up being very harsh on those who do not comply with its norms; the integrationist state is paternalistic, forcing people into employment and back into mainstream society on its terms, not theirs; and the social democratic state starts with a commitment to equality but this also ends up underpinning social conformity rather than the freedom to be 'equal but different'.

State welfare serves the interests of capitalism, but even so, working people deserve the best services they can get, and good services can challenge capitalism. Education is an example. Why does the state provide schools and colleges? The radical position doubts whether this is because of a genuine desire to help children and adults learn and develop. It accepts that individual policy-makers and teachers may be motivated by this (it does not want to dismiss the integrity and hard work of individuals, although it does challenge careerism and inflated salaries), but it does not see the *system as a whole* as altruistic. The system provides education in order to meet the needs of the economy. Schools have a triple function in this respect. First, they teach children the skills they need to get jobs in the modern economy (competence in maths and writing, the ability to use a computer). If the economy required more manual labourers than computer operators, different skills would be emphasised and the school leaving age might be different. Second, schools act as a childminding service, so that their parents can go to work. Third, even the children who fail or drop out of school are, in a sense, being prepared for work – for unskilled, low-wage jobs (Willis, 1977). The education system labels some children as successes and others as failures, perpetuating inequality. But a radical perspective is certainly not an excuse to give up trying to raise educational standards. Working-class children are not well served by poor schools and limited educational opportunities. Good education can give young people the skills and knowledge they need to do well themselves; but, more than that, to change society. It can begin to undermine capitalism. The radical approach calls for a revitalised role for the state, actively to promote the interests of the working class, to provide high-quality services for the poorer groups in society, to redistribute wealth and power on a much greater scale than the social democratic approach envisages.

For the radicals, social problems are not the result of individual choices or moral weaknesses, but of deep-seated, structural divisions in society – class, race, gender, age and disability are the main examples. These features, rather than people's individual actions or attitudes, determine their outcomes in life. Welfare services, as they currently operate, do little if anything to redress these imbalances: indeed, they may even reinforce them, because of the tendency for the middle classes to take better advantage of social services, both as recipients and as employees. Further, state welfare can disguise the depth of these inequalities, by giving the impression that services and opportunities are open to all. Formally they may be, and some young people from poor families do go to top universities and do get top jobs. But the power of these deep structural forces is such that most people live and die in the same social class in which they are born; and those in the poorer social groups live in worse health and die sooner.

Looking at welfare benefits, the radicals go further than the social democrats in calling for even higher levels of taxation to fund payments to those in need, and an end to stigmatising needs and means tests. They would also want to see greater equality of income before taxes, and might pass legislation to raise minimum wages and prohibit excessive salaries and bonuses. But at the same time as calling for reforms of the benefits system, the radical viewpoint remains sceptical about the whole enterprise: after all, the money has not permanently been given to the poor. They will have to spend it – and so it goes back into the pockets of businesses, keeping the capitalist system ticking over.

Pause for reflection

Before reading further, think what social work would be like under each of the four models. What would be its distinctive values, what sort of work would it be doing, in what sort of organisations, and with whom?

The implications for social work

Under the minimalist model, social work is likely to take on the residual, safety net character of other welfare services. The key words that capture the approach are 'rescue' and 'control'. It is likely to focus on people who are considered a risk to themselves or others, taking on a policing role. It will also provide services for people in severe need, people with the most intractable problems, but these are likely to be fairly basic services. People whose needs are at lower levels would be expected to sort them out for themselves, or with the help of their families. If families cannot provide directly, the next expectation is that people purchase services privately, or perhaps rely on charities – but charities themselves are likely to be hard pressed (they get little if any state support) and to have high eligibility criteria. Social workers might offer advice to people about where to go for assistance, and might act as brokers in arranging services. For the neediest people, who cannot or who are not allowed to manage for themselves, social workers might purchase services on their behalf, using tightly limited state funds, from private or voluntary agencies.

Social workers might work for state agencies, charities or private welfare agencies, or they could set up as a business themselves, providing freelance social work services. As freelance workers, their services may well be purchased by state welfare agencies – for example, they might be commissioned to undertake assessments or to provide specialist help. Those who are directly employed by the state sector are especially likely to be involved in the more coercive aspects of social work. They are likely to have few resources, and will have to ration services carefully, with strict eligibility criteria.

In the integrationist model, the key words are 'treatment' and 'reintegration'. There are still the elements of control and rescue, but help comes a bit sooner, and control a bit more subtly. The emphasis is on getting people back into mainstream society, to live according to accepted social norms. This means employment, education or training, bringing up children in acceptable ways, caring for members of one's family. It is a conservative approach, with traditional views about family life, so expectations tend to fall heavily on women as mothers, partners and daughters to provide care for family members. It is also corporatist, so state agencies will not provide all the services themselves: rather, they will work together with private, voluntary and other statutory agencies.

Social workers, then, might be working for state agencies, but also for charities or private businesses. Churches and other religious institutions may well be significant partners in welfare provision, so social workers may be employed by faith-based organisations. State-employed social workers are likely to be involved in purchasing or coordinating services provided by other agencies, rather than arranging direct provision by state organisations.

For the social democratic approach, the emphasis is on even earlier intervention, to prevent needs arising in the first place. There will be an emphasis on working at a community level, with groups rather than individuals, and in ways that are voluntary rather than compulsory. Even when people's needs increase, there is still an effort to work in cooperative ways, to try to empower people to keep or regain control of their lives. There is an emphasis on listening to people's views, trying to involve them in decisions about what happens to them, and in planning services more generally. The key words are 'prevention', 'participation' and 'partnership'. Social workers are likely to work for state agencies, but in contrast to the minimalist model (and, to an extent, the integrationist approach) these will be well resourced and well respected by society.

When difficulties go beyond the preventive level, social workers would continue trying to work in positive and voluntary ways. An example is state care for children. Rather than seeing it as a last resort to be avoided if at all possible (and kept as short as possible), the social democratic approach sees it as a positive service to help children and families (Thoburn, 2007). Children are likely to be admitted sooner, before their needs become overwhelming; but equally, young people in trouble with the law are likely to be sent into care rather than custody. There is an emphasis on having highly qualified, skilled staff to help the children. An approach known as social pedagogy is popular in continental Europe, described as 'education in its broadest sense', with an emphasis on child development, group work and therapeutic relationships (House of Commons CSFC, 2009: para. 102). It underpins a much more optimistic view of residential care and more creative ways of working with the young people. There are currently proposals to introduce this approach in England (DfES, 2007: paras 3.59–60; House of Commons CSFC, 2009: paras 101–10).

Chapter 1

It is worth noting, though, that there are tensions in the social democratic model. On the one hand, it talks of empowerment and the importance of service users' views; on the other, it is very centralised and top-down, with a tendency to require social conformity (and, as was discussed in Chapter 1, welfare is a subtle way of achieving this).

The radicals make that point, of course. For them, all forms of state intervention are ambiguous – they may offer help, but they are also repressive. Social workers who operate from this perspective would be passionate advocates for the people they work with, arguing hard to make sure they receive the full benefits to which they are entitled and the highest-quality services. They would emphasise service users' rights, and might well work with organisations like claimants' unions and disability rights groups to campaign for welfare reforms. At the same as taking this advocacy and adversarial approach, they would be engaged in 'consciousness-raising' – that is, explaining the controlling aspects of welfare, helping service users to see that even if they get their full entitlements, they are still losing out in the wider capitalist system. Radical social workers would be trying to change the way that people understand themselves and their lives, encouraging them to work for radical social change. The role of feminist workers in the Women's Aid movement provides an excellent example of this approach (Fraser, 1989). For them, women who come to refuges because of domestic violence are not seen as victims, but as survivors and potential activists. Radical workers can help the women to understand what has happened to them not in individual terms (their own behaviour or the features of their relationship), but in wider terms of male–female power relations in society. Radical social workers are unlikely to work in statutory agencies, but if they do they would probably be seen as mavericks, and may often find their position an uncomfortable one, in conflict with their colleagues and managers.

Box 3.3 Radical social work

There is a long tradition of radical critiques of welfare services and the role of the state, even from those working within them, going right back to opposition to the Poor Law and the controlling aspects of charity. There is also a long tradition of radical social work, and while it has never been accepted wholesale into mainstream local authority services, it has had an important impact, over the years, in challenging and changing aspects of social work policy and practice.

The core notion of radical social work is its strong mistrust of the individualised casework approach, which it criticises for denying the wider social, political and economic realities that constrain people's lives, notably poverty, class, race and gender (different versions emphasise different oppressions). Casework, whether with individuals or families, focuses on *them*, their thoughts and behaviour, and so reinforces the idea that they are to blame for their own misfortune. Its message is that they have to change, behave responsibly, in order to fit back into society. In contrast, radical approaches argue that the emphasis should be on understanding people's lives in terms of wider social structures, and seeking to change society, not just individuals.

An important UK book to popularise the ideas of radical social work was Bailey and Brake (1975). The emphasis at that time was on social class as the main structural factor that limited people's lives. At the end of the book is the manifesto of a group called Case Con, which sought to promote a radical approach to social work. The manifesto is critical of the Seebohm report for shifting responsibility for welfare from the state to the family. It is highly critical of attempts to professionalise social work, regarding these as self-serving. It calls for social workers to work with trade unions in the struggle for a workers' state. The Case Con Manifesto (1975) is also available on the internet (www.radical.org.uk/barefoot.casecon.htm).

Parts of the Case Con Manifesto seem very dated now, but its central message, to see the bigger picture and not to individualise people's problems, is as relevant as ever. It is reflected in the more recent publication of a new manifesto, entitled *Social Work and Social Justice: A Manifesto for a New Engaged Practice* (known as the Social Work Manifesto: Jones *et al.*, 2004). This new manifesto highlights the organisational challenges and frustrations facing many social workers in the UK today (managerialism, marketisation, financial restrictions, increased bureaucracy), and speaks of the 'current degraded status of social work'. It calls for a social work committed to social justice and to challenging poverty and discrimination. It sees seeds of hope in the growth of user movements and in the wider global anti-capitalist protest movements.

The latter seems a very long shot. Anti-capitalist movements remind us that there are alternative visions of society, but it is far from certain that they would want to support social work – they may well see it as part of the problem. The optimism about the 'innovation and insight' of service user movements may be better grounded. These have certainly challenged and reinvigorated social work in the UK; but even so, this needs a much more balanced approach. There is nothing in the Social Work Manifesto about legal and moral duties to protect vulnerable people from harm, sometimes overruling people's wishes, about balancing competing rights and responsibilities, about weighing up the interests of different individuals and groups, about the ambiguities and complexities of notions such as participation, justice, equality and diversity (some of the values it lists as 'anti-capitalist').

Radical social work has been criticised for being unrealistic and unable to give a satisfactory account of what social workers should actually do differently when faced with individuals in distress or in need of protection. Nevertheless, its ideas have an important part to play in counterbalancing minimalism and individualism, helping social workers to practise in ways that are better informed and more sensitive to the difficulties that individuals face (Collins, 2009; Ferguson and Woodward, 2009). In that sense, radical social work is good social work.

The ambiguity of social policy

Reality is a complex mixture of the approaches, with overlaps and tensions between them. Some countries may be nearer to one model than another, but there are always competing viewpoints. Even within political parties there is a range of opinions, and individuals too are likely to have a mixture of beliefs, not always consistent. A central challenge for politicians and policy-makers is to 'sell' their policy proposals so that they appeal to all viewpoints, all at the same time. Policies that achieve this are most likely to be accepted, at least initially, but it means that policies can be highly ambiguous. This section highlights three prominent policy themes that are especially relevant to social work, and which typify this ambiguity – community care, social inclusion and personalisation.

Community care appeals to all perspectives because it seems to meet most people's wishes better than institutional care. For the minimalists, the added attraction is that they can see the potential for reducing the role of the state and cutting state expenditure by closing residential facilities and replacing them with community-based alternatives that are cheaper and supplied by non-state agencies. Community care appeals to integrationists partly because it returns people to, or keeps them in, mainstream society, and also because of the links between the statutory, voluntary and private sectors, with the state commissioning services from different agencies. Community care is also attractive to social democrats, because it can offer lower-level preventive services as well as better meeting the wishes of service users. Even the radicals find community care attractive in so far as it meets service users' rights and wishes.

But all are going to be disappointed. For the minimalists, it never saves enough money and still leaves too big a welfare machine; for the other groups, it is flawed by insufficient funding, the scarcity and often inadequacy of the services available, and the burdens it can place on family carers.

Social inclusion is another policy area rife with ambiguity. Levitas (1998) illustrates it brilliantly. She shows how the three discourses of MUD, SID and RED interweave in the ways that New Labour has developed and marketed its policies on tackling social exclusion. There are some elements of the moral underclass discourse, the rather judgmental approach to making people responsible, for example in the ways that teenage pregnancy and antisocial behaviour have been given such high profiles. There are other elements that chime with the social integrationist discourse, getting people back into society, for example through neighbourhood renewal and community-based schemes like Sure Start Children's Centres; and there are elements of a redistributionist discourse, such as the minimum wage, tax credits and the commitment to end child poverty. Getting people into work hits all three buttons. Even the radicals find some aspects attractive, for example participation, in so far as they really do respond to people's rights and wishes.

Once again, though, inevitably, all will be dissatisfied, because no one gets everything they want. Services cannot deliver what both minimalists and social democrats would prefer; and they will certainly not satisfy the radicals, who are extremely critical of the authoritarianism of New Labour's approach to social inclusion (Butler and Drakeford, 2001).

Personalisation is another example of the way that a policy can, on the face of it, appeal to all perspectives simultaneously. Most people would like to have at least a say in the services they get, and some would welcome full control. Most people would prefer support that is tailored to their individual circumstances, rather than an inflexible, one-size-fits-all service. Social democrats welcome it in so far as it empowers service users and communities; even the radicals see some potential here. Integrationists welcome it because it brings the promise of new roles for the voluntary and private sectors, as advocates and supporters of service users, planners along with the local authorities, and as providers of services. Minimalists like it because it gives responsibility back to the individual.

On the other hand, there are some highly sceptical critiques of personalisation. Important criticisms, from a radical perspective, are set out by Iain Ferguson (2007, 2008). He argues that personalisation as currently proposed has more to do with minimalism than social democracy, and is certainly not radical. For him, it is based on individualistic, consumerist notions of choice; it underplays the realities of poverty and vulnerability which constrain people's capacity to be independent consumers; it stigmatises those who cannot, or do not wish to, be independent; and rather than giving or sharing responsibility, it is likely to force it on to people and so risks making their situations worse. Of course, the supporters of personalisation do not accept these criticisms, and argue that people will not be forced to take on responsibilities they cannot manage, and that there will be personalised support to help them with their new independence. Personalisation certainly offers much that is potentially positive and exciting; but, as Ferguson concludes, it is not something that social workers should accept uncritically.

Conclusion

This chapter has described three mainstream models of state welfare, and the fourth, radical approach. It has pulled out the relevance and implications for social work. The radical model is more than a fourth point along the spectrum; it is also a new way of looking at the other three. As a fourth point it may seem unrealistic, but as an ever-present critical perspective, always pushing us to think anew about our practice and the underlying policies and assumptions, it is invaluable. It can be awkward and unsettling, which is why it is so important.

The other main point in this chapter has been about the ambiguity of social policy, and how a policy can be 'sold' by seeming to be all things to all people. Personalisation currently fits this very well. The difficulty is that people do not all support it for the same reasons. They use the same words, but mean different things. So, after the immediate popularity wears off, longer-term disillusionment and conflict are inevitable. It will not save as much money as some hoped, it will not be as well funded as others hoped, budgets will be tight and inter-agency relationships will still be strained. Some may see a subtle expansion of state activity and control, as voluntary agencies become tied to local authority contracts and funding, while others will see the withdrawal of the state from welfare provision.

Questions for reflection

- Which of the four approaches appeals most to you, and why? Discuss the ideas with colleagues, and try to explain your view.

- Which approach do you think is dominant in your country at the moment? If you cannot say one, where and how can you see the different strands?

- Think of a social work setting where you have worked or been on placement. Can you see any signs of the different models? How did they overlap, or compete? Was there any evidence of a radical perspective? How was this regarded?

Box 3.3

- Read the Case Con Manifesto and the Social Work Manifesto (see Box 3.3). Identify the similarities and differences. What do you think about them?

Useful websites and further reading

The *Guardian Society* website is an excellent way to stay informed about wider political and social policy developments in the UK. You can register for a daily e-mail to keep you up to date with the latest stories: http://society.guardian.co.uk.

Radical perspectives on social work in the UK are available through the Social Work Action Network (SWAN: www.socialworkfuture.org – which has the Social Work Manifesto) and The Barefoot Social Worker website (www.radical.org.uk/barefoot – which has the Case Con Manifesto). There are also radical social work websites in other countries – google 'radical social work' to find them.

For the MUD, RED and SID models:

Levitas (1998; 2nd edn 2005) *The Inclusive Society? Social Inclusion and New Labour.*

Two useful books on the political contexts of social work are:

Jordan with Jordan (2000) *Social Work and the Third Way: Tough Love as Social Policy.*

Powell (2001) *The Politics of Social Work.*

For thought-provoking accounts of the radical perspective, see:

Ferguson (2008) *Reclaiming Social Work: Challenging Neo-Liberalism and Promoting Social Justice.*

Ferguson and Woodward (2009) *Radical Social Work in Practice.*

Part 2
Key issues

This part of the book discusses a number of key issues for social policy generally and social work in particular. The chapters uncover more of the tensions behind the core models of social work, social policy and the state, and offer further models for pulling out the underlying issues. A theme across all the chapters is the complexity and ambiguity of the terms – needs and rights, inequality and poverty, participation and choice. All of them carry different meanings and implications according to people's views about the purposes of social policy, the roles of the state, and the functions of social work.

Chapter 4 considers needs and rights. Need has traditionally been at the heart of social work and social policy, but rights is a new and pressing language. But what counts as a need, and what counts as a right? Who decides, and on what basis? How are those decisions influenced by risks, resources and responsibilities? The chapter offers two models for thinking about need – Jonathan Bradshaw's (1972) taxonomy and the image of a pyramid. It discusses the significance of human rights for social work, distinguishing between different types of rights. It looks at the role of international treaties and the Human Rights Act 1998. It ends by considering recent developments in the debates about rights and responsibilities.

 Chapter 5 discusses inequality and poverty. There are basic questions about what we mean by these words, and why they are important – and great disagreement. What do we mean by inequality, and why does it matter? How do we define poverty, and whose responsibility is it? The chapter focuses on social class, taking health inequalities and educational attainment to illustrate the issues and interactions. It also looks at the issue of child poverty. The conclusion highlights the professional and personal implications for social workers.

Chapter 6 looks at participation and choice. Again, what do we mean by the terms, why are they important, what are the limitations, what are they for? The chapter uses the models of two ladders to illustrate the ambiguities and challenges of participation. It identifies a number of key questions about choice. It summarises recent research into the implementation of individual budgets to show the opportunities and dilemmas in practice.

4 Needs and rights

Need has traditionally been at the heart of social work and social policy. Social workers say that their goal is to meet the needs of their service users; the stated goals of social policies are to ensure that people's needs are met. Need has a central role in the major legislation that shapes social work policy and practice in England and Wales. The Children Act 1989 gives the definition of a 'child in need', and specifies the duties of the local authority to such children and their families. The NHS and Community Care Act 1990 sets out a two-stage process of assessing need and then arranging necessary services, the idea being to separate these two processes so that the assessment is led by the person's needs, not by the services available. But even if a child or an adult is assessed as being in need, there is no guarantee that they will receive a service from the local authority.

Not all need gets a service, or at least not a particular service from a particular agency. Difficult decisions have to be made about priorities and the rationing of limited resources. The government guidance on the Children Act is clear that local authorities are not expected to meet every individual need, but have to identify the extent of need in their area and decide about priorities accordingly (DH, 1991b: 7). Government guidance in the field of adult care is equally clear on the importance of prioritising. The *Fair Access to Care Services* (FACS) guidance for local authorities in England (DH, 2002)

Box 4.1

specifies four bands of need – low, moderate, substantial and critical (see Box 4.1) – and most authorities restrict their services to people in the higher categories (in 2007–8, 72 per cent of councils set their eligibility criteria at the substantial or critical levels: CSCI, 2008b: para. 2.21).

So we begin to see that need is highly contentious. Two fundamental questions arise. First, *who* defines need and *how*? Second, how are different needs prioritised? The following sections offer two models for thinking about these issues. The second part of the chapter considers the implications of the new policy language of rights.

Defining social need

A well-established and widely used model for thinking about the ways that needs are identified is Bradshaw's (1972) 'taxonomy of social need'. It gives us some further angles on the social work diamond, about the relationships between service users and social professionals in saying what a person's needs are. Bradshaw distinguishes between four ways of identifying need:

- Felt need;

- Expressed need;

- Comparative need;

- Normative need.

Felt need is the need that individuals and groups perceive for themselves – they feel hungry, they feel the need for more money, better jobs, warmer homes, better schools. The difficulty of relying on felt need as the test of whether someone really is in need or not is that people have very different perceptions about their own needs. Some people feel a need much quicker than others. This may be because of other factors – for example, a person with asthma will feel the need for a dry house sooner than someone who has no breathing problems – but sometimes it is just because different people have very different tolerance levels. Some can put up with very difficult circumstances, even thrive on them, whereas others would feel the need for help much earlier.

Some felt needs become expressed needs when they are turned into demands: 'I need help looking after my husband'; 'The children round here need a playground.' But not all felt needs are expressed – people may keep quiet out of a sense of shame, or because they are afraid of the consequences of asking, or because they cannot imagine anything being any different – 'What's the point of asking? That's just the way things are.' Not all expressed needs are met. Some may be 'bounced back' to the person doing the asking – 'It's up to you to do something about it.' Sometimes the need might be expressed to the wrong person – 'I'd love to help you, but it's not my job.' Or the need may be refused because it is not considered a sufficiently high priority, or it may be put on a waiting list.

Comparative and normative need do not require the person or people in need themselves to feel or express their need. In the former, need is identified by comparing the situation of some people to that of others – so, children in some schools do not achieve as good exam results as those in others, adults in some neighbourhoods have poorer health than those in others. But how to deal with those differences? The children may need extra help, or their parents, or their teachers. What sort of problem is it – a problem of the children's abilities or attitudes, poor parenting, poor teaching? How we define the problem determines what services we offer. Some may say schools need closer inspection and monitoring, others that parents need more help. As for adults in poor health, they may need extra health advice, or better housing, or better jobs, or improved health services. Some comparisons can be misleading: for example, to compare school performance simply by looking at exam results. This does not take account of the backgrounds of the children, whether one school is serving a very deprived area while another takes pupils from more prosperous households.

Normative need is need decided by professionals and experts, in accordance with their norms and standards. For example, experts might decide what people need for an adequate lifestyle, and then calculate the level of income this requires. This approach overcomes a potential difficulty with expressed need – that those who express their views loudest might get a service, while less forceful groups may not get the help they need. It would also deal with one of the challenges of felt need, the different tolerance levels of individuals, by giving an objective standard of need. However, it has its own drawbacks. Experts do not always agree, standards change over time, and why should an external opinion be privileged over someone's own views about their situation and what they need?

There are different combinations of these categories of need, and some combinations may be more likely to get a service than others – so, a need that is felt and expressed, and also comparatively and normatively supported, is more likely to be met than one that lacks comparative and normative backing. There are thought-provoking implications. A person may need professional help to express their need, but this could then be trumped by the professional's view of what they 'really' need. A powerfully expressed view might prevail against experts' opinions, but it is always vulnerable to being dismissed as a 'want' rather than a 'need', or not really in the person's best interests. Or it could be dismissed as unrealistic – 'in an ideal world, you might get that service (say, extra home care), but given the high levels of demand and limited resources, you're jolly lucky to get anything at all'.

Levels of need

The notion of different levels of need is crucial for making those difficult prioritising decisions, and brings in the state and organisational points of the social work diamond. Whether and how different types of need are met reflects different beliefs about the role of the state, the tasks of different welfare organisations and the best use of resources. It is not just about rationing, although in practice that has become a major part of it, but also about targeting the work and skills of a particular agency at the level where they are likely to be most effective, and about organisations cooperating to ensure that even if they do not provide a service for a particular need, there is another agency locally that does, so they can refer the person to them. Hardiker *et al.* (1991) proposed an early model of levels of need in children's services, which has been revised and developed in subsequent publications (see Hardiker, 2002). This section draws on that work.

The concept of different levels of need has often been illustrated by the image of a triangle or pyramid. As examples, a version is used in the *Every Child Matters* green paper (HM Treasury, 2003: 21), and another in the Welsh Assembly Government's 2007 strategy for social services in Wales (WAG, 2007: 41–2). Hardiker refers to her model as a grid or a map, but the image of a pyramid has gained wide currency because it conveys the idea that more people are in the lower bands, and fewer at the higher levels. There are many different versions of the model, some with just three levels and others with seven, nine or even more. The principle behind them is the same: that as need increases more specialist services are provided, either instead of or in addition to the lower-level ones.

The general goal is to match the right sort of service to the person's needs, and prevent needs increasing. Often the aim is to help people move down again to the lower levels. If this is not possible, for example with long-term conditions, the aim is to manage the needs and (if possible) stop them increasing, or slow down the increase. The new policy drive for personalisation highlights what should

Box 4.4

always have been the case: that all this should be with regard to the person's choices and rights, as well as their needs. If people's choices have to be overruled, this must be on the basis of evidence and assessment, in accordance with the law and only to the extent that is necessary and proportionate to the risks involved (see Box 4.4).

Figure 4.1 shows a five-level version, based on Hardiker's (2002) model, with universal needs at the bottom, then four levels of increasing need. Roughly, these represent vulnerability, specific additional needs, severe needs or risk, and harm. As one goes up the pyramid the focus tends to move from groups to individuals, and from voluntary to compulsory forms of involvement with statutory agencies.

In thinking about the model it is important to distinguish between needs, services and the take-up of services. It is also important to realise that pyramids from different agencies may not match up because of different priorities. One of the central problems of inter-agency working is that a case that is high priority for one service may be a lower priority for another. Furthermore, there are no sharp lines between the different bands, but rather a gradual progression; and we should also recognise that a person may have high-level needs in some aspects of their lives, but be able to manage their affairs very well in others. A one-off and one-dimensional picture of need will not be adequate, and services have to be able to respond flexibly.

The bottom level of the pyramid represents the basic needs that everyone has: for sufficient education, decent housing, a reasonable income and good health. Individuals and families meet many of these needs for themselves; and, as we have seen, current policy aims to encourage that independence and self-responsibility, to buy their own homes, earn an income, care for family members. But we should not underestimate the role of the state at this level. It provides basic but essential public services that all require, such as sanitation, refuse collection, police, roads, parks. Economic policy affects the number of jobs that are available. Legislation sets an overall framework for people's safety and wellbeing, for example to protect them from crime, and to ensure that all children receive a sufficient education. There are state schools to meet the universal need for education. Most families use these, although take-up is not compulsory. Families may use private schools or teach their children at home, but the state

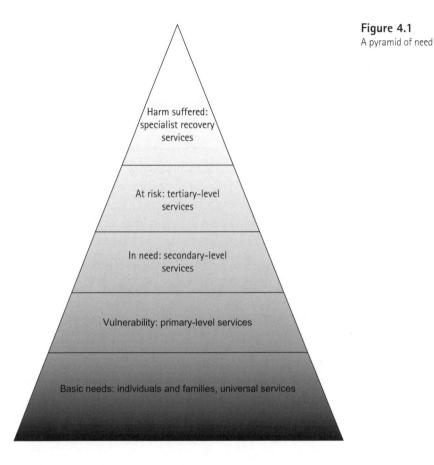

Figure 4.1
A pyramid of need

Harm suffered: specialist recovery services

At risk: tertiary-level services

In need: secondary-level services

Vulnerability: primary-level services

Basic needs: individuals and families, universal services

requires that parents ensure their children are educated. State intervention at this level also includes public information and advice, for example about the importance of a healthy diet and exercise.

But, for some, this will not be enough. For a variety of reasons, they will have additional needs, and the first step up is to a level where people may be seen as vulnerable. This includes those with extra needs because of young or old age, on low or insecure incomes, in poor health, unlikely to do well at school. Voluntary and community services, such as mother and toddler groups, after-school clubs and home visiting programmes from agencies such as Age Concern or Home Start might meet needs at this level. Other typical services at this level would be advice centres or adult education classes to help people look for jobs or learn new skills, or to manage their money better (e.g. Citizen's Advice Bureaux). If we apply the pyramid idea to income maintenance, this level would include payments such as the state pension for older people, child benefit for families with children, and tax credits for people on low wages.

From a health point of view, this level includes common medical needs that are typically dealt with by general practitioners, dentists, opticians and community nurses. It would also include advice and preventive services such as walk-in centres and 'well woman' clinics. These are often described as 'universal services' because they are open to all who need them, even if not all use them. It is also important to note the way that the UK health sector uses the terms 'primary care' and 'secondary care'. Primary care includes all community-based services, however intensive or frequent they may be, in contrast to secondary care, which is hospital-based. So, from a health point of view, even regular visits from community nurses would be regarded as primary services; but in terms of the patient's *needs*, he or she may be much higher up the pyramid.

Most people's needs will be met at the first two levels. But some have higher-level needs – people with chronic illnesses, disabled people, families where the parents are struggling to cope. This is the next level up, where more specific need emerges out of vulnerability. So some parents will need additional support with parenting skills, some disabled people will need assistance and adapted housing to live at home, some people caring for relatives will need extra help or respite care. In terms of income maintenance, we now have additional payments for people with no or very low incomes because of unemployment, disability or retirement (but often with eligibility criteria such as needs and means

Chapter 3

tests, as discussed in Chapter 3). On the whole, take-up of services at this level is still voluntary, although there may be strict eligibility requirements. Services would be specifically aimed to meet the extra needs of the identified groups, such as children's centres, parenting classes, day centres, home care, meals on wheels, community nurses.

This specific needs level is where, in the UK, local authority social work and social care services tend to start being involved. This is not to say that local authorities are not involved at the earlier levels, because they have general powers to promote the wellbeing of people in their area (Local Government Act 2000) and duties to ensure cooperation between different agencies. This means that they may well be providing or commissioning lower-level services, but probably not as an explicit part of their social work/social care services.

The next level up is when needs become more severe, and social workers may now talk of risk, 'need of protection', or 'safeguarding'. By now, intervention is increasingly focused on individuals, although there may still be group activities, and it is increasingly likely to be compulsory, perhaps because it is required by the courts or simply because there is no alternative – the person cannot manage without the service. Choice is more constrained, and in some cases support will be mixed with monitoring. So, children may be the subject of child protection plans, and there may be court proceedings if the risks are not reduced. For older people, there may be an intensive package of home care support, adaptations to their home or specialist housing, and telecare facilities (e.g. sensors to detect movement around the house, linked to a monitoring service). People with mental health problems are likely to be receiving medication and in touch with a community mental health team. Young people in trouble with the law may be on court orders that require them to attend advice or training sessions, intended to prevent reoffending.

At the top of the pyramid, harm has occurred and now the services are aimed at managing or reducing the long-term consequences. This may be by arranging for people to move to new living situations, or by helping them to return to their homes and families but with extra support. For children, the options include foster care and then return home, longer-term foster care, residential care, or adoption.

Specialist therapeutic help may be required in any of those settings. For adults, options could be hospital care followed by a return home or a move to supported housing or residential care. Even prison could fit into this model, if services are in place while people are serving their sentence to help them learn new skills for, say, anger management and employment.

An important point, stressed by Hardiker (2002: 66), is that the name of a service is not a reliable guide to where it sits on the pyramid of need. It is necessary to look at the values and methods of the service. For example, a service called a 'family centre' could be working at the lower levels if it has a community focus, provides drop-in services, information and advice; or at the third or fourth level if it focuses on specialist assessments, expert-led intervention and cases referred by social workers or the courts. The same family centre *could* provide services at both levels, but it is important to be clear about the differences if the services are to be used effectively.

Box 4.1 *Fair Access to Care Services* (DH, 2002)

This is statutory guidance from central government to local authorities in England for determining eligibility for adult social care services. It reflects a pyramid approach to need. Councils have to follow the guidance, which was intended to lead to a more consistent approach across the country. However, each council has to make its own decision about where its eligibility level is, and what services are provided. They are supposed to take a longer-term, preventive view of individuals' needs, but they have to keep within their resources and are therefore also expected to focus help on those in greatest immediate or longer-term need. There are four bands representing 'the seriousness of risk to independence or other consequences if needs are not addressed'. Some of the criteria for each of the levels are:

Critical

- life is, or will be, threatened;
- little or no choice and control over vital aspects of the immediate environment;
- inability to carry out vital personal care or domestic routines;
- vital family and other social roles and responsibilities cannot or will not be undertaken.

Substantial

- only partial choice and control over the immediate environment;
- inability to carry out the majority of personal care or domestic routines;

- the majority of family and other social roles and responsibilities cannot or will not be undertaken.

Moderate

- inability to carry out several personal care or domestic routines;

- several family and other social roles and responsibilities cannot or will not be undertaken.

Low

- inability to carry out one or two personal care or domestic routines;

- one or two family and other social roles and responsibilities cannot or will not be undertaken.

In January 2008, CSCI's annual report on social care in England raised grave concerns about the operation of FACS. It was especially concerned about what happened to people who did not meet the criteria, who might then become 'lost to the system' and experience great hardship without adequate support (CSCI, 2008a). The government subsequently commissioned CSCI to undertake a fuller review. This concluded that the difficulties were not just to do with consistency and the clarity of decisions, 'cutting the cake fairly', but that the cake itself was too small. Limited resources and the emphasis on risk undermined the wider preventive aims, and

Chapter 9

were incompatible with the personalisation agenda (CSCI, 2008b; Hudson and Henwood, 2008). The government undertook to update the guidance (Hope, 2008), but more substantial reforms will have to wait for the wider review of the funding of social care (discussed in Chapter 9).

Thinking about current policies for personalisation in the light of the pyramid raises two particular issues. One is the emphasis on lower-level prevention; the other the emphasis on service users' rights and choices.

The preventive agenda is well captured in a paper about services for older people entitled *All Our Tomorrows: Inverting the Triangle of Care* (ADSS and LGA, 2003). This argues that the pyramid should be re-envisaged, so that instead of specialist, recuperative care being seen as the top level, the highest priority should be community-based strategies to promote the wellbeing of older people, such as improved housing, accessible services, life-long education, and closer partnerships between service users, professionals and agencies.

The emphasis on choice means a new approach to working with service users and carers to help them understand risks and *manage* them, rather than automatically seeking to remove risk, which may not be what the person wants – for example, it could be too restrictive for how they wish to live (see the government guidance on decision-making, choice and risk: DH, 2007a). The issue is reflected in *Safeguarding Adults* (DH *et al.*, 2008), which is a consultation document about government guidance on protecting vulnerable adults from abuse (known as *No Secrets*: DH and Home Office, 2000). The consultation document argues that service users 'should be seen as active citizens with a right to choose the type of care they receive, together with a right to have a say in the risks they are comfortable with' (DH *et al.*, 2008: 25). This approach points to the challenges of balancing needs and rights. Now we go on to look at human rights and their implications for social work.

What are 'human rights'?

If need is the traditional heart of social policy, rights are its new blood. That is not to say that rights are a new idea, but the language of rights has become much more widespread in recent years, and in the UK particularly since the implementation of the Human Rights Act 1998, in 2000. Rights are a very powerful form of language, more so than need: compare 'I need help looking after my husband' with 'I have a right to help looking after my husband'. The latter is much more insistent, and this underpins the wide range of rights-based movements – women's rights, children's rights, disabled people's rights, service users' rights and so on. But for all that, rights are no less complex than needs, with just as many ambiguities and contradictions, and just as many difficult balances to be struck.

Not all rights are human rights, but many 'lesser' rights – for example, consumer rights – have at their core ideas about fairness, honesty and treating people with respect that are certainly consistent with broader human rights; and those principles are thoroughly consistent with the values of traditional relationship-based social work. The language and ideas of rights reaffirm something old about social work, but also bring new dimensions and challenges. The international definition of social work states that 'Principles of human rights and social justice are fundamental to social work' (IFSW/IASSW, 2001), and Ife (2001) has argued that social work should be seen as a human rights profession. If that is the case, it is essential to consider what we mean by human rights, and what the implications might be.

United Nations international treaties about human rights may sound a long way removed from the day-to-day realities of social work, but in fact the different rights that they specify are of direct and powerful relevance to social work practice. Social workers do not have to be human rights campaigners or activists to be doing human rights work – they do it every day by working with people whose rights are challenged by poverty, ill health or harm, and the quality of their practice is a vital factor for making sure that people's rights are upheld. This will often involve weighing up competing rights, with hard decisions about overruling some in order to uphold others. International treaties provide widely accepted statements of what human rights are, and are a useful foundation for thinking about how rights apply in practice.

Two core human rights treaties are the International Covenants on Civil and Political Rights and on Economic, Social and Cultural Rights. They have their roots in the 1948 Universal Declaration on Human Rights and were written in order to give more detail and force to that declaration. They were adopted by the UN General Assembly in 1966, and both came into force in 1976, after sufficient countries had ratified them (ratification is a binding commitment to respect them). The UK ratified both treaties in 1976, but they are not directly part of UK law (unlike the European Convention on Human Rights, discussed below). Rather, they are principles that should be reflected in all legislation and policy.

The distinction between these two broad types of rights is long-standing. Civil and political rights have been called 'first-generation rights', and have their roots in libertarianism, where the state has a small but strong role to defend people's individual freedoms (the minimalist approach described in Chapter 3). Economic, social and cultural rights have been called 'second-generation rights', and have their roots in egalitarianism and social democracy. They imply a much more active role for the state to ensure that they are achieved, not just to defend them. First-generation rights are sometimes called 'negative rights', because they limit the powers of the state (it must not infringe them except in certain

exceptional and clearly defined circumstances), in contrast to the 'positive' second-generation rights, which bring many more duties and tasks for the state. While there is some merit in this distinction, on the whole it underestimates the power of first-generation rights, which can be used to argue that states have positive duties to protect and promote people's civil and political rights. Box 4.2 shows a selection of the rights that come under each heading.

Chapter 3 and Box 4.2

The box shows the clear differences between the two approaches to human rights, although there are also some overlaps and a key principle of human rights work is that all rights are interdependent and indivisible – so, progress in achieving one is likely to lead to improvements in others, and a violation of one will have a harmful effect on others. Even so, it is not hard to see the likelihood of strong political conflict about the importance of these different sorts of rights.

There is also a third-generation of human rights, which are more collective and belong to communities, societies and nations rather than to individuals. Examples are the right to benefit from economic growth, a harmonious society and a healthy, clean environment. There are overlaps with the earlier rights and it is clear that all are interdependent, because individuals benefit from these rights as well as communities. Also, the first- and second-generation rights have communal aspects, such as freedom of assembly and the rights of ethnic minorities; and many of them, such as education and an adequate standard of living, require provision on a collective level, even if they can be claimed by individuals.

Ife (2001) argues that first-generation rights have traditionally been met through the law (e.g. bills of rights and international treaties), and defended by legal action through the courts, the work of legal professionals and campaign groups. Second-generation rights have typically been delivered through the policies of national welfare states, voluntary and private sector agencies, and the direct work of welfare professions such as social work. The third-generation rights are achieved through economic development schemes, community projects, environmental campaigns, and the work of community development workers.

Box 4.2 Human rights

Civil and political rights	Social, economic and cultural rights
First-generation rights	*Second-generation rights*

No discrimination.	No discrimination.
Right to life.	Right to work; fair wages; equal pay for work of equal value; safe and healthy working conditions; reasonable working hours and paid holidays.
No one shall be subjected to torture, or to cruel, inhuman or degrading treatment or punishment.	Right to join trade unions and to strike.
No one shall be held in slavery.	'The widest possible protection and assistance should be accorded to the family'; special protection for mothers, children, young people.
Right to liberty, no arbitrary arrest.	
Liberty of movement and freedom to choose one's own residence.	Right to social security.
	Right to adequate standard of living.
Right to a fair trial: all entitled to the equal protection of the law.	Right to freedom from hunger.
No unlawful interference with a person's privacy and family life.	Right to the highest attainable standard of physical and mental health.
Freedom of thought, conscience and religion, and of expression.	Right to education.
Right of peaceful assembly, and of freedom of association.	States undertake to take steps, individually and through international assistance, to the maximum of their available resources, to achieve progressively the full realisation of these rights.
Right of people from ethnic, religious or linguistic minorities to enjoy their culture, religion, language.	
From the International Covenant on Civil and Political Rights (1966).	*From the International Covenant on Economic, Social and Cultural Rights (1966).*

In fact, social work has a part to play in all three dimensions. The importance of civil and political rights for social work has been brought home by the Human Rights Act 1998, which is discussed further below. The third-generation, collective rights may be detected in area-based approaches to tackling social exclusion, such as neighbourhood renewal, economic regeneration schemes and the promotion of strong communities (CLG, 2006). As noted in Chapter 2, the contribution of social work to such initiatives has been undervalued in England in recent years, but there is a long history of social workers

Chapter 2

doing community development work, although often in agencies outside local authorities. Even so, casework social workers have a part to play, because they work with individuals and families in the most deprived communities and can help their service users get involved in local schemes (Collins, 2009).

Box 4.3 The force of UN human rights treaties

The force of UN human rights treaties is primarily political and moral, to raise awareness about rights and to pressure governments to respect them. As such, they are often used by non-governmental organisations (NGOs) as a basis for campaigning for changes to law and policy. As well as this potential at *national* level, they are very useful as a source of ideas to review the policies and practices of one's *organisation*, and to audit one's own *practice*. Alongside the Universal Declaration and the two covenants, the core UN human rights treaties are:

- *International Convention on the Elimination of All Forms of Racial Discrimination* 1965 (ICERD), ratified by the UK in 1969;

- *Convention for the Elimination of All Forms of Discrimination against Women* 1979 (CEDAW), ratified by the UK in 1986;

- *Convention against Torture and Other Cruel, Inhuman or Degrading Treatment or Punishment* 1984 (CAT), ratified by the UK in 1988;

- *Convention on the Rights of the Child* 1989 (CRC), ratified by the UK in 1991;

- *International Convention on the Protection of the Rights of All Migrant Workers and Members of their Families* 1990 (CRMW), still to be ratified by the UK;

- *International Convention on the Rights of Persons with Disabilities* 2006 (CRPD), ratified by the UK in June 2009.

There is a UN committee for each convention, which periodically reviews the progress being made by each country that is a party. Governments are required to write a report for the review, and NGOs can also send reports. The committee considers the reports and questions representatives of the different bodies, and then produces a final report with recommendations for

---

action, known as its Concluding Observations. These are powerful documents, publicly challenging governments to change law, policy and practice.

The CRC is probably the best known of the UN treaties in the UK, although it is only relatively recently that levels of awareness have risen, together with greater understanding of its implications for the UK, not just the poorer countries of the world. The UN committee considered the most recent UK report on children's rights in 2008, and published its concluding observations in October that year (UN Committee on the Rights of the Child, 2008). While acknowledging progress in some areas, it called for further action on a range of issues, including:

- The 'general climate of intolerance and negative public attitudes towards children' (para. 24);

- Deaths of children in custody (para. 28);

- Greater support for families (paras 44–5);

- Fuller inclusion of disabled children in society (paras 52–3);

- Treatment of asylum-seeking children and young people (para. 71);

- The low age of criminal responsibility and the high number of children in custody (paras 77–8);

- The use of antisocial behaviour orders against children, and their potential to bring the children into the criminal justice system (para. 79).

The Human Rights Act 1998

The Human Rights Act (HRA) 1998 incorporates the European Convention on the Protection of Human Rights and Fundamental Freedoms into UK law (usually known simply as the European Convention on Human Rights, ECHR). The ECHR was written in 1950 and the UK signed it in 1951; since 1965 people who considered that their rights under the Convention had been infringed have been able to apply for a remedy to the European Court of Human Rights in Strasbourg, France. So, the ECHR was not new to the UK, but the Human Rights Act 1998 introduced three vital changes. First, UK courts can now hear ECHR cases (although complainants are still able to apply to Strasbourg after they have exhausted all domestic routes). Second, all UK legislation since 2000 should be compatible with the ECHR, and all legislation (whatever date) should, if possible, be interpreted and applied in such a way as to be compatible with the ECHR (HRA 1998, s. 3). Third, and crucially for social work, it is unlawful for a public authority to act in a way which is incompatible with a Convention right (HRA 1998, s. 6). A 'public authority' includes central and local government, NHS trusts, the courts, police and prisons, and private businesses and charities when they are fulfilling 'public functions' (there is still some uncertainty about the limits of this, but under s. 145 of the Health and Social Care Act 2008, it now definitely includes residents in care homes whose placements are funded by local authorities).

The rights in the ECHR are limited to first-generation rights. Also, the ECHR applies only to states, and it is not possible for a person to take legal action for violation of ECHR rights against another individual, or against a private business or charity, if there is no state involvement (although there may be other legislation that they can use to uphold their rights). So, at the moment, self-funded residents in a care home are not covered by the ECHR but local authority-funded residents are. The government has said it will resolve this anomaly, but in the meantime all residents are covered by the systems of regulation and inspection under the Care Standards Act 2000, and beyond that, if abuse occurs, the criminal law.

Box 4.4 highlights three key articles from the ECHR in order to demonstrate the relevance of Convention rights to social work and the complexity of the balancing acts involved. However, other articles have far-reaching implications too, notably: Article 2, the right to life (e.g. for treatment of severely ill or disabled people); Article 5, freedom from unlawful detention (e.g. for people with severe mental health problems or limited mental capacity, children and adults in care settings – for example, action under the ECHR has led to the introduction of 'deprivation of liberty safeguards' for adults with limited mental capacity: DH and OPG, 2009); and Article 9, freedom of thought, conscience and religion (e.g. diet, daily activities and participation in acts of worship for people in care settings or receiving community care services).

Box 4.4 Three key articles for social work in the European Convention on Human Rights

Article 3: Prohibition of torture

'No one shall be subjected to torture or to inhuman or degrading treatment or punishment.'

Examples of relevance to social work: protection of children and adults in their own homes, the community and in care settings (care homes, day care, children's homes, foster care). Includes humiliating treatment. Creates a positive duty to take action if the public authority knows about the situation.

Article 6: Right to a fair trial

'In the determination of his civil rights and obligations ... everyone is entitled to a fair and public hearing within a reasonable time by an independent and impartial tribunal established by law.' (Press and public may be excluded in certain circumstances, including the interests of juveniles and the protection of private life.)

Examples of relevance to social work: child care proceedings, mental health tribunals. Note that the text refers to a *hearing* not just a trial – so administrative meetings which affect people's rights under the ECHR are likely to be covered. This includes, for example, child protection case conferences and looked after children reviews. If hearings do not comply with all the Article 6 requirements (e.g. independence), there must be a route of appeal to a court or tribunal that does. Core requirements of fairness, impartiality and transparency apply to all decision-making processes.

Article 8: Right to respect for private and family life

'Everyone has the right to respect for his private and family life, his home and correspondence. There shall be no interference by a public authority with the exercise of this right except such as is in accordance with the law and is necessary in a democratic society in the interests of national security, public safety or the economic well-being of the country, the prevention of disorder or crime, for the protection of health or morals, or for the protection of the rights and freedoms of others.'

Examples of relevance to social work: support for families, preservation of family links for children and adults in care settings. Possibility of rehabilitation to family. Also includes right to physical integrity (one's body), sexuality, clothing and appearance, and confidentiality of information and records. Interference in these rights is allowed under the specified conditions, which include protecting the rights and freedoms of others, but any intervention must be lawful, necessary and proportionate (the catchphrase is 'don't use a sledgehammer to crack a nut').

If we look at Box 4.4 and think about child and family social work, we can see how social workers have to deal with complex balances between rights and responsibilities all the time. They have to balance the responsibilities of the state to protect children from harm, and the rights of children to be brought up in their own family (Articles 3 and 8). They have to balance parents' rights to bring up their children as they decide, and children's rights to safety (again, Articles 3 and 8). They have to balance the responsibilities of the state to support families, and the responsibilities of parents to care properly for their children. They have to respect the responsibilities of the local authority to act fairly and proportionately at all times, and the rights of children and parents to a fair hearing (Article 6). In adult care work, there are parallel responsibilities to support people's rights to choose, to help (or oblige?) them to exercise their own responsibilities, to protect them and others from harm and – more than that minimalist approach – to promote their wellbeing. Wider debates about the Human Rights Act reflect these tensions and dilemmas, and help us see the bigger policy context of social work practice.

Rights and responsibilities

The government published a review of the implementation of the Human Rights Act in 2006, which concluded (among other things) that the Act 'promotes greater personalisation and therefore better public services' (DCA, 2006b: 1). The review considered that the Act had not seriously impeded action against crime and terrorism, and that its overall impact had been beneficial. It concluded that the ECHR does allow suitable balances between individual rights and public safety, but there are many myths and misunderstandings about it, and people need to be more aware of the protection aspects (pp. 39–42).

The government published a green paper entitled *The Governance of Britain* in 2007, and suggested new legislation about human rights, which would:

> provide explicit recognition that human rights come with responsibilities and must be exercised in a way that respects the human rights of others. It would build on the basic principles of the Human Rights Act, but make explicit the way in which a democratic society's rights have to be balanced by obligations.

> (MoJ, 2007: 61)

The idea of a new bill proved very controversial. The Parliamentary Joint Committee on Human Rights (JCHR) undertook an investigation and reported in August 2008. It discussed what sort of rights should be included, and what force a new bill of rights should have – that is, whether it should it be more like a declaration of general principles, or give individuals the right to take cases to court. It argued that human rights 'cannot be made contingent on the prior fulfilment of responsibilities' (JCHR, 2008: 71), and suggested that any new bill should be called a Bill of Rights and Freedoms, rather than Rights and Responsibilities.

The government would not be budged and published a green paper in spring 2009 entitled *Rights and Responsibilities: Developing Our Constitutional Framework* (MoJ, 2009). The purpose was to launch a consultation about a UK Bill of Rights and Responsibilities. The government accepts that rights are not dependent on responsible behaviour, but holds that both are necessary for a healthy society:

> The challenge is how better to remind people of the importance of individual responsibility and give this greater prominence. Individual rights must be promoted and protected without losing sight of the essential contribution of responsibilities to collective harmony and prosperity.

> (MoJ, 2009: 18)

The green paper rejects the idea of any new economic, social and cultural rights that could give rise to individual claims in the courts. It argues that these are matters for Parliament to decide, not the courts, because they involve political decisions about spending public money. It considers that the Bill could express the principles of the welfare state without creating any individually enforceable legal rights (MoJ, 2009: 43, 57). It suggests that the Bill could include a right for children to achieve wellbeing, but in this broad aspirational way, as a general principle, rather than bringing individual entitlements. It links this idea with a proposal that the Bill could also specify the mutual responsibilities of parents, society, the government and young people themselves (pp. 21, 46–8). The debates about the Bill will be an intriguing issue to follow over the coming years, with profound implications for all public services.

Conclusion

This chapter has discussed the central social policy themes of needs and rights, showing that beneath the easy phrases about 'meeting people's needs' and 'respecting people's rights' are complex challenges, such as who decides and on what basis, and difficult decisions – for example, how are resources taken into account, how are competing claims evaluated? The issues go back to the core models in Part 1 of the book. They reflect different views about the balances between welfare, responsibility and the economy (What sort of services can we afford? Where should we target them?), and disputes about the proper role of the state. These large-scale debates about needs and rights are reflected in social work practice, in the tensions between service users' choices and professional judgments, organisational responsibilities and resources, and statutory duties (the four points of the diamond). We can see that social work decisions are shaped by wider policy debates. The issues are not just about

social work, but about the sort of society we would like to live in, such as how rights and responsibilities are to be balanced, and what responsibilities the state is to take for meeting people's needs, enabling them to exercise their rights and helping them to fulfil their responsibilities.

Questions for reflection

- Think back to Bradshaw's taxonomy of need. What are the lessons for social work practice?

- Think back to the pyramid of need, and to the models of state welfare in Chapter 3. Where would the different models focus their services, in terms of the pyramid? Why?

- Think of an agency or team where you have worked or been on placement (or know about). Where were its services aimed, in terms of the pyramid of need? How effective were its links with agencies or teams providing services at the levels above and below?

- Look back at Box 4.2, which shows the examples of civil and political rights and economic, social and cultural rights. Think about an individual or service user group that you have worked with. What rights are involved? What are the implications of a rights-based approach to social work with them?

- Think of an agency or team where you have worked or been on placement. Do the staff talk about their work in terms of human rights? If so, in what ways? If not, what difference might it make if they did?

- What do you think are more important – rights or responsibilities? What are your reasons, and what implications do these have for the way that social work is undertaken?

Useful websites and further reading

A number of clear guides to the Human Rights Act with helpful examples of the sorts of issues that the Act covers are available on the internet:

Audit Commission (2003) *Human Rights: Improving Public Service Delivery.*

British Institute for Human Rights (BIHR) (2008) *The Human Rights Act: Changing Lives,* 2nd edn.

Department for Constitutional Affairs (DCA) (2006a) *Human Rights, Human Lives: A Handbook for Public Authorities.*

Department of Health (DH) (2008b) *Human Rights in Health Care: A Short Introduction.*

Equality and Human Rights Commission (EHRC) (2008) *Ours to Own: Understanding Human Rights.*

It is worth reading the green paper *Rights and Responsibilities* (MoJ, 2009).

Many special interest groups and campaign groups adopt a human rights perspective in their work. Examples are the Children's Rights Alliance for England (CRAE, www.crae.org.uk), the Mental Health Alliance (www.mental healthalliance.org.uk) and Age Concern/Help the Aged (www.ageconcern.org.uk).

The following books are useful accounts of the implications of human rights for social work:

Ife (2001) *Human Rights and Social Work: Towards Rights-Based Practice.*

Reichert (2003) *Social Work and Human Rights: A Foundation for Policy and Practice.*

Reichert (2006) *Understanding Human Rights: An Exercise Book.*

5 Inequality and poverty

This chapter looks at the subjects of inequality and poverty. It builds on the last chapter, because poverty is a particular form of need, and equality is a core part of the human rights discourse. Saying that raises some problems. If we think of poverty in terms of the pyramid, at what level should the state intervene? If we think of equality in terms of rights, what about responsibilities too? Who is responsible for people's poverty, and for doing something about it? It is another contentious and ambiguous area of social policy, with strong parallels and implications for social work.

Social work's professional values, as described in the BASW code of ethics, include respect for all persons, including 'service users' beliefs, values, culture, goals, needs, preferences, relationships and affiliations'; and a commitment to social justice, including 'the fair and equitable distribution of resources to meet basic human needs' (BASW, 2002: 3.1.and 3.2). So there are two aspects, respect and resources, and given these assertions one would expect inequality and poverty to be central concerns of social work. There is indeed a huge body of literature about tackling discrimination and working with disadvantaged groups. For all that, social work is often criticised for having more rhetoric than reality on these matters, for not appreciating the extent and impact of poverty on the lives of service users, individualising their problems rather than seeing the bigger social picture, and being part of the state apparatus that controls poor people (the radical social work critique).

Likewise, in social policy there is plenty of talk about promoting equality, and tackling social exclusion and poverty, but there is great ambiguity and conflict about what the terms mean, and what policies should follow from them (Lister, 2001). Tackling poverty has, after all, been a goal of social policy since

Chapter 3

the Poor Law – the title shows it – but different political perspectives have very different views about why and how, as shown in Chapter 3. Some people want social policy to eradicate poverty and inequality; others think a bit of poverty and inequality is a good thing; others that state welfare perpetuates them.

This chapter focuses on socio-economic inequality – social class and poverty – rather than the other equality strands of race, gender, disability, sexuality, age, and religion and belief. That is not to say that these are less important, and the interweaving of all of them is crucial to a proper understanding of inequality. The chapter shows some of the differences for people from different minority ethnic groups. These complex interconnections are currently the subject of an investigation by the National Equalities Panel, which is due to report at the end of 2009.

The interaction of inequalities is reflected in the following extract from the government's guide to its Equality Bill, launched in April 2009:

> We know that inequality does not just come from your gender or ethnicity; your sexual orientation or your disability; your age, or your religion or belief. Overarching and interwoven with these specific forms of disadvantage is the persistent inequality of social class – your family background or where you were born.

> (GEO, 2009: 9)

If passed, the Equality Bill will create a new duty for public sector bodies, including central government departments, local authorities and primary care trusts, to have 'due regard' to reducing socio-economic disadvantage when making strategic decisions – for example, about programmes and spending (i.e. the duty does not apply to individual cases: GEO, 2009: 10). The Bill is intended to consolidate and strengthen anti-discrimination legislation. Public authorities currently have duties to promote equality of opportunity for race, gender and disability (i.e. positive duties that go beyond not discriminating), and the Bill extends these to sexuality, age, religion and belief, gender reassignment and pregnancy and maternity.

But what exactly do we mean by inequality, and why does it matter? The following sections discuss these questions, and then the chapter goes on to look at social class and poverty to illustrate the debates and current policies. The conclusion highlights the relevance for social work, especially the personal implications for social workers.

Defining inequality

The report of the government-commissioned, but independent, Equalities Review (2007) gives a clear and wide-ranging picture of inequality in the UK, and identifies ten areas in which the effects of discrimination and disadvantage may be seen. These are listed in Box 5.1.

The Equalities Review does not specifically include income or wealth in its list, although it mentions income when it discusses 'standard of living'. But the list makes it clear that much more than income

> ## Box 5.1 Ten dimensions of inequality
>
> - *Length of life*, including freedom from premature death.
>
> - *Physical security*, including freedom from violence, physical and sexual abuse.
>
> - *Health*, including wellbeing and access to high-quality health care.
>
> - *Education*, including acquiring skills and qualifications, access to lifelong learning.
>
> - *Standard of living*, including nutrition, housing, warmth, clothing, social services.
>
> - *Productive and valued activities*, including employment, work/life balance, being able to care for others.
>
> - *Individual, family and social life*, including self-development, equality in relationships.
>
> - *Participation, influence and voice*, including participation in decision-making and democratic life.
>
> - *Identity, expression and self-respect*, including freedom of religion and belief.
>
> - *Legal security*, including non-discrimination and equal treatment in the criminal justice system.
>
> (Equalities Review, 2007: 18)

is involved. The quality of public services, social life and legal protection must also be considered. It is a useful checklist for thinking about the opportunities and experiences of people who use social care services.

Another way of thinking about the different aspects of inequality is to distinguish between equality of outcome and equality of opportunity or treatment. We can cross-reference this with the Equalities Review's ten dimensions, so that we think about opportunities and outcomes for each of them.

For some, equality of outcome is impossible and undesirable – people are different, with different talents, interests and choices. Instead of trying to enforce dull uniformity, we should recognise that people have individual responsibility for creating and taking opportunities, and celebrate difference. Others would say that equality of outcome has nothing to do with making everyone the same, but rather that greater equality in things such as income, health and educational achievement is a fundamental requirement for freedom and diversity (e.g. Tawney, 1931, quoted in Mount, 2008: 4).

There are different aspects to equality of opportunity. One is that everyone should be treated exactly the same (so, for example, criteria for jobs or university places are the same for all applicants, regardless of background: Equalities Review, 2007: 15), while the other is that, because of the existing inequalities in society, some people need extra help to enable them to take advantage of opportunities that come easily to others (and are taken up sharply by others, notably the middle classes). So, in some cases it is not about exact equality of treatment, but 'positive action' is needed to redress deep-seated disadvantage.

Of course, opportunities and outcomes are closely connected. As the Equalities Review (2007: 15) puts it: 'in the real world, outcomes are dependent on opportunities and opportunities on outcomes. If your family is poor, your educational potential is less likely to be realised; and if your educational achievement is lower, you are likely to earn less.' In other words, policy has to address both angles; but the test of whether opportunities really are more equal is whether, eventually, outcomes become more equal.

The New Labour way emphasises equality of opportunity, and there is little sympathy for those who do not take advantage of the opportunities. They are likely to be subject to 'sanction escalation', as we saw in Chapter 2. There is a focus on outcomes as well – see the outcomes for children and for adults in Chapter 2 – but the prime responsibility for securing these is with individuals, with government making sure the opportunity is taken.

Chapter 2

It is challenging to think about what equality of opportunity/treatment means for the organisational point of the social work diamond. The concept of 'institutional discrimination' draws attention to the way that the structures and practices of an organisation can treat people unfairly, not just the attitudes and behaviour of individuals.

This understanding came to prominence with the use of the term 'institutional racism' in the Macpherson report (1999) on the failed police investigation into the racist murder of Stephen Lawrence, a young black man. The report defined institutional racism as:

> The collective failure of an organisation to provide an appropriate and professional service to people because of their colour, culture or ethnic origin. It can be seen or detected in processes, attitudes and behaviour which amount to discrimination through unwitting prejudice, ignorance, thoughtlessness, and racist stereotyping which disadvantages minority ethnic people.
>
> (Macpherson, 1999: para. 6.34)

The important point about institutional discrimination, as the Equalities Review (2007: 35) emphasises, is that it is not just about the prejudices of individuals, but about the culture, systems and routines of an organisation. It is not saying that everybody in an organisation is racist, sexist, or prejudiced against a particular group of people, but nor is it saying that discrimination is confined to just a few 'bad apples in the barrel'. It is more subtle than both of those extremes, and is a powerful concept for evaluating organisational policies, norms and practices.

A striking example is a 2007 report by Mencap, *Death by Indifference*. This argued that institutional discrimination in the NHS against learning disabled people had led to the unnecessary deaths of six people. In response, the government set up an independent inquiry into health care for people with learning disabilities, which found 'some appalling examples of discrimination, abuse and neglect across the range of health services' (Michael, 2008: 7). A joint investigation by the Local Government Ombudsman and the Parliamentary and Health Service Ombudsman (2009) upheld most of the complaints about the six deaths, and commented that they were a 'shocking indictment of services which profess to value individuals and to personalise services according to individual need' (p. 17).

Why *does* inequality matter?

The short answer to this question, as the discussion has already begun to show, is that different aspects of inequality matter differently to people from different political and philosophical perspectives.

We can see this if we think back to Chapter 3, the four welfare approaches: the minimalist, integrationist, social democratic and radical perspectives bring very different understandings and emphases – but as we noted there, most countries and most people have a mixture of these beliefs.

For the minimalists, poverty and inequality are essential parts of a free market and a free society, inevitable but also useful to motivate individuals to work hard. They would accept that people have basic rights to fair treatment (i.e. civil and political rights against discrimination), but would not support positive action to redress inequalities of opportunity. People have to make and take their own opportunities. They would argue that maximum freedom is essential for economic growth, so that talented people can make lots of money, and then (they believe) the benefits will trickle down to all.

For the integrationists, the worst extremes of poverty are unacceptable, and they would support policies and taxes to tackle them. However, they would consider some degree of inequality valuable as a reward for hard work, to keep the economy going and to ensure social stability (for them, this means securing the support of the middle and wealthier classes). So, they would support equality of opportunity, and limited forms of positive action to redress the worst inequalities. They would not support larger-scale action to redistribute wealth and achieve equal outcomes.

From a social democratic point of view, there should be greater efforts to end inequality as well as poverty. This should go beyond legal protection against discrimination and unequal treatment, and beyond small-scale positive action, to much wider policies for redistributing wealth and opportunity (the interest is in social and economic rights, as well as civil and political). The radicals look for this but more so. They argue that civil rights tend to uphold privilege (e.g. rights to private property are far more use to those who own property), and look for an end to the unequal social relations that inevitably go with capitalism (you cannot have capitalism without inequality – it runs on some people making money out of others).

The mixture of the approaches and the rhetoric that goes with them is shown in the way that politicians use the different discourses at different times. After New Labour was elected in 1997, Peter Mandelson, one of party's leading figures, promised that after ten years in office one of the signs of its success would be a more equal society, although not only by redistribution of money, which he regarded as a 'limited version of egalitarianism' (Mandelson, 1997, in Compass, 2007: 3). His point was that tackling inequality is more than a matter of taxing the rich: it is also about improving public services, regenerating neighbourhoods and getting people into work, all well-known New Labour themes, typical of the integrationist approach. But in 1998 Mandelson also famously said that New Labour was 'seriously unconcerned about people getting filthy rich as long as they paid their taxes' (Mandelson, 2008). This gives a nod to redistribution, but the lightness of the taxation regime for the wealthy makes this much more like the minimalist position (heavy taxes would give a very different message). The banking scandals of 2007–9 have demonstrated that governments ought to be concerned about some people getting filthy rich, and political rhetoric has changed recently. Whether anything will change in practice remains to be seen.

Mandelson's comments reflect the political need to appeal to all the perspectives. The current government approach gives three reasons why equality is an important social objective, which combine the different elements:

- for the individual, in terms of his/her legal and human rights, to be free from discrimination and prejudice;
- for society, because a more equal society is more cohesive and more at ease with itself;
- for the economy, because it ensures the widest labour pool and helps the nation to be competitive in the global economy.

(GEO, 2009: 1; CLG, 2009c: 8)

The emphasis on individual rights and opportunities, and a strong economy, should appeal to the minimalists, even if they are not convinced by the value of a more equal society. The economic aspects should appeal especially to the integrationists, along with the idea of a cohesive society. The idea of an equal society and non-discrimination should appeal to the social democrats and (as much as anything from the state ever can) the radicals.

There is evidence that more equal societies have higher overall standards of health, less violence and fear of crime, and enable more people to reach their full potential. Wilkinson and Pickett (2009) show that inequality does not just affect the poorer section of society, but has a damaging impact on the richer groups too (and see Wilkinson and Marmot, 2003; Wilkinson, 2005). They suggest that the stresses of living in unequal societies lie behind this – the pressures affect the better-off as well as the poor (Wilkinson and Pickett, 2009: esp. 180–93). From this perspective, there is a practical as well as a moral argument for greater equality – everyone does better.

So did New Labour achieve its goal of a more equal society in ten years? The main findings are good progress in some aspects but not in others; slower progress in many areas over the second half of the period; and there is still a long way to go (e.g. Compass, 2007; Palmer *et al.*, 2008; Hills *et al.*, 2009b). Hills *et al.* (2009a: 357) conclude that there were notable reductions in child and pensioner poverty, improvements in children's educational achievements, some closing of the large gaps between some minority ethnic groups and the white British population. But they go on to say:

Where significant policy initiatives were undertaken, the outcomes generally moved in the right direction, if not always as rapidly as policy makers and other observers might have hoped . . .The problem is that the scale of the action was often small in relation to the underlying inequalities, and the momentum gained by the middle of the period had often been lost by the end of it. Problems were often harder to tackle than the government appears to originally have assumed, and less amenable to a one-off fix.

(Hills *et al.*, 2009a: 358)

To explore the issues in more detail, the following sections look at social class and poverty.

Social class

Social class is another term that seems obvious at first sight, but turns out to be conceptually complex and tricky to define. How many classes are there? How would you classify different people – for example, a waitress who happens to be the daughter of a duke? Where would you put a plasterer? But what if they earn more than, say, a school teacher – who should go higher? What is your basis for deciding? In everyday conversation people might talk about 'working class', 'middle class' and 'upper class', and are likely to ascribe different people to those categories for a variety of reasons. What jobs or how much money people have may be less important than their family background, how they talk, dress and where they live (so someone who is perceived as 'upper class' is likely still to be seen that way, even if they lose all their money).

Sociologists, social researchers and social policy analysts need to have a clear and shared framework for social class categories if they are to monitor social trends and the outcome of social policies. Occupation is usually taken as an indicator of social class, despite the occasional anomalies it produces. The scheme most widely used in official statistics until 2001 was a five-class system, based on occupation, known as the Registrar General's scheme. Class I was professional occupations (e.g. doctors, lawyers); Class II was managerial and technical occupations (which included social workers and nurses); Class III was skilled occupations, split into IIIN (non-manual work, such as retail staff) and IIIM (skilled manual work, for example bricklaying); Class IV was partly skilled occupations (including care assistants); and Class V was unskilled work, such as labouring.

A revised system was introduced in the national census in 2001, known as the National Statistics Socio-Economic Classification (NS-SEC). Many social policy documents will still use the old scale, but the newer one will become more widespread over time. Table 5.1 shows the new categories and examples of the occupations that come under each.

Table 5.1
National Statistics Socio-Economic Classification

1.	Higher managerial and professional occupations:	
	1.1 Employers and managers in large organisations	e.g. senior managers in national or local government, health service managers, senior police officers
	1.2 Higher professionals	e.g. university lecturers, doctors, solicitors, architects
2.	Lower managerial and professional occupations	e.g. social workers, nurses, teachers, librarians, professional sports players
3.	Intermediate occupations	e.g. secretaries, electricians, computer engineers, nursing auxiliaries
4.	Small employers and own account workers	e.g. child minders, shopkeepers, carpenters, decorators
5.	Lower supervisory, craft and related occupations	e.g. bakers, train drivers, TV engineers, motor mechanics
6.	Semi-routine occupations	e.g. care assistants, sales assistants, call centre workers, caretakers
7.	Routine occupations	e.g. sewing machinists, packers, labourers, refuse collectors
8.	Never had paid work/long-term unemployed	
	Unclassified	includes full-time students, and cases that cannot be classified for various reasons

Source: Based on ONS (2005)

The social gradient

The challenges of defining social class might lead one to suspect that the notion is of little practical use. This is not the case, for despite the conceptual difficulties, SEC (socio-economic classification) is an extremely powerful predictor of one's life chances. There is a strong 'social gradient' of inequality, which holds across all aspects of life and death (Wilkinson and Marmot, 2003). As examples, people in the higher groups are more likely to live longer and be in better physical and mental health, while their children are more likely to do better at school and go on to higher education. They are less likely to be disabled, overweight, smokers, or the victims of accidents or crime, and their children are less likely to die in infancy. It is not just that the richest group does better than the poorest, but at each step along the way, the higher-placed SEC group nearly always does better than the one below it.

An example is the death rates of working-age men in England and Wales, 2001–3, shown in Figure 5.1. Men in routine occupations are nearly three times more likely to die before the age of 65 than men in higher professions – 513 deaths per 100,000 compared to only 182 – and the slope across the different

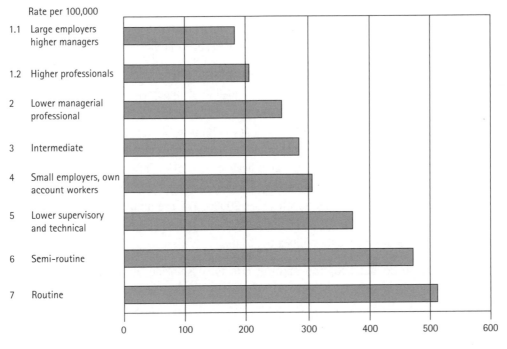

Figure 5.1
The social gradient
Age-standardised mortality rate by NS-SEC: men aged 25–64, England and Wales 2001–3.

Source: ONS, 2007. Crown copyright. Reproduced under the terms of the click-use licence.

groups is clear to see (ONS, 2007). It is worth pointing out that we are talking about trends across populations, not an inevitable fate for individuals – but those trends are strong, reflecting the powerful impact of inequality and poverty on people's lives.

Social class, health and choice

New Labour made tackling health inequalities a political priority soon after it was elected in 1997 by commissioning an independent review of the issues. This became known as the Acheson report (1998), and it stressed the importance of tackling health inequalities both 'upstream' and 'downstream' – that is, to address the structural and social determinants, such as poverty, employment and education, but also to address individual behaviour, such as smoking. The government published a white paper, *Saving Lives: Our Healthier Nation*, in 1999, which set out the goals of improving overall health while reducing the health 'gap' between the richer and poorer sections of society (DH, 1999b). In 2003 the government published *Health Inequalities: A Programme for Action*, which specified two particular goals: to reduce inequalities in life expectancy and infant mortality (DH, 2003b). In 2008, a progress report found that while life expectancy had risen for all groups, including the poorest, it had risen faster for the better-off groups – so the gap had actually widened. The same had happened with infant mortality – it had fallen for all groups, but not as much for the poorest, so the gap had widened (DH, 2008d; and see Sassi, 2009). In late 2008, the government announced an independent review to advise on strategies for tackling health inequalities from 2010 (the Marmot review, due to report in late 2009).

The 2008 progress report recognises that health inequalities are a reflection of wider inequalities in income, housing and education, and in turn linked to inequalities in opportunities and aspirations (DH, 2008d: 29). However, it focuses attention on the importance of people's own choices and behaviour, especially smoking, heavy alcohol consumption and poor diet. The social gradient comes into play again. The report shows that high-risk health behaviours, especially those big three, are more prevalent in lower SEC groups. The report highlights the significance of smoking, although this is not a new theme – for example, it was emphasised in the 1999 *Saving Lives* paper. It is the main cause of the social class differences in premature death rates (DH, 2008d: 47). The progress report argues that 'reducing the socioeconomic gradient in smoking is probably the single most effective thing the Government can do to reduce inequalities in health' (p. 48).

While there can be no doubt about the harmful effects of smoking, it is again necessary to counterbalance this focus on individual behaviour. Yes, people make choices, and it is important not to deny that, but they make choices in circumstances that are not always of their own choosing, moulded by powerful social and economic forces. The close links with social class show that it is not a simple matter of individual choice, otherwise smoking would be equally distributed across the SEC groups. Child and family social workers are likely to be more concerned about parents using illegal drugs than smoking, but the point is the same, to understand people's behaviour in the wider context of limited opportunities, stress and poverty, not simply (accusingly) as individual choice. Graham (2007: 179) makes the following comment about seeing health behaviour as a lifestyle choice:

> Such a perspective casts poorer groups as the problem: it implies that if they only modified their lifestyles and parenting practices to be more like richer groups, all would be well. It is a perspective which locates cause and solution at the 'downstream' end of the causal pathway. Such an approach leaves upstream determinants intact and undisturbed. However, the evidence suggests that it is the persistence of these inequalities – inequalities in the structural institutions of society, like the labour market and people's positions within them – which underlies the persistence of health inequalities.

To be fair, the DH progress report does talk about a wide range of interventions to tackle health inequalities, many of which are upstream, at the universal and primary levels, especially support for parents and young children, getting people into work, and better coordination and commissioning of services. It avoids direct talk of poverty, speaking more euphemistically about 'disadvantaged communities'. The endurance of health inequalities, despite all the programmes and policies, shows what a hard upstream task it is to reduce them.

Social class, race and education

How does social class interact with race? School attainment illustrates the complexities. The social gradient holds true for GCSE results (ONS, 2004), but within that there are different patterns of performance from young people of different minority ethnic backgrounds.

From 2005 to 2009, the government's race equality strategy was called *Improving Opportunity, Strengthening Society* (see CLG, 2009a, 2009b). In February 2009 the government published a discussion document on renewing the strategy (CLG, 2009c). These three documents identify areas where progress has been made, where more needs to be done, and differences between outcomes for different minority ethnic groups. The 2009 report shows that school achievement of minority ethnic pupils has generally improved, but there is great variation behind this (CLG, 2009a: 19). In 2008, 64 per cent of pupils nationally achieved five or more GCSE passes at grade C or above. For Chinese young people, it was 84 per cent; for black Caribbean pupils, 54 per cent (up from 33 per cent in 2003); black African, 60 per cent (up from 41 per cent in 2003); and Bangladeshi, 62 per cent (up from 45 per cent in 2003). For Travellers of Irish heritage, it was 17 per cent, and for Gypsy/Roma students, 16 per cent.

But are these differences because of race or socio-economic background – or can we say anything about the interaction of these factors? The CLG discussion document (CLG, 2009c: 22) refers to research by Strand (2008), and his analysis gives two important answers to this question. He finds that the major differences are to do with socio-economic group rather than race. The biggest gaps of all were not *between* the racial groups, but *within* the white British group, between children whose parents were long-term unemployed and those who were in professional and managerial jobs. Strand assesses the interaction of race, gender and class, and finds that the three lowest-performing groups are white boys, white girls and black Caribbean boys, all from low SEC homes. He stresses that we should not see the findings as an argument to concentrate more on the white groups: rather, 'the substantial gap between high and low socio-economic status is an equity issue for *all* ethnic groups' (Strand, 2008: 4; emphasis in original).

But class does not explain all the difference. Strand's second finding is that black pupils from middle and high SEC homes, particularly black Caribbean and black African boys, underachieved compared to white pupils from the same class backgrounds. Strand identifies four crucial factors for school success: parents' educational aspirations for their child, pupils' aspirations, pupils' academic self-concept, and the frequency of completing homework. These help explain why some children do better than others, but given that children in the higher SEC groups are likely to share these features, they do not explain why black children from these groups do less well than their peers. Strand (2008) suggests looking at teacher expectations (and see Strand, 2007). This is not to accuse teachers of being consciously racist, but it gets us back to the difficult issues of unconscious attitudes and institutional discrimination.

Poverty

Reducing poverty is crucial to improving people's physical and mental wellbeing and creating a more equal society. In New Labour policy, the main way of doing so has been to get people into work, with a system of tax credits to boost the take-home pay of people in low-paid jobs or with large families. Getting more parents to work also requires the widespread availability of good-quality day care for pre-school children, and early morning and after-school provision for school-age children. For older people, the main way is to encourage private savings and pension plans.

But before we can talk about reducing poverty, we are back to the issue of definitions. We need a clear understanding of what 'poverty' is. Is it simply lack of money – if so, how much do people need to stop being poor? Or should we consider other aspects of life, not just income? These questions are crucially important, because unless we are clear about what we mean by poverty we will not know what we have to do to tackle it, or when we have been successful. Four approaches to understanding poverty are outlined in Box 5.2.

Box 5.2 Four questions about poverty

1 Absolute and/or relative poverty?

Where is the 'poverty line'? Should it be the minimum income necessary for survival, or should it be the amount of money to have a generally acceptable standard of living in one's society? Who decides how much money is needed for either of these poverty lines? How? (For example, what counts as part of a 'generally acceptable standard' – subscription television channels, holidays, new clothes or second hand, alcohol?)

2 Income and/or opportunities?

Should poverty be measured simply in terms of the income and financial assets of an individual or household, or should it include other factors like educational attainment, health, employment, standard of housing? Access to services such as decent schools and health care? Quality of neighbourhood life, low crime rates?

3 Individual and/or social causes?

How do we understand the causes of poverty? Individual misfortune, individual choices? Intergenerational or community attitudes and cultures? Lack of effective services and support? Wider structural causes (e.g. social class, gender, race)? The exploitative relations of capitalism?

---

4 Material and/or social consequences?

Do we measure poverty solely in terms of the material impact (poor diet, clothing, health, housing, education), or do we also look at the impact on social relations (shame and stigma, disrespect and humiliation, powerlessness, stereotyping)? Lister's (2004) 'wheel of poverty' has the material aspects at the centre and the non-material, symbolic and relational aspects round the edge.

The first approach is to distinguish between absolute poverty and relative poverty. Absolute poverty is usually taken to be such a shortage of income and other resources that a person's physical existence is in jeopardy. This level of poverty is relatively unusual in the countries of the developed world, which makes it tempting for some people in England to claim that we do not have real poverty here (the experiences of immigrants and asylum seekers must give us pause for thought). The response to this is the notion of relative poverty. The best-known definition is from Peter Townsend (1979: 31):

> Individuals, families, and groups in the population can be said to be in poverty when they lack the resources to obtain the types of diet, participate in the activities, and have the living conditions and amenities which are considered customary, or at least widely encouraged and approved, in the societies to which they belong.

This definition focuses attention on the wider social context, but raises as many questions as it answers. Which things should be included, and who is to say? And how much money does that require?

The government uses a low-income line of 60 per cent of the UK median income, adjusted for household size (because larger families need more money to avoid being in poverty). The figures are published in the annual *Households Below Average Income* report (DWP, 2009), which uses weekly disposable income (i.e. after taxes and benefits), and gives the figures before and after housing costs, BHC and AHC. The government prefers the BHC figure, but the Child Poverty Action Group argues that AHC is a better measure of disposable incomes (CPAG, 2008: 5).

In 2007–8, the national median income (i.e. half the population above and half below) was £393 BHC, or £332 AHC. This is taken as the standard for a couple with no children. Table 5.2 shows what this means for the median and low-income lines, before and after housing costs, when it is adjusted for different types of household.

In 2007–8, there were 13.5 million people in the UK below the 60 per cent line, AHC (DWP, 2009: 40, 42). That is 23 per cent of the population, but the rate varies substantially for different ethnic groups. It is 20 per cent for white British people, but 25 per cent for Indian people, 31 per cent for black Caribbean, 45 per cent for black non-Caribbean, and 61 per cent for Pakistani and Bangaldeshi people (DWP, 2009: 38).

Table 5.2

Median weekly income and low-income line for different types of household, UK 2007–8, before and after housing costs

	Median BHC	60% of median BHC	Median AHC	60% of median AHC
Couple with no children	£393	£236	£332	£199
Couple with two children ages 5 and 14	£601	£361	£537	£322
Lone parent with two children ages 5 and 14	£472	£283	£398	£239
Single person with no children	£263	£158	£192	£115

Adapted from DWP (2009: 18)

The report notes that the distribution is skewed by a substantial number of individuals with very high incomes, and there is a large concentration of people around the 60 per cent mark (DWP, 2009: 12–13). This means that many people will be living on the edge, just getting by, always vulnerable to falling below the line. This makes it important to understand poverty over time, and recognise that it may be a transient experience for some, recurrent for others, and persistent for still others.

Another aspect of defining poverty is to consider a person's access to opportunities and services, not just their cash income. This approach directs attention to the importance of good-quality local facilities such as schools, health services, shops, banks, parks, sports and social centres; the availability of jobs, easily reached from people's homes and paying decent wages; good housing; protection from crime and antisocial behaviour; and access to reliable, safe and frequent public transport.

It is important to recognise the resilience and coping strategies of many poor people, and not to cast them as passive victims (Lister, 2004). Having said that, we must also recognise that the struggle to manage on a low income, week after week, wears people out, physically and mentally. There are powerful impacts on health (the social gradient) and also on self-esteem and confidence, knowing that one is poor and not able to take part in the things that 'ordinary' people do. These social consequences are felt early by children, and they shape their expectations accordingly, 'learning to be poor' (Shropshire and Middleton, 1999). The sense of exclusion is transmitted to children in many ways, through television, shops, remarks by other children, even, inadvertently, how their parents explain things. When shopping with a child, better-off parents tend to explain why they are not going to buy something by saying it is not good value, not worth the money; poorer parents are more likely to say that they cannot afford it (Shropshire and Middleton, 1999: 23–4). The language gives a strong message to the children about their power to make choices, and their place in society.

Box 5.3 'Modest but adequate'

One approach to the question of trying to define relative poverty is to think in terms of a modest but adequate standard of living (e.g. Parker, 2002), and then work out how much money this would require.

- What would you include in a modest but adequate lifestyle for a family of two adults and two children (aged 14 and 5)? For example, think about food, possessions, personal space and time, family activities, friends. The exercise works best when you are very specific about what is included.

- Or for a married couple, in reasonable health, aged 80 and 76?

- How much money do you think this would cost per week?

- Look back to the 60 per cent of median income figures. Do you consider them generous, sufficient, or inadequate?

- Find out the current income support levels for these two households (DWP website). What do you think of them?

- It is useful to discuss these questions in a group, if possible. What things do you agree about, and on what matters do you disagree? What are the reasons for any disagreements?

Child poverty

When New Labour came to power in 1997, the UK had one of the highest rates of child poverty in the industrialised world (Stewart, 2009: 47). Well over a quarter of all children were living below the 60 per cent low-income line, BHC (3.4 million, 27 per cent; it was 33 per cent, AHC: DWP, 2009: 72, 74). In 1999, Tony Blair pledged to end child poverty by 2020, with an interim goal of halving it by 2010. Although it now seems certain that the 2010 target will be missed, it is important to acknowledge that this was an ambitious and unprecedented commitment. Even in 2009, as the difficulties for achieving the targets became clearer and the economic crisis magnified them, the government proposed to put the 2020 goal into legislation with a Child Poverty Bill (HM Government, 2009a: 9).

If we think about the social policy triangle, we can see why the promise was an effective political move, even if surprising. New Labour's main method of tackling child poverty is getting their parents into work, so it achieves welfare goals at the same time as enforcing responsibility and economic participation. Also, it is designed to reduce the long-term costs of child poverty, shown in poor educational achievement, low employment rates when they grow up and higher risks of early childbearing for young women (e.g. Ermisch *et al.*, 2001). So, it is about helping children now, but also about making them better workers in the future (Williams, 2004). This policy breadth makes it politically powerful (and who could vote in favour of children being poor?), and explains why even the Conservative Party has accepted the goal as an 'aspiration' (Letwin, 2006, in Stewart, 2009: 58).

Having said that, the specificity of the targets was risky, and set off a lengthy process to work out how to define child poverty. The government now uses a three-part measure: 'relative poverty', the current 60 per cent of median income, BHC; 'absolute poverty', which compares the current poverty line to the line in 1998–9 (i.e. not the strict starvation-level definition of absolute poverty); and 'material deprivation and low income' (DWP, 2003; HM Treasury *et al.*, 2008: 5). The test of material deprivation is rather like the concept of a modest but adequate lifestyle. It includes a list of possessions and activities, and asks parents if they and their children have these; and if not, if this is because they choose not to or cannot afford them. One example is keeping the house warm: 1 per cent of richer families said they could not afford this, compared to 18 per cent of the poorest (DWP, 2009: 69–70).

In 2007–8, there were 2.9 million children living below the relative poverty line, BHC, 23 per cent (31 per cent, AHC: DWP, 2009: 74). This is a disappointingly small decrease since 1997, but we have to appreciate that it is a moving target, and (like health inequalities) if the better-off do better, then it is harder for the poorest to catch up. Over half a million children have been taken out of poverty since 1998–9, and the number in poverty would have been far higher if nothing had been done. Looking behind the overall figures shows significant drops in the number of children in persistent poverty, and among the children of lone parents (Stewart, 2009: 55, 57).

There are great variations according to region and ethnicity. In inner London, the proportion in poverty, AHC, was 44 per cent, far higher than the 31 per cent national average. Children from minority ethnic backgrounds were more likely to be living in poverty than white British children: the AHC figures were 27 per cent of white British children, 34 per cent of Indian children, 39 per cent black Caribbean, 53 per cent black non-Caribbean and 67 per cent of Bangladeshi and Pakistani children (DWP, 2009: 66–7). There are some well-known risk factors for child poverty – large families, lone-parent families, workless families, families with a disabled member. Platt (2009) shows that these explain some of the differences, but even so, minority ethnic children are more likely to be in poverty than white British children in apparently similar family circumstances.

The immediate causes of child poverty are their parents/carers having low income or being out of work, but the factors behind that are 'multiple, complex and overlapping' (HM Treasury *et al.*, 2008: 7). What is necessary? It needs the upstream activities, such as raising educational levels so that people can get better jobs, but it needs immediate action too (see CPAG, 2009, for a detailed set of proposals). Hirsch (2008), summarising a number of research studies funded by the Joseph Rowntree Foundation, proposes three broad aspects: *support, opportunity* and *behaviour*.

- *Support* includes improved financial help, such as raising benefit levels, improving the operation of the tax credit and benefit systems, and raising the minimum wage. It also involves skilled support and guidance for helping people find and start jobs, and help for gaining skills and qualifications. This echoes Harker (2006: 61), who argues for a welfare to work system that is more tuned into parents' needs and helps them to make progress in jobs, not just to find jobs.

- *Opportunity* includes good-quality childcare, jobs with family-friendly hours, flexible working and jobs which offer training and progression.

- *Behaviour* is important too, but the question is how can the government facilitate and encourage the behaviours it wants (such as more parents in work, or gaining skills)? This needs a shift to a partnership approach, recognising people's different circumstances without blaming and punishing them.

Conclusion: the relevance to social work

Why are these debates about poverty and inequality so important for social work? One answer is that the people we work with tend to be from the poorer groups in society, so we need to understand the challenges they face, the broader social trends and the policies that are in place. As an intellectual profession we need to understand the issues; as a practical profession, we will want to use this knowledge to do something about them. We have those professional values about respect and fair distribution of resources.

But what can we do as social workers? There is little scope in mainstream local authority social work for campaign work and public protest, but there is ample opportunity and challenge in one's day-to-day practice to help secure better opportunities and outcomes for service users and their families. Yet, as was noted at the start of the chapter, social work is sometimes criticised for being part of the blaming and controlling state system, despite our aspirations and our rhetoric.

Humphries (2004: 105) is especially critical of the gap between talk and practice. She goes so far as to say: '[Social work] needs to stop pretending that what it calls "anti-oppressive practice" is anything but a gloss to help it feel better about what it is required to do, a gloss that is reinforced by a raft of books and articles that are superficial and void of a political context for practice.'

Humphries is talking about social work's role in immigration cases, but her general point could apply to all rhetoric about equalities. In a similar vein, McLaughlin (2008: 56) speaks of 'a new professional middle class who use anti-oppressive terminology to gain some sense of moral superiority, while simultaneously establishing more forms of control over various sections of society'. We have to take the criticisms seriously but not be defeated by them. The messages are that we need to be wary of easy talk, and also have a critical awareness of the big picture behind social work if we are to avoid individualistic and oppressive practice – the power of structural inequality, the impact of poverty, the politics and the policies.

Another reason why social divisions and equalities are so important in social work is that they all affect us personally. We all have our own class background, race, gender and sexuality, we are able-bodied or disabled, and many will have personal experiences of disadvantage or discrimination. This leads to complex, personally and professionally challenging situations. For example, social workers may be working with black families who have suffered racism, or with people who have racist attitudes. How does our own racial group affect how we are perceived by these service users, how we understand their experiences, interact with them, and feel about working with them?

There may be particular tensions between social workers' own class backgrounds and social work's position in the socio-economic classifications (Table 5.1). By getting a degree and a professional job, social workers are, on the outside at least, middle class. But how do we feel about that on the inside? Such questions add another dimension to the social work diamond – alongside our responsibilities to service users and to the organisation, our professional values and our state role, there are our personal

Table 5.1

experiences, understandings and values. So, in a book about social policy, we still have to think about our personal beliefs, and we still have to think about practice with individuals and families, not just social trends and statistics. Of course – the personal, political, social and practice dimensions are indivisible.

Whatever the causes, people experience problems downstream and help at that moment can be a good thing. It might only be a 'sticking plaster', but that could be just what is needed. Concentrating only on the upstream factors can be as unhelpful as looking only at the immediate, pressing situation. We need both. The bigger picture is essential, even if we are not radical activists ourselves. It can help us avoid simplistic and blaming responses, and look for new ways to offer support, create opportunities and work in partnership with people, to help them change behaviours that may be harmful or distressing to themselves or others.

Questions for reflection

Box 5.1

- Look back to the ten dimensions of inequality given by the Equalities Review (2007), shown in Box 5.1. Think of an individual or family you have worked with. How do their opportunities and experiences relate to that list? What are the lessons for social work?

- Look back to the discussion of institutional discrimination. Use the ideas to evaluate the policies and practices of an agency where you have worked or been on placement, towards a particular service user group. What are the lessons?

- How do you think your social class background has shaped the person you are today? Have you changed class? Do you think you could – and would you want to? How do you relate your personal sense of class to where social work is in the NS-SEC?

- What about your race and gender, sexuality and whether you are able-bodied or disabled? How did these aspects interact with your social class when you were growing up, and now? How do you think they shape the way that you work with service users, colleagues and other professionals?

- How much allowance do you make for the effects of poverty when assessing and understanding the situation and behaviour of social work service users? How much should you?

Useful websites and further reading

There are many research and campaign groups with specialist interests in different aspects of inequality and poverty. Important organisations on poverty are:

- *The Poverty Site* (www.poverty.org.uk) has statistics and research about poverty in all four countries of the UK. It is produced by the New Policy Institute with support from the Joseph Rowntree Foundation. Both of these organisations have websites with invaluable research and policy analysis about poverty: www.npi.org.uk and www.jrf.org.uk.

- *Child Poverty Action Group* (CPAG): the leading campaign, research and policy analysis group on child and family poverty: www.cpag.org.uk.

- *End Child Poverty* campaign: www.endchildpoverty.org.uk.

Specialist government units include:

- *Government Equalities Office* (GEO): a cross-departmental body to coordinate the government's equality strategy: www.equalities.gov.uk.

- *Child Poverty Unit*: the inter-departmental unit responsible for child poverty strategy in England and Wales: www.dwp.gov.uk/childpoverty.

- *DH Health Inequalities* site: www.dh.gov.uk/en/Publichealth/Healthinequalities.

The chapter referred to a range of reports and reviews about inequality and poverty, many of which are available on the internet. The report of the Equalities Review (2007), *Fairness and Freedom: The Final Report of the Equalities Review*, is recommended.

Look out for the reports of the National Equalities Panel and the post-2010 strategic review of health inequalities, both due in late 2009.

Recommended books are:

Alcock (2006) *Understanding Poverty*, 3rd edn.

Lister (2004) *Poverty*.

Toynbee (2003) *Hard Work: Life in Low-Pay Britain*.

Graham (2007) *Unequal Lives: Health and Socioeconomic Inequalities*.

Hills *et al.* (2009b) *Towards a More Equal Society? Poverty, Inequality and Policy since 1997*.

Wilkinson and Pickett (2009) *The Spirit Level: Why More Equal Societies Almost Always Do Better*.

6 Participation and choice

Participation and choice, along with themes of empowerment and control, have become central concepts in modern social policy. They underpin the drive to transform adult social care (HM Government, 2007; DH, 2008c), but are fundamental to a wider vision of personalising public services as a whole, making them more accountable to service users, responsive and imaginative. Beyond that, there is a vision of broader social change, greater involvement of service users and citizens, a new culture and new roles for local government and social professionals, and stronger, supportive communities (PMSU, 2007; CLG, 2006, 2008c). All this is a very ambitious agenda, fraught with difficulty and complexity. It raises the usual questions. What do we mean by 'participation' and 'choice'? Why are they important? What are the limitations? And, behind all the rhetoric, what and who are they for?

As regards participation of service users and carers in social care, there are three aspects:

- participation in decisions about their own situation and the services they receive;
- participation on broader issues about planning, delivering and evaluating services; and then more broadly still,
- participation in society.

There is potential for a productive interplay of ideas and strategies between these three levels, and between practice and policy. The goal of ensuring genuine empowerment, not just tokenism, should be the same whether one is working with an individual on their own care or support plan, or with a group of service users at a wider planning level. At all levels, though, there are dilemmas of balancing other rights and responsibilities, managing risk and working within available resources.

The first part of the chapter identifies different meanings of participation, using the models of 'ladders of participation'. The second section discusses the significance of participation from different social policy and social work perspectives. The third part links participation to the current programmes to personalise social care, and identifies key principles for policy and practice.

Ladders of participation

Sherry Arnstein's 'ladder of citizen participation' (1969) has become a well-known and highly influential model for describing and analysing participation. It has been a starting point for other ladders, and many complementary or alternative models. This section outlines Arnstein's model and another famous ladder, by Roger Hart, for children's participation.

Arnstein's ladder of citizen participation

Arnstein's (1969) ladder was based on her study of the involvement of local people in urban regeneration programmes in large American cities in the 1960s, and is shown in Figure 6.1. She was primarily concerned with the participation of groups in political processes, rather than individuals and casework, but the framework can easily be applied to the involvement of individuals in decisions about their own situation.

On the lower rungs of Arnstein's ladder are forms of participation that are not truly participative at all. The bottom rung is 'manipulation', when people are invited on to committees, or asked to give their views about proposals, simply to confirm decisions that have already been made. It is merely the appearance of involvement. The next rung up is 'therapy'. This is where the experts recommend that someone, or some group of people, should be involved in planning or running a service, or perhaps in the appointment of a member of staff, because 'it will be good for them'. This might be in the sense of teaching them some new skills, or building their self-esteem. It is not that there is anything wrong with these things, but if they are the sole reason for encouraging participation, the balance of power has not shifted at all.

Arnstein calls the next three steps 'degrees of tokenism'. First is 'informing'. This is when people are told in advance about what is planned, but not invited to express a view or assisted to do anything about it. It is important that information is honest, full and given clearly, avoiding jargon, otherwise it is not participatory at all. It may be rather 'take it or leave it', but at least being informed gives people the opportunity to consider the proposals and take action themselves if they decide to do so. Above that comes 'consultation'. Here, people's views are sought at the planning stage, but there is no guarantee that they will be acted on. Decisions are still made by the professionals, and professionals still control

Figure 6.1
A ladder of citizen participation
Adapted from Arnstein (1969: 217)

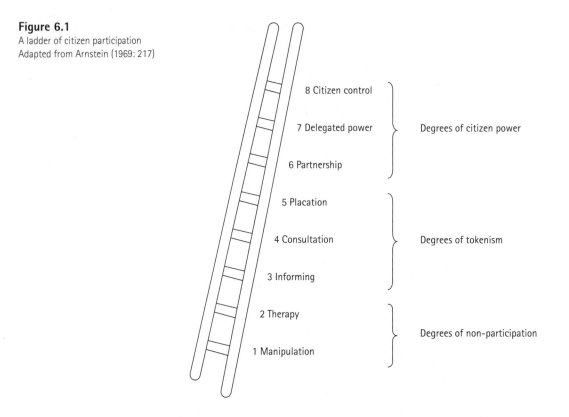

the implementation of the plans. Level 5 is 'placation'. This is where people are invited to get involved, perhaps to sit on a committee, but the purpose is to head off dissent, rather than listen to alternative views. At this level, the people invited to participate might be local figureheads, or the usual service user representatives, well known to the planners or service managers and easily manageable by them. The representatives might be allowed to vent their frustrations, and some concessions may be made, but essentially this is just about smoothing the way for the existing plan. Open meetings and residents' surveys or opinion polls may also be placatory, depending on the circumstances.

Moving up, the top three rungs represent 'degrees of citizen power'. Level 6 is 'partnership'. This is when local people or service users share in decision-making with the professionals, and the agreement of both parties is necessary for the plan to proceed. Not all partnerships are equal, however, and it may be that the views of one group can be overruled by the other. The key points for effective partnerships are that the residents or service users are fully informed about the issues at stake, have access to independent advice, and are aware of any external limits that constrain the project (e.g. budgets, legislation, timescales). Level 7 is 'delegated power'. This is where the residents have full control over an issue – but only that issue, as delegated to them by the programme managers. So it tends to be a rather limited aspect of the project – choosing the furniture for the community centre within a specified budget, for example. Further, there is always the risk that the experts will take the power back if they are not happy with how it is being exercised. At the top of the ladder is 'citizen control', when the residents are fully in charge. Here, there may not be a role for professionals; but if there is, it could be as adviser, enabler, advocate, facilitator.

Hart's ladder of children's participation

Arnstein's ladder has been adapted by Roger Hart (1992, 1997) to illustrate the different aspects of participation for children and young people, as shown in Figure 6.2. His focus was on involving children in community development and environmental projects, but it can be applied to other situations and adapted as necessary.

The bottom three rungs of Hart's ladder are examples of non-participation, and are unacceptable. The first is 'manipulation', for example when children's artwork is used in a publication but the children were not involved in any decisions about the book or the use of their pictures – and if people are told that the children were fully involved in the project, Hart would consider this deception. Next is 'decoration'. An example is when children go on a protest march but have no idea what they are

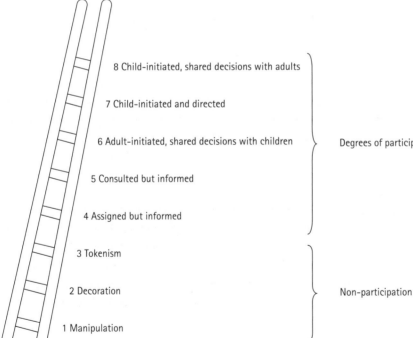

Figure 6.2
A ladder of children's participation
Adapted from Hart (1992: 8; 1997: 41)

protesting about. It is a step up from manipulation because there is no pretence that the children are running the march, but it is not truly participative. 'Tokenism' is the next level. Here, children may be called to talk at meetings, but those who get invited are often the charming, photogenic ones. They are not selected by other children, and it is not clear whose views they represent.

Moving into degrees of participation, level 4 is 'assigned but informed'. This is when children are told about a project and asked to take on a specific role or task. They do have information about what is involved, and a choice whether to participate, but no choice about how the project is run or what their role is. The next rung is 'consulted and informed', which means that the children's views are sought at the planning stage. The children's views will be taken seriously at this level (otherwise it would be at one of the first three rungs), but even so there is no guarantee that they will be acted on. The plan is finalised by the adults, and the children's roles are fixed by them. Level 6 is when the plans are initiated by the adults, but the decisions are shared with the children. The challenge for the adults here is to ensure that the children are properly informed and really do take part in all aspects of the project. Next comes 'child initiated and directed' and the highest rung of all is 'child-initiated, shared decisions with adults'. At first sight this order seems odd – surely, 'child-initiated and directed' should come highest? Hart's answer is that while this might look like full participation, it tends to be limited to specific areas, for example play activities. So it is rather like Arnstein's 'delegated power' – the children do have control of the scheme, planning and implementing their project, but it is only in a relatively modest context. Hart holds that he is not a separatist, and that children can actually achieve more, be involved in bigger schemes, if they do so with adults – but here, at the top of the ladder, the roles of the adults are those of advisers, enablers, facilitators.

Hart notes that it is not always necessary to aim to be at the top of the ladder – some children, in some circumstances, may choose to stay on the lower rungs, and that may be appropriate for them. The important thing is to avoid operating at the bottom three rungs.

Complementary models

Arnstein's and Hart's ladders are helpful models for thinking about participation at group and individual levels, but they have been criticised for being overly rigid and one-dimensional. There are many adaptations and alternatives (for useful summaries, see Adams, 2008; Thomas, 2007), but here I shall highlight two complementary models: Emmanuelle Abrioux's (1998) circle and Nigel Thomas's (2000) climbing wall. Both are writing about children's participation, but their ideas are useful for thinking about and implementing participation more generally, not just with children and young people.

Abrioux worked with girls and young women in Afghanistan. The social and political climate there at the time was strongly against women's open participation in society. Abrioux makes the point that aiming for the higher rungs in those circumstances could have been very dangerous for the girls. She argues that we need a more contextual understanding of participation. We need to be sensitive to different starting points, and the risks to participants. An initiative that might be considered tokenism in one environment could be a constructive step forward in other circumstances. She does not reject the idea of a ladder, but suggests we balance it with the idea of a circle, in which the important idea is to keep moving round. It is not about reaching the top, but about recognising the value of small steps and continually moving on. Participation is a process, not a one-off achievement.

Thomas looked at children who are looked after by local authorities in England (usually placed in foster homes or residential care). There are regulations that require regular reviews of the children's progress and the plans for them, and Thomas studied their participation in these reviews. He uses his observations to ask incisive questions about the ladder model:

> Is a child who attends a meeting because s/he is told that s/he must, and then takes a very active part in the discussion, higher or lower on the ladder of participation than one who attends as a free choice but then says nothing? Is a child who takes a very active part in dealing with all the matters on the agenda, but who does not realise that she could have asked for other things to be discussed, a 'participant' or is she merely being 'consulted'?
>
> (Thomas, 2000: 175)

Thomas argues that there are different aspects of involvement, and we can think of them like bricks or pillars in a wall. He suggests six key aspects: the level of *choice* that a child has over his/her participation; the amount of *information* they have about their situation; the degree of *control* that they have over the decision-making process; how much *voice* they have in the discussion (how much are they allowed to say?); the level of *support* that they receive; and the degree of *autonomy* that they have (that is, freedom to make decisions independently of what others say).

Thomas puts these different dimensions into a diagram, like a bar chart – so, if a child receives a lot of support, that will be a tall column, but if they have little autonomy, that one will be short. This gives a picture of the different aspects and levels of involvement, and Thomas calls it a 'climbing wall' to distinguish it from the idea of a wall as a barrier. The idea is that there is more than one route up it – increasing different aspects will lift the child's overall level of participation and control over his/her own life. Thomas's model shows us that participation is multifaceted, and it is an extremely useful guide for practice, to ensure that we offer appropriate support on all six dimensions.

The ladders and the complementary models are useful for generating questions about the practices of participation. For example, timing: at what stage are service users involved, and how are their views obtained? Are they involved in identifying the problem, designing the service and implementing it, or only afterwards, to assist in evaluation? People may have very different views beforehand, in the middle of a process, and afterwards. Second, are people invited to contribute, or do they have to force their way in? How are meetings publicised, where are they held and at what time of day? Third, what efforts are made to get the views of the 'hard to reach' or 'seldom heard' groups? (Robson *et al.*, 2008, discuss four particular groups: homeless people with addiction problems, people from black and minority ethnic communities, people with communication impairments and people with dementia.) What methods of involvement are used, and what are their strengths and weaknesses (e.g. neighbourhood committees, user-led organisations, user representatives, group discussions, one-to-one interviews, questionnaires, evaluation forms, complaints procedures)? The implications for social work practice and organisations are discussed further below in the section on 'whole systems' change (notably Box 6.1), but first I shall consider more of the underlying dilemmas and debates.

The politics of participation and choice

As the ladders have shown, participation and choice are two more of those words with many different meanings, and many different implications for practice. That is why they have become so widespread in current policy – everyone can sign up to them. For the minimalists, they are a way of restraining the power of overbearing welfare state professionals, and shifting control to service users and citizens. They also welcome the shift of responsibility to individuals and families, and the possibility of reducing state expenditure, as people take on new roles and responsibilities for managing their own welfare. It brings marketplace principles of choice to the public services. The integrationists aim to target services more effectively, and service users' views should help them to do this. They also like the idea of a range of welfare suppliers and people being able to choose between them. They see choice and participation as important ways to get vulnerable people back into society, and also more broadly to regenerate community life, building social cohesion and social capital. The social democrats value participation and choice because they are aspects of citizenship and equality. They may be less concerned than the others about people having a choice of supplier, or about saving money: for them, the priority is to get higher-quality services and a more integrated society. Even the radicals like the ideas of participation and choice, giving power to the people, but they are very suspicious of the motives behind the rhetoric, seeing it as a vehicle for privatising services, saving money and reducing state help to vulnerable families. More than that, they mistrust it as a subtle but powerful form of social control, window-dressing that tricks people into participating in a system that oppresses them (Carey, 2009).

Participation and choice also have profound implications for the social work diamond, unsettling the traditional roles and relationships between state, organisation, profession and service users. Some see the prospect of a new role for the state, to become an 'enabling state', creating the conditions for individuals to make the right choices for their own wellbeing and the wellbeing of others – for example, to adopt a healthy lifestyle, get a job, spend and save their money wisely. The state should become a platform on which citizens can build their own lives, supported by professionals if necessary to 'co-produce' services (Leadbetter, 2004). The radicals, of course, see this sort of talk as diverting attention from the real issues of inequality and power, but still want to see genuine participation and empowerment. Welfare organisations will have to be redesigned to facilitate this new approach – and

this will involve substantial changes of culture, structure, practice and review systems (see Box 6.1). Professional roles should change, to be less the experts assessing needs and allocating services as a 'professional gift' (Duffy, 1996), and instead seeing service users as citizens and supporting them to make their own decisions and achieve their own goals.

The political arguments are well set out in the report of the House of Commons Public Administration Select Committee (2005), *Choice, Voice and Public Services*. It highlights six contentious aspects:

- *Public attitudes*: the question here is whether people really want choices, and if so, what sort. The Committee considers that people are less likely to be concerned about having a choice of provider, but more about the *quality* of the service and *practical choices* that have a direct impact on their lives. To link this to social care, it may be less important to a service user whether their care worker is employed by a local authority, a private agency or themselves; the important thing is having control over when the person comes, what they do, how they do it. Flexible and tailor-made public services are likely to be expensive, which raises political questions about whether the public would be prepared to pay the necessary level of taxes.

- *Choice and capacity*: if people are to have choices, the system has to have enough options. On this point, the Committee warns that government rhetoric about choice has become overblown and misleading. Parental choice about schools is a good example. The truth is that popular schools are oversubscribed and not everyone gets their first choice, but unrealistic expectations can lead to great disappointment and anger. Once again the underlying issue is about the overall standards of the service, for all options to be of a high quality. A choice between poor suppliers is no choice at all.

- *Choice and equity*: the issue here is that participation and choice may not empower everybody, but only those who already have the knowledge and skills to take advantage of them. This tends to be the middle classes, and in this way participation and choice can reinforce inequality rather than redress it. The Committee considers that this is not inevitable, but it needs explicit and determined action to prevent it: 'choice can be consistent with equity if schemes are well designed and motivated by a desire to reduce unfairness' (House of Commons PASC, 2005: 43).

- *Markets and the private sector*: the Committee rejects the idea that the private sector is always better, pointing to the contracting-out of hospital cleaning services as an example of how it has brought worse results. It is also concerned about 'cream-skimming' – that is, the private sector takes the easier and more profitable cases, leaving the most difficult ones to the state sector.

- *Choice and efficiency*: there is tension between these two values. If people are to have choice, there has to be spare capacity, which is inefficient. This could be justified if the overall result were to raise standards, but the Committee is not convinced that it does.

- *Choice and standards*: the Committee concludes that any evidence that choice of providers raises standards is 'sparse and inconclusive' (House of Commons PASC, 2005: 43). It questions whether choice of provider is being promoted primarily to give control to service users, or rather to introduce markets into public services.

Five key questions

Greater participation and choice for service users and carers could be an inspiring vision or an alarming one, depending on one's personal and political points of view. It has the potential to go either way, and there are many challenges for policy and practice. For a start, different people will have different priorities and may make incompatible choices. Who decides, and how? Resources are limited. Who decides, and how? People may not make the 'approved' choice, or their choice may be unsafe. Who decides, and how? Five dimensions are especially important.

Human rights or consumer rights?

It is important to analyse the extent to which programmes for greater service user involvement support it from a standpoint of human rights or consumerism. The latter approach is far more limited. It gives some rights, for sure – to express a view, be consulted, make complaints – but the risk of a consumerist approach is that participation is restricted to fine-tuning services in order to make them more efficient. Rather than encouraging collective action from service users and a revitalised role for state services, it reduces the issue to one of individual choice, a 'supermarketised vision' of involvement (Cowden and Singh, 2007: 6). This diminishes the potential for radical change in the ways that services are designed and delivered, and for challenging discriminatory attitudes and practices. A cost-saving agenda is also characteristic of a consumerist approach, although this is often downplayed. The unspoken idea is that devolving control to individual service users, say through direct payments or individual budgets, will save the state (i.e. the taxpayer) money. The danger here is that participation and choice become ways of passing difficult rationing decisions down the line, to the users themselves (Hoggett, 1996: 20).

There are also grounds to question whether an approach that sees social care service users simply as customers does justice to the complexity of the relationships and responsibilities involved – for example, that some service users are not there voluntarily, and that sometimes their wishes may not be met because of concerns for their own safety or the safety of others. In contrast, a human rights approach recognises the wider implications of participation, that it will entail a new role, not necessarily a reduced one, for state welfare services; and human rights provide a crucial underpinning for legal and procedural safeguards when wishes do have to be overruled.

Cloak or dagger?

For some, participation is a sharp instrument to change public services and beyond that the nature of the relationships between the state and the citizen (e.g. Leadbetter, 2004). Other analysts, though, have identified ways that it can be used as a cloak for decisions that have already been made, or as a handy weapon in political or professional battles. Barnes *et al.* (2003) speak of user involvement being reduced to a 'technology of legitimation', giving the appearance of democratising services, and of how professional groups can sometimes 'play the user card' to try to win arguments ('We know better than you what the users want'). Equally, if service user views go against what the professionals want, they may then play another card, dismissing them as 'unrepresentative' or 'unrealistic'.

Cowden and Singh (2007) point out that government ministers and managers can use the rhetoric of 'listening to users' and 'increasing choice' to criticise and control the practice of front-line workers, by implying that the workers do not really know what the public wants, or are resistant to change. In this way, 'it is easy for service user critiques of professional practice to be simply incorporated into an agenda dominated by performance management, audit and evaluation' (Cowden and Singh, 2007: 19–20).

Process or outcome?

Another important dimension is whether the aim is to encourage participation for its own sake, because the process itself is necessary and worthwhile, an aspect of citizenship, regardless of any benefits it brings; or whether better outcomes are the litmus test. Outcomes include benefits such as enhanced confidence and self-esteem, and improvements to the services. Often these different aspects will go together, *intrinsic* and *extrinsic* benefits (Doel *et al.*, 2007), but they need not. Wonderful cooperative work might not achieve the result the group desires – for example, the local hospital might still be closed. Was it worth it? One disappointing result may not invalidate the personal benefits or the whole principle of participation, but many of them certainly will.

Linked with this 'process or outcome' aspect are questions of whether the goal is greater participation in everyday activities and choices, or in decisions about 'bigger' issues. Robson *et al.* (2008: 7) make the point that participation in the activities and routines of everyday life is 'the bedrock of involvement in other aspects of services'. Staff need to be listening to service users, creating opportunities for them to make choices and exercise control, but that is not sufficient by itself to ensure that service users play a wider part in the development and management of services. Organisations must also enable service users to have access to, and influence in, decision-making structures and processes.

Why do people not always participate?

The fourth key dimension is to understand the possible reasons for non-participation, and work to counter them; but at the same time to respect people's choices not to express their views or get involved in particular projects. Some may be cynical that anything will ever be any different, some may fear repercussions if they complain, and some may be apprehensive about the burdens of taking on too many responsibilities. The important thing is to have worked hard in listening, explaining and creating methods that enable people to play a part and express their views; and just because some people choose not to participate, not to write them off for next time, or to give up on participation altogether.

One reason why some people may take up chances of participation more readily than others is that they are more comfortable with roles in decision-making (this may apply especially to individual budgets, if people have prior skills and confidence in managing financial affairs: see Leece and Leece,

2006). The middle classes may be better placed to take advantage of the new opportunities for personalised services than people from lower SEC backgrounds or other disadvantaged groups. Some people come with a long history of being told what to do by professionals, lacking confidence, skills and (in some cases, understandably) trust to take a different role. For some, saying nothing is the best way of exercising choice, or showing resistance. Others will welcome the opportunity to have their say and possess ample determination to express their views.

There is the other side too: that the biggest cultural and attitudinal change is not for the service users, but for the staff. One explanation for the very slow expansion of direct payments was that there was often reluctance to trust service users to manage the funds properly or safely, the systems were too bureaucratic, and practice was shaped by assumptions that certain people would not be interested or able to manage (Ellis, 2007).

Cooperation or conflict?

The fifth key issue concerns the relationships between workers and users. Are the two groups locked in irredeemable conflict? The consumerist approach can sometimes make it seem like that, but Beresford and Croft (2004) call for closer links and alliances, seeing this as the way forward for a new, more emancipatory social work. Their argument is that the service user movement, and especially service user organisations, have had a great impact in society, well beyond social work and social care, in culture, politics, legislation and social policy. As a movement, it has not been confined to narrow consumerism, but has emphasised the human rights of service users, and a more democratic approach to running public services. Although it has challenged social work, it has done so 'from a progressive and liberatory position' (Beresford and Croft, 2004: 62). If social work is to move away from a controlling role towards a more liberating one, practitioners need to work together with service users and local people.

Carr (2004) sounds a warning. She highlights the extent of the changes that service user involvement demands in social care agencies, and says that it challenges 'the very fabric of the institutions in which it is taking place' (2004: 268). As such, resistance and conflict are inevitable. Carr is hopeful that shared understandings and alliances between service users and practitioners may be achieved, but the road will be difficult. Conflict must be anticipated and worked through, not suppressed. Differences should be valued, and debated openly and honestly.

'Whole systems' change

SCIE has published a wide range of material about participation, including Carr (2004); Begum (2006), Wright *et al.* (2006), Moriarty *et al.* (2007), Doel *et al.* (2007), Robson *et al.* (2008), and Carr and Robbins (2009). One of the common themes is that participation has far-reaching implications for the organisational point of the social work diamond. Social work organisations will need to change their ethos, structures and practices if participation is to be more than tokenistic. Box 6.1 shows the four parts of the jigsaw that need to be addressed.

Box 6.1 A 'whole systems' approach to participation

Culture

Culture includes the beliefs, values and norms of an organisation. It is not static but something that can change over time. Building an effective culture for participation includes:

- establishing a shared understanding of participation;

- leadership – ensuring managers actively support and sustain participation;

- ensuring that all staff are committed to participation (training and support);

- developing a participation charter, as a public promise about participation;

- showing evidence of participation in organisational policies and documents, such as policies and manuals;

- publicising commitment to participation (e.g. leaflets, posters).

Structure

Participation can create change or improvement only when people can influence decision-making processes. Structures must enable service users to become active participants. This includes:

- development of a participation strategy, to include training for staff and service users/ participants, roles in key meetings and committees, changes to make meetings more appropriate (time of day, style of meeting), payment;

- partnership working with other organisations – for example, service user organisations, advocacy and support groups, and other agencies, to promote participation and learn what they do;

- identification of 'participation champions', specialist workers or teams, to coordinate and promote participation;

- provision of adequate resources for participation (e.g. training, equipment, interpreters, expenses and payment, suitable venues).

Practice

Practitioners need to be able to work in a way which enables participation and ultimately brings change or improvement. Good practice on a day-to-day basis is essential to ensure that people have a positive experience of becoming involved. This includes:

- involvement of all, including children and young people, older people, and people from groups that are seldom heard;

- ensuring safe participation, which includes informed consent, not making people feel embarrassed or anxious, awareness of cultural or religious factors, confidentiality;

- creating an environment for participation (e.g. being welcoming, layout of rooms, avoiding jargon, showing respect, thanking people);

- using a variety of flexible and creative approaches, such as focus groups, questionnaires, non-verbal methods, informal meetings, internet;

- understanding the different mechanisms for involving people in organisational development as well as individual decision-making processes (e.g. formal committees, strategy groups, recruitment processes, research);

- providing opportunities for practitioners and service users and carers to develop their skills, knowledge and experience.

Review

The process of monitoring and evaluating the participation of service users and carers. It is important to show how participation has helped change or improve services. This includes:

- systems to provide evidence of the *process* of participation (i.e. what the organisation is doing to involve people) and the *outcomes* (i.e. what has changed as a result);

- clear identification of proposed outcomes (unless you have clear goals, you will not know if you have achieved them) with service user participation in setting them;

- service users and carers should be involved in defining the aims, objectives, processes, and the ways and means of measuring them;

- feedback to service users;

- adequate resources for review systems.

Sources: Based on Wright *et al.* (2006) and Moriarty *et al.* (2007)

Personalisation and self-directed support

The goals of greater choice and control for service users lie behind the development of personalisation and self-directed support in social care. Individual budgets (or 'personal budgets', which is now becoming the more usual term) are among the most important ways to achieve these goals. There are now plans for personal budgets in health care (DH, 2008a and 2009b).

Individual budgets have their origins in the campaigns of disabled people for greater control over the services and support available to them, one result of which was the introduction of direct payments under the Community Care (Direct Payments) Act 1996. Centres for Independent Living, which are user-led organisations for disabled people, have been especially prominent in developing direct payments in the UK, and supporting people to use them. The 1996 Act allowed local authorities to give disabled service users (aged eighteen to sixty-four) a cash sum in place of services, to spend on the services and support they chose. Implementation and take-up were slow and highly variable across the country. People aged sixty-five and over were added in 2000, and then carers, parents of disabled children and disabled young people aged sixteen–seventeen. In 2003 the government made it mandatory to offer direct payments (people can still decline), and made take-up a performance indicator for local authorities, to increase the pace of change (Spandler, 2004; Leece and Leece, 2006; Leece and Bornat, 2006; Ellis, 2007; Glasby, 2007; Scourfield, 2007; Glasby and Littlechild, 2009).

Individual budgets build on the principles of direct payments but bring greater flexibility and incorporate other funding streams as well as social care. In 2005–7, these included housing-related support (Supporting People funds), and DWP disability budgets. They did not include health budgets. The organisation In Control, established in 2003, has been especially prominent in developing the concept of individual budgets, designing a system to operate them and campaigning for their wider adoption (see Poll et al., 2006; Poll and Duffy, 2008). It initially focused on people with learning disabilities, but now works for all groups of social care service users. The report from the Prime Minister's Strategy Unit (PMSU, 2005), *Improving the Life Chances of Disabled People*, proposed that individual budgets for disabled people should be rolled out nationally by 2012, subject to piloting and evaluation. It also proposed that every area should have a user-led organisation to support disabled people to make use of these schemes, modelled on Centres for Independent Living. The green paper *Independence, Well-being and Choice* (DH, 2005) extended the idea of individual budgets to older people. The government published an independent living strategy in 2008, which emphasised that this does not mean living alone or without support, but having choice and control over the assistance or equipment needed, and having equal access to housing, transport, health, employment, and education and training (ODI, 2008: 11). It asserted the government's aim of transforming social care to give 'maximum control and power' to service users (p. 16), including greater use of individual budgets and direct payments, more early intervention and prevention, development of user-led organisations, and better services for information, advocacy and support.

The core principles of independent budgets are that service users should play a greater part in assessing their own needs, and specifying the outcomes they wish to achieve. They should be told what resources they are entitled to, expressed as an amount of money, and have support in planning how to use it, and then using it. There should be a variety of ways of helping people to spend their entitlement, from giving them the cash directly to managing it on their behalf. In Control has a seven-stage process, summarised in Box 6.2.

Box 6.2 In Control's seven-stage process for self-directed support

1 Set individual budget

The person's eligibility for support and the amount of the IB are calculated using a transparent, rational system, and the person is told what the amount is. Currently, the person has to meet the FACS criteria for their local authority, and there will also be a financial assessment. In Control has designed a 'resource allocation system' (RAS) where the assessment of needs gives a points score, and then (if the person is eligible) funding is given on a price-per-point basis. In Control argues that an effective RAS should eventually do away with the need for a FACS-style assessment (Duffy and Waters, 2008).

2 Plan support

The person plans how they wish to use the money to meet their needs and achieve the outcomes they want, in a way that suits them best. The person may be assisted in the planning process by family and friends, a social worker, or a specialist supporter or broker.

3 Agree plan

The plan is checked and approved by the local authority and any other funding provider. This gives an opportunity for issues such as safety and risk to be assessed. Some areas use risk enablement panels to consider these issues. Plans may be amended as a result.

4 Manage individual budget

The person decides on the best way to manage their IB. The person could take all of the IB as a cash payment, but does not have to. Some or all of it could be managed by a local authority care manager, a third party, a trust, or a service provider – but the important point is that it is the person's allocation, ear-marked for them.

---

5 Organise support

The person organises the services and support they want, with assistance as necessary – for example, hiring a personal assistant, purchasing equipment, transport, housing adaptations, leisure activities.

6 Live life

The person uses the services and support to live a full life with family and friends in the community.

7 Review and learn

The plan is reviewed to see if the person is achieving their goals, and changes made if necessary. Minor amendments can be made within the existing plan; major changes may require a reassessment, new resource allocation and new support plan.

Sources: Based on Poll *et al.* (2006: 28);
Poll and Duffy (2008); Glendinning *et al.* (2008a, 2008b)

The government's pilot of individual budgets took place in thirteen local authorities from November 2005 to December 2007. The independent evaluation was published in October 2008 (the Individual Budgets Evaluation Network, IBSEN: Glendinning *et al.*, 2008a and 2008b). In Control has undertaken two evaluations (Poll *et al.*, 2006; Hatton and Waters, 2008). CSCI also undertook an evaluation of personalised support for people with multiple and complex problems (Henwood and Hudson, 2008; reported in CSCI, 2009).

It should be noted that many of the individual budget holders interviewed by the IBSEN evaluation had held their budgets for a very short period of time, and that In Control stresses from its evaluations that people tend to appreciate the benefits of individual budgets more as they become more used to them (Hatton and Waters, 2008). Workers' attitudes are likely to change too, as they gain experience and knowledge of the new system, so the evaluation results need to be seen as a snapshot of an early stage in an evolving process. That said, there are four aspects of individual budgets which are especially relevant to the wider discussions about participation and choice. These are to do with the relationship between choice and need, choice and risk, added burdens, and the implications for professional roles.

Choice and need

The IBSEN study found that most people used at least part of their budget to purchase traditional services, such as home care, personal care and day care (Glendinning *et al.*, 2008b: 15–16). Bearing in mind that people had to meet the FACS criteria, and in most authorities this is set at substantial or critical, it is not surprising that most of the money has to go on these essential services. To put it simply, people cannot manage without them. They may have more choice than before about who provides the care (they can hire the person) and as employers more control over when the person comes, what they do and how they do it; but there was not much of a choice about whether to have these services. 'Choice' is therefore limited by need, and while there are gains in the greater control, this does create challenges for the wider goals about people's aspirations and wishes. There are tensions between the needs-focused FACS approach and the outcomes-oriented approach of self-directed support. These tensions are a prime example of the challenges for participatory approaches of restricted resources and high levels of need and risk.

Choice and risk

Staff were greatly concerned about the risks to service users, notably about them employing people who were not suitable or even dangerous, spending the money on the 'wrong' things and not meeting their essential needs, not getting good value for money and not coping with the additional responsibilities (Glendinning *et al.*, 2008b: 33; 2008a: 171–82; CSCI, 2009: 152–5). There were also concerns about fraud. These may be justifications that social workers use to avoid giving power to service users and the extra, or different, work that this might involve (Ellis, 2007), but local authorities do have duties to safeguard vulnerable people from harm, and to spend public money appropriately, so these concerns are not unreasonable. The IBSEN study found that systems were developing to deal with them. These included panels to check the plans (which offer protection to the service user and the individual worker), revised policies and guidelines, regular reviews, and training for staff. The wider point for participation is that changing attitudes to risk requires whole systems change, as shown in Box 6.1 (and see the government guidance on decision-making, choice and risk: DH, 2007a). However, changes will have to go beyond local authority social care, to other agencies and more generally in society, if workers are to feel confident about managing risk.

Added burdens

The IBSEN study found that, overall, people with individual budgets reported feeling more in control of their lives, the help they had and how it was delivered (Glendinning *et al.*, 2008b: 20). Within that, there were differences for different service user groups. Outcomes were generally positive for people with mental health problems, physically disabled people and people with learning disabilities. The outcomes were more mixed for older people. Those who had individual budgets reported lower psychological wellbeing than those who did not. The study found that many older people saw planning and managing their own support as an additional burden (Glendinning *et al.*, 2008b: 19). In terms of the wider lessons for participation, this shows the importance of recognising differences between different groups, looking at the specific needs of individuals, listening to their views, appreciating how difficult and daunting it can be for some people, and designing services and support accordingly.

Professional roles

Individual budgets had changed workers' roles, and they were spending much more time on the assessment and planning stages (Glendinning *et al.*, 2008b: 35; 2008a: 186–90). There was a great range of views about the changes, with some workers welcoming them as a chance to get back to core social work skills, and others complaining about yet more forms and the fragmentation of the social work role. The In Control research found that most people had help from a social worker in making their support plan, and in general this was associated with better outcomes, notably for older people (Hatton and Waters, 2008). In Control concludes that a wide range of support is essential, especially from family and friends. Not everyone may have close family and friends who are able to assist, and in such cases the role of independent organisations and support brokers is vital. The lessons here are that participation is no short cut and involves hard work in preparation and supporting people; and that there is nothing inevitable about its impact on social work. It could be reinvigorating, or it could become another bureaucratic procedure. Social workers can make the difference through their approach to the tasks.

Conclusion

This chapter has debated some of the ambiguities, tensions and conflicts about service user participation and choice. Individual budgets exemplify the issues. Individual budgets and direct payments have helped some service users to create improved packages of support for themselves, tailor-made and more flexible, to achieve a much better quality of life and a greater sense of wellbeing and independence. There are inspiring examples in the literature and on the In Control website. At the same time, there are concerns that the forces driving personalisation are those of cost-cutting, privatisation, consumerism and shifting the burden of responsibility to individuals. One response to these dangers is to support a more communal, collective approach, so that participation and choice are not restricted to individual cases, but the issues are widened by involving advocacy and support groups, especially user-led organisations, bringing their shared experience, strength and insights.

Service user participation and choice are such powerful, flexible and ambiguous concepts that they can be used, simultaneously, in different ways (Spandler, 2004; Scourfield, 2007). They can challenge long-established ways of doing things, patronising attitudes and unimaginative practice. At the same time, that powerful potential can be diluted if it is only given lip-service, and kept at the lower rungs of the ladder. More than that, it can distorted, if it is taken over and used for political purposes about cutting back the welfare state, or to satisfy managerial goals about budgets and organisational compliance, or as a card to play in inter-professional arguments. At the same time again, there are challenging issues of limited resources, restricted supply (will there be enough people with the right skills who want to be personal assistants?), fairness between different groups and between individuals, safety and legal responsibilities. Political rhetoric based on simplistic notions of consumer rights or customer behaviour does not do justice to these complexities. Taking participation and choice seriously means recognising all sides, the positives and the risks. This is not to be overwhelmed by confusion, but to help us put them into practice in ways which are creative, fair and enhance service users' human rights.

Questions for reflection

- Think about times when you have tried to involve adults or children in planning or running services, or in making decisions about their own lives (if you have not done it in work, think about examples in your personal life). Use Arnstein's or Hart's ladders to analyse what happened. Would you do anything differently next time?

- On the basis of your experience, could you suggest any adaptations to the ladders, or any alternative models of participation?

- Where on the ladders would you put the following? What factors shape your answers – and could they be changed to move things higher up the ladder?
    - *Individual/personal budgets for social care service users*
    - *Social services' complaints procedures*
    - *General elections*

- Use the four elements of whole systems change in Box 6.1 to think about the way that participation was being implemented in an agency where you have worked or been on placement. What areas could be developed further?

Box 6.1

Useful websites and further reading

In Control: www.in-control.org.uk

National Centre for Independent Living: www.ncil.org.uk

Shaping Our Lives (user-led organisation): www.shapingourlives.org.uk

DH personalisation website:

www.dh.gov.uk/en/SocialCare/Socialcarereform/Personalisation/DH_079379

SCIE has a large number of papers about participation on its website: www.scie.org.uk

The two papers which are used in Box 6.1 are especially recommended:

Wright *et al.* (2006) *The Participation of Children and Young People in Developing Social Care.*

Moriarty *et al.* (2007) *The Participation of Adult Service Users, Including Older People, in Developing Social Care.*

Also, for SCIE, Carr and Dittrich (2008) *Personalisation: A Rough Guide.*

A recommended book is Warren (2007) *Service User and Carer Participation in Social Work.*

Part 3
Current topics

The chapters in Part 3 look at crucial aspects for the delivery of high-quality welfare services and social work: professionalism and inter-professional working, organisation and regulation, and funding. All of these demonstrate the challenges of the three core models (the roles of social work, social policy and the state), and exemplify the tensions of the key issues. For example, the themes of needs and rights run across the chapters – how professionals can best respond to these, what organisational structures will work best, what principles should apply to raising money and paying. Equally, the issues of poverty and inequality, and participation and choice, have deep implications for social work's professional roles, approaches to safeguarding service users' interests and the question of paying for care.

Chapter 7 explores social work's identity as a profession, and the challenges of inter-professional working. Social work has an uncertain status as a profession, and the chapter considers some of the reasons behind this. Despite moves to strengthen its professional characteristics in recent years, there are other trends working against this, including political ambivalence, increasing bureaucratisation and the rise of the term 'social care'. The chapter discusses the relationship between professionalism and bureaucracy, and some of the implications of partnership and inter-professional working.

 Chapter 8 describes the organisational and regulatory structures for social work in the UK, and considers the underlying principles. The arrangements are complex and prone to frequent change, and this instability reflects competing beliefs about the best ways of delivering social work and ensuring high-quality standards. Some of the approaches have been discussed in previous chapters (rights, user participation, professionalism, bureaucracy), and this chapter adds managerialism, markets, the mixed economy of welfare, law and politics.

Chapter 9 discusses the finances of social care. It describes the current system for funding local authority social services in England, and how the money is spent. It also discusses the thorny issue of who should pay for social care, and how. This is highly controversial because of the rising demand for social care, means-testing, the tricky boundary with health care, and the problems of the 'postcode lottery'. The chapter describes the current approach in England and compares it to Scotland. It identifies the main issues and principles that need to be addressed by the review of long-term care funding.

Chapter 9

7 Professionalism and inter-professional working

This chapter explores the uncertain and contested nature of 'professional social work', and how this reflects underlying ambivalence and tension about its role in society. Four aspects stand out. The first is that it has long been seen as a profession in crisis, and we need a balanced understanding of why this might be. Second, while many practitioners, academics and leading figures in the occupation have argued hard that social work should be afforded proper professional status, others remain ambivalent about this objective. Third, there are the tensions of being professionals in highly regulated, bureaucratic organisations. Fourth, in recent years social work in the UK does appear to have achieved some of the features of professional identity, but at the same time there are ambiguities in the rise of social care, para-professional roles and multi-professional teams.

As for inter-professional working, a central theme in current social policy in England is to develop better partnership working between different professionals and different agencies. This is regarded as crucial to delivering services more effectively, both at the top end of the pyramid of need, the 'at risk'

Chapter 8

cases, and at the lower end, the earlier preventive work. It is one of the imperatives behind the major organisational restructurings that social services departments, and other public services, have undergone in recent years, and behind new legal requirements for closer inter-agency working. This chapter focuses on the implications for professional roles, and the following chapter looks at the organisational structures.

It might seem that social work is well placed to take a leading role in these interdisciplinary ways of working, because it has been described as, arguably, '*the* joined-up profession – a profession that seeks to liaise, to mediate, and to negotiate' with other professionals and with service users (Frost *et al.*, 2005: 195). 'Working together' and 'partnership' have long been watchwords in social work. However, the frequent criticisms for failing to achieve this suggest that it is much easier said than done. The perceived shortcomings lead to regular exhortations to do it better, further organisational changes, and ever more detailed and prescriptive procedures and regulations – what Howe (1992) has called 'the bureaucratisation of social work'. So, the policy context of joined-up working is ambiguous, offering opportunities and risks for social work.

Social work – a profession in crisis?

Social work's public image in the UK has been dominated over the years by heavy criticism of poor practice in child protection cases. The two most recent cases in England have been those of Victoria Climbié, where Lord Laming's inquiry (2003) led to the Every Child Matters programme and the Children Act 2004; and 'Baby P' (Peter) in 2008. However, there is a much longer history. High-profile inquiries into the deaths of children at home go back to the case of Maria Colwell in the early 1970s (DHSS, 1974), and reached a crescendo in the 1980s with a succession of cases, notably the murders of Jasmine Beckford, Kimberly Carlile and Tyra Henry (respectively, Brent, 1985; Greenwich, 1987; Lambeth, 1987). The criticisms for not intervening either soon enough or decisively enough were then countered by criticism for taking action too soon, too strongly, in the Cleveland sexual abuse crisis (DHSS, 1988). Summaries of these and other inquires are given in DHSS (1982), DH (1991a) and Reder *et al.* (1993). During the 1990s the focus of concern shifted to the abuse of children in residential care (e.g. Utting, 1997; Waterhouse, 2000; and see Corby *et al.*, 2001) but returned to the protection of children in their families in 2000–3, with the case of Victoria Climbié.

The Baby P trial in 2008 provoked exceptional levels of antagonism from the popular press. The *Sun* newspaper collected a petition calling, successfully, for the sacking of the director of children's services where the child had lived. The injuries suffered by this young boy were truly dreadful, but the reactions of the press and the government show that more was at stake than just what had gone wrong in this one sad case. Like the earlier cases listed above, it was seen as a window to wider problems about welfare services and social work in particular. The government responded by ordering a progress report from Lord Laming into the effectiveness of the changes he had recommended in the Climbié inquiry, and by setting up a Social Work Task Force (SWTF) to analyse the problems faced by the profession and make recommendations for change.

Lord Laming's progress report was published in March 2009, and the SWTF first report in May 2009 (Gibb, 2009: its full report is due in October 2009). Both reports found major problems with excessive workloads, staff shortages, cumbersome bureaucracy, inflexible and unhelpful IT systems and the poor public image of the profession. One extract from Laming's report illustrates the difficulties:

> Frontline social workers and social work managers are under an immense amount of pressure. Low staff morale, poor supervision, high case-loads, under-resourcing and inadequate training each contribute to high levels of stress and recruitment and retention difficulties ... Public vilification of social workers has a negative effect on staff and has serious implications for the effectiveness, status and morale of the children's workforce as a whole. There has been a long-term appetite in the media to portray social workers in ways that are negative and undermining ... However, without highly motivated and confident social workers the reality is that more children will be exposed to harm.

(Laming, 2009: 44)

Following Laming's report the two ministers responsible for adult and children's social care wrote a joint letter to social workers in England, expressing their appreciation of social work and their commitment to putting it 'on a new footing, one which reflects its true value' (Balls and Johnson, 2009; and see DCSF, 2009). There may now be an opportunity for the renewed political focus on child and family social work to chime with the personalisation drive in adult services, to bring new support and resources and reinvigorate social work.

It has to be said, however, that we have been here before. The sense of social work being in crisis is not at all new, and even the Conservative Party, hardly traditional friends of welfare services and social work, recognised the need for recovery and revitalisation before the Baby P case (Conservative Party, 2007; and subsequently, 2009). But long before that, research undertaken in the early 1990s found social services 'working under pressure' (Balloch *et al.*, 1999b), and Jones and Novak (1993: 196) spoke about social work then experiencing 'a degree of demoralization unparalleled in its history'. And even further back, in 1979, Carole Satyamurti opened a chapter with the sentence 'In recent years, the notion of "crisis in social work" has become a cliché' (1979: 89). One hopes that things will be different this time, but New Labour's record on social work is not too encouraging: as we have seen, social work has

Chapter 6

been treated as a failing profession and very deliberately excluded from the government's major social inclusion programmes. Personalisation may be a sign of change, but as we discussed in the previous chapter even this is rather ambiguous, carrying risks of privatisation and the fragmentation of professional roles.

In 2001, Mark Lymbery wrote that social work was 'at the crossroads', with important choices to make about its core functions and tasks. If that was the case then, it is more so now. Yet we have been at similar junctions before. The Barclay report of 1982 and the Seebohm report of 1968 were crossroads of their time, holding out visions of transforming social work, recognising what it has to offer and enabling it to serve people better. The point of recalling this is to remind us that social work's role in society is *always* in dispute, shaped by those enduring debates about what it is for and who it is for.

It is also to observe that we are still here, and celebrate social work's capacity to survive. Jordan (2004) holds that it has survived at a cost, by becoming more investigative, procedural and finance-led, but even so he argues that social work still can and does help people (Jordan, 2007). But it is important not to confuse resilience with indestructibility (Balloch *et al.*, 1999a: 184), and in the current situation revitalisation is certainly needed.

One of the proposals in the SWTF first report (Gibb, 2009: 7) is for 'a refreshed and easy to understand description of the purpose of social work'. This is a sorry reflection on the success of the General Social Care Council (GSCC) roles and tasks statement, published only a year before, but perhaps the point is that the process is more important than the outcome. As we noted in Chapter 1, no statement will

satisfy everyone, and it is better to think of them as provisional frameworks for continuing reflection and debate. The notion that social work can be reduced to one 'easy to understand description' risks reducing it to the banal, missing the complexity of the job and the ambiguities of the policy context.

There are two ways of refining Lymbery's (2001) metaphor about social work being at the crossroads. One is to say that we are always at a crossroads – every day, every policy and every decision involve balancing legal duties, service users' wishes, resources and professional judgments about wellbeing and safety. Another way, thinking about the historical and political context, is to be wary about talk of major changes of direction, taking totally new roads. Instead, it is probably better to think that the road we are on has bends, ups and downs, bumpy stretches here and smoother surfaces there. And it is a ring-road – the same issues come round again and again. Furthermore, we do not have full control over how we travel along the road – there are many other people in the car fighting to get their hands on the steering wheel. It is also not an easy vehicle to drive – it was built by many different people, not all with the same design in mind, it has got an old chassis with different parts added at different times, of varying quality, some working and some not. On top of that, we did not build the road and we have not got a very clear map. But we got into the car, and we have to play our part in keeping it on the road.

Social work's ambiguous professional status

Social work has always had a rather marginal professional status. Its characteristics as a profession are uncertain when compared to the traditional professions of medicine and the law, which has led to it being called a 'semi-profession' (Toren, 1977). The traditional model of a profession includes the following elements (Johnson, 1972):

- Specialist skills based on a distinct body of theoretical knowledge;

- Its own organisation/governing body, independent of employers;

- The professional body provides or regulates training and education, and controls entry to the profession;

- Professional examinations/qualifications at the point of entry and afterwards ('continuing professional development');

- Its own code of conduct;

- A service ethic, putting the best interests of the client first.

The picture of skilled and knowledgeable practitioners, working in the interests of service users, not self-interest, and with standards overseen by a professional body, is, for many, powerful and attractive. In the UK, the British Association of Social Workers has long argued for the professional status of social work – its code of ethics opens with the claim that 'Social work is a professional activity'. The BASW claims to speak for social work as a profession as well as for its individual members, but it is not a regulatory body and there is no requirement that social workers belong to it – indeed, the great majority do not.

Becoming a profession?

Looking at the key features of the 'ideal' profession, social work has often been perceived to fall short of these requirements. In particular, it has been criticised for not having its own distinctive and authoritative theoretical base, for not having its own, sufficiently rigorous entry requirements, and for not having a system of professional registration to uphold standards. Instead, critics point out that its knowledge is drawn from other disciplines, and that its application to practice is weak and uncertain (the critics see evidence of this in the succession of child abuse scandals – although such criticisms fail to recognise the complexities of the issues, the legal and ethical balances that cannot be reduced to the simple application of knowledge). Although social work education has long been established at university level, until recently most social workers qualified at sub-degree level, and a qualification was not a legal requirement to become a social worker. Further, occupational standards and disciplinary measures were the responsibility of employers, not an independent professional body. (For summaries of the issues, see Foster and Wilding (2000); Lymbery (2001); Orme (2001); Harris (2008).)

Recent changes in the UK have been part of New Labour's drive to modernise social services (DH, 1998). The GSCC was established in England in 2001, with parallel organisations in the other countries

(see Chapter 8). There has been a greater emphasis on promoting and disseminating social work evidence about 'what works', notably through the Social Care Institute for Excellence (SCIE). Since 2003, social work qualifying education has had to be at degree level (Bachelor's or Master's level degrees).

It might appear, then, that social work has at last achieved professional status in the UK. However, the situation is not that clear, and other trends point against it. There is political ambivalence about social work's role and status, reflected in the way that the term 'social work' is played down in many policy initiatives, with 'social care' being the preferred phrase (see further below). With regard to social work's knowledge base, the emphasis on evidence-based research and theory is important, but a simplistic focus on 'what works' can mask important questions about 'from whose point of view?', about the framing and funding of research projects, and about the resources available to support good practice (Trinder, 1996; Gray and McDonald, 2006).

There are further reasons to do with critical understandings of professionalism. The critique is that rather than those attributes, or traits, being the *basis* of professional conduct and status, what happens is that some occupations achieve a higher standing because they have access to wider sources of social, economic and political power, and *then* they try to preserve their position by adopting the standard professional traits – so the traits are a symptom, not a cause, of professional status (Howe, 1986: 96; Abbott and Meerabeau, 1998; Hugman, 1998). Professional status brings *control* over work – with whom one works, what the aims are, how it is done. When we think of professionalisation in terms of control of work, we can see why it is so ambiguous in social work. It is problematic because of social work's location (in the UK) in public sector bureaucracies, the emphasis on inter-professional working, the resistance of service users and radical voices within social work itself. All of these set limits on the control that social workers have over their own work, and moreover the nature of the work itself creates problems for social work's professional status.

The nature of the work

One model that sheds light on the reasons why social work is in a weak position to achieve full professional status is the notion of 'dirty work' (Hughes, 1958). There are physical, social and moral aspects of dirty work (see Ashforth and Kreiner, 1999). Physical dirty work is to do with rubbish, death and effluent, or unpleasant working conditions. Social dirty work is work with stigmatised groups, such as poor people or offenders, or work that puts people in a servile relationship (e.g. personal care). Moral dirty work is work that is seen as 'sinful' or morally dubious, or where the job involves intrusion into private life. Social work involves all of these. At times it is physically dirty (some home visits for example: Ferguson, 2004) but the social and moral aspects are more significant. We work predominantly with people who are stigmatised in society – older people, disabled people, poor people. By going into the heart of people's private and family lives, we infringe an important social principle about privacy, and we open up aspects of life that are deeply disturbing for the general public. It is work that needs doing, but it provokes very ambivalent feelings in society, and people who do society's dirty work are tainted by it.

Some of the established professions do dirty work too, of course, but not to the same extent. For example, doctors and lawyers work across all social classes, and social work's role is different in that it is particularly intrusive and ambiguous (the care and control dilemmas). Also, there are splits within professions between those who do more or less of the dirty work, and less is higher status. Having the power to pass the dirty work on to someone else reflects higher professional standing (e.g. doctors to nurses, nurses to nursing auxiliaries). The relatively low status of social work with older people compared to child and family social work (Lymbery, 1998) may be understood in terms of it being perceived as 'dirtier' work, because older people are the more socially stigmatised group.

Challenging professionalisation

Another reason why social work has found it hard to achieve full professional status is that there are those who argue it ought not to get caught up in a quest for professional status at all. These views link with the criticisms of the professional traits, and come from both the right and left wings of politics, the minimalists and the radicals. Critics on both sides argue that the lists of professional attributes are nothing more than covers for self-interest – they are what professionals say about themselves in order to justify their claims to special treatment, deference, high salaries or fees, social status.

From a radical, left-wing perspective, the arguments against professions are powerfully set out by Illich (1977: 19–20):

> Professionals assert secret knowledge about human nature, knowledge which only they have the right to dispense. They claim a monopoly over the definition of deviance and the remedies needed . . . Gravediggers become members of a profession by calling themselves morticians . . . Morticians form a profession when they acquire the muscle to have the police stop your burial if you are not embalmed and boxed by them. In any area where a human need can be imagined these new professions, dominant, authoritative, monopolistic, legalised – and, at the same time debilitating and effectively disabling the individual – have become exclusive experts of the public good.

The growth of the service user movement challenges the elitism and exclusionary tendencies of professionalism, and shifts the expectations of what professionals do – no longer the expert who knows best, but working with service users to empower them, to respond to their wishes and aspirations. One danger is that the skills for this new way of working may not be considered as demanding as the old model of technical expertise, diagnosis and treatment. However unfairly, this approach can be portrayed as less rigorous, simply helping people, more common sense than specialist knowledge.

Criticisms come from the right wing of politics too, where social professionals are accused of incompetence, encouraging dependency, and being a drain on the economy. Welfare professionals were one of the targets of the New Right attacks on the welfare state from the 1970s to the 1990s, and mistrust about their willingness to adapt to new ways of working has continued under New Labour. It has led to the growth of extensive regulatory regimes such as performance indicators and inspections, and social work has felt the force of these bureaucratic and controlling responses, further diminishing its professional standing.

The rise of social care

The rise of the term 'social care' is a strong indicator of the wider political and social ambivalence about social work, the reluctance to recognise it as a full profession. 'Social care' carries a number of meanings (see Payne, 2006: 4–5, 30–1, 46–7). It may be seen as:

- distinct from social work;

- part of social work;

- incorporating social work.

In the first sense, social care is different from social work – it is the term used for residential, day care and domiciliary services, perhaps assessed and commissioned by a social worker, but not (necessarily) delivered by a qualified social worker. It is more direct, hands-on care (dirtier work) than social workers usually provide. In the second sense, social care is part of social work – social workers plan it and arrange it, and it is an important aspect of the whole service that they provide, even if they do not deliver it directly themselves. This is the sense in which it is used in the Barclay report (1982), where part of the social worker's job is 'social care planning'. In the third sense, social care is a general term used for the whole range of personal social services (rather like 'health care' is used for all types of health services), and social work is only one part of that – and in terms of numbers a very small part.

It is hard to get an accurate figure for the size of the social care workforce in England, as definitions of who is included or excluded vary. Adding together estimates of the workforces for adults (CSCI, 2009) and children (CWDC, 2009) suggest it could be as high as 1.7 million. The number of registered social workers in November 2008 was just over 81,000 (CSCI, 2009: 173), but not all of these would have been employed as social workers. It is important to remember this bigger picture of the people who do so much of the direct work with service users, but the implications of swallowing up social work in social care are threatening for social work's professional identity.

In this context, it is notable that in England we have a General Social *Care* Council, not a General Social *Work* Council, and a Social *Care* Institute for Excellence, not a Social *Work* Institute for Excellence. For a government that is ambivalent about social work, the ambiguity of the term 'social care' works well, to include social work but also to put it in its place. The dominant image of care work is of semi-skilled, routine work – still important for people's welfare, but not involving the same level of decision-making or requiring the same level of formal education as professional social work. 'Social care' is a softer, more publicly acceptable term than 'social work', but its prominence serves to diminish the intellectual challenges of social work, to portray it in much more limited terms.

Role fragmentation and para-professionals

A further factor is the fragmentation of social work tasks and the increasing number of para-professional jobs. These arise when some of the tasks undertaken by a professional are identified as being suitable for workers who do not have a full professional qualification, as long as they have relevant training and are supervised by a qualified professional. It is a widespread trend across the public services, and examples outside social work include teaching assistants, nursing auxiliaries, legal executives and police community support officers. These jobs may develop their own qualifications and occupational associations. In children's social services, the growth of posts with titles such as 'child and family support worker' is part of this wider trend. In adult social services, there are posts such as 'community care practitioner'. The role of 'care manager' itself may well be open to people who do not hold social work qualifications, but may have other professional backgrounds, such as nursing.

The growth of these new jobs brings benefits and risks for qualified social workers. There are the advantages of reducing some of the workload, the tasks that one does not need a professional social work education to undertake. It could be a way of shifting the dirty work and raising professional status, but for some social workers it can seem as though the para-professional has taken the parts of the job that attracted them (the social workers) to it in the first place. The para-professionals may well have more direct contact with the service users, while the social worker's role is one of commissioning services and coordinating the work of others.

Furthermore, breaking up the job into its constituent parts, labelling some as complex and others as straightforward, and delegating some to other workers, risks losing a clear picture of the whole. It certainly makes it vital to keep good records and have clear lines of accountability, so the bureaucratic tendencies are advanced. Fragmenting the social work role like this may not actually raise its professional status but rather de-professionalise it, by de-skilling it and moving it towards a production-line style of working, with different people doing different parts of the work, and possessing limited competence in only that area (Healy and Meagher, 2004). It is a process that has been called 'the McDonaldization of social work' (Dustin, 2007). The seven-stage process of self-directed support (see Box 6.2) is especially amenable to this, with one worker doing the

Box 6.2

assessment, another the support plan, another helping to purchase the support, another conducting the reviews. Given the importance that service users regularly attach to continuity of worker and knowing who to go to, this is likely to cause as many problems as it solves.

Professionals or bureaucrats?

Stereotypically, bureaucrats and professionals are opposites. The professional uses his/her individual judgment, carries individual responsibility for his/her work, and is only answerable to his/her professional peers, because they alone can really understand the complexities of the job. In contrast, the bureaucrat follows procedures, is accountable for his/her work via the organisational hierarchy, and is answerable to line managers. It is not unusual for professionals to complain that organisational structures and procedures limit and even undermine their professional judgments.

The words 'bureaucracy' and 'bureaucratic' are often used in negative ways, as criticisms of slow, cumbersome organisations and ways of working, and the tem 'bureaucrat' is an insult for someone who is seen as petty-minded and inflexible. Yet the terms have a more neutral meaning, without those pejorative connotations, as identified by the German sociologist Max Weber (1864–1920) (see Weber, 1947). In his model, bureaucracy is a technical way of organising an enterprise so that it runs in a rational, legal and orderly manner. It typically involves an organisational hierarchy shaped like a pyramid, with a post at the top, such as 'director' or 'chief executive', carrying overall responsibility for the service. Underneath the director come assistant directors, then senior managers with responsibilities for, say, particular geographical areas or services. Underneath them are team managers, then assistant team managers, then field-level workers. Some organisations may have many tiers, others might be much flatter, but the principles are the same: each worker knows his or her role and the extent of his or her authority, and will pass work up or down the pyramid accordingly. There are procedures, criteria and systems to guide staff in their work, and when in doubt they should ask their line manager. In turn, their manager has authority to tell them what to do. The manager possesses this authority by virtue of their position in the hierarchy, not their personal characteristics, or whether or not the staff member likes them (so, you have to go to your manager – you cannot, or should not, go to someone else). There are clear lines of accountability and communication. Bureaucracy is, in theory, a rational, legal, fair, transparent and efficient way of organising things.

Local authority children's services and adult services departments are striking examples of bureaucratic structures, and many of New Labour's strategies for modernising public services are classic bureaucratic techniques, even if they would shrink from using the word 'bureaucratic'. The specification of goals and targets, the measuring of performance against them, the issuing of procedures and guidance, even the continual reorganisations, all reflect a faith that the right structure and systems, when finally identified and put into practice, will resolve all the problems of public services and ensure effective working and clear communication.

Reality does not always live up to those expectations, for a multitude of reasons. However rational the system aims to be, pressures of unlimited demand and limited resources will affect the way that people do their jobs, as they try to cope with workload pressures and balance fair service for all with high-quality service to the individual (Lipsky, 1980). Personal likes and dislikes will come into play, and personal ambitions. The aims of the organisation may not always be clear, or not always compatible, and different groups within the organisation may have different goals to others (e.g. for some it may be important to deliver a basic service for all, for others a quality service for a few; for some to save money, for others to deliver the best service now, even if that means financial difficulties later). The standard bureaucratic responses to these problems are more rules, more procedures, tighter management, new organisational structures. But rules still need to be interpreted and applied to particular situations, and there is always the 'gap' of direct practice, how workers relate to and work with service users and their families (Evans and Harris, 2004; White, 2009; Evans, 2009).

Despite the tensions, there are many professionals who do work in bureaucracies, social workers in local authorities being a notable example. Professional qualifications are often an essential requirement for a particular post in the bureaucracy, so the two models are not incompatible, even if sometimes uncomfortable. One model to explain this is the notion of 'bureau professions' (Parry and Parry, 1979). Here, the idea is that the profession gives up an amount of autonomy in return for the security of a guaranteed clientele and a salary (rather than relying on fee-paying clients who may choose to take their custom elsewhere). Some bureaucratic elements may even help professionals, because rules and procedures can mark out a particular area of work as exclusively theirs (Roach Anleu, 1992).

Supervision in social work may be seen as an intriguing practice in which the two approaches are brought together, a mixture of professional consultation and organisational accountability (Pithouse, 1998). Traditionally, social work managers have tended to be qualified social workers, so they should still understand the professional dilemmas as well as carry organisational responsibility. This blurring may be less effective as managers become more driven by businesslike concerns with hitting targets and balancing budgets (Harris, 2003; Harris and White, 2009), and as social workers increasingly find themselves working in multidisciplinary teams, with managers from other professional backgrounds. In these circumstances, tensions between professional responses and bureaucratic responsibilities may become more prominent.

Julian Le Grand's model of knights and knaves, pawns and queens is an intriguing way of thinking about questions of who controls the work of social professionals, and on what basis – the tensions between professionalism and bureaucracy, and between professionals, managers, politicians and service users. His ideas are summarised in Box 7.1.

Box 7.1 Knights and knaves, pawns and queens (Le Grand, 2003)

There are tensions about the motivation and capacities of people who work for public services (e.g. doctors, civil servants, social workers). Are social professionals knights, guided purely by altruistic motives, or are they knaves, motivated by self-interest (not necessarily in a criminal sense, but in terms of salary, status, or just not doing any more than they have to)? Should front-line practitioners be seen as pawns, who need to be told what to do by the policy-makers and their managers, or as the most powerful piece on the board, queens, who should be able to exercise professional judgment and make autonomous decisions?

Equally, what about service users? Should they be seen as knights (happy to wait their turn, to pay taxes to support others) or as knaves (out to get the most they can for themselves from public services)? Are they to be thought of as pawns, who should gratefully accept whatever they are offered by the experts, or as queens, who should have a say – *the* say – in what services they receive?

For Le Grand, the post-war welfare state treated professionals as knights and service users as pawns. Right- and left-wing critiques of the welfare state, from the 1970s onwards, challenged this view – professionals may not always know best, may be more motivated by self-interest than altruism; service users are active agents rather than passive recipients, and they should have the final say in what services they receive (the service user as customer).

Le Grand stresses that the reality is more complex than the simple stereotypes suggest – people can be both knightly and knavish, and in different circumstances one or the other might come to the fore. People may want to be in control of some aspects of a service but not others – and all of us have times when we are not up to taking control and just want to be looked after. For Le Grand, one aim of policy should be to use the knavish instincts for knightly purposes – for example, to pay people well enough to ensure that they work hard in the interests of others. In this sense, Le Grand's model is controversial because it underpins his support for the increasing privatisation of welfare services, as shown by his role in promoting the idea of 'social work practices' for children looked after by local authorities (see Box 8.4). (Interestingly, the idea of

Box 8.4

turning self-interested instincts into socially productive behaviour by paying people more seems not to apply to poorer people or the unemployed. For them, the dominant view is that minimal pay or low benefits will be an incentive to work hard.)

Le Grand makes the point that even though real life is more fluid and unstable than his model implies, stereotypes can be very powerful, and he warns that policies and services may be designed around stereotypes rather than complexity. This is an important warning for social policy and social work generally.

Inter-professional working

A further important aspect of the policy context for social work's professional identity is the growth of inter-professional working, and in particular multi-professional teams. These offer opportunities for social workers to gain new professional roles and tasks, and to apply their professional skills in new ways. At the same time, they also present new threats to social work's control over its work and its continuing existence as a distinct profession.

Inter-professional work may occur within an agency (for example, social workers and lawyers who both work for the same local authority: Dickens, 2006a), or across different agencies (e.g. local authority social workers and health visitors). Inter-professional working can occur at a strategic level, to coordinate the policies and services of different organisations (e.g. between a local authority and a primary care trust), in multi-professional teams (see below), and in cooperation on individual cases (e.g. medics and social workers working together to plan a patient's discharge from hospital). It may involve 'co-location', sharing the same workplace, although this does not guarantee improved relationships (White and Featherstone, 2005; see below).

Better inter-professional working is often portrayed as the solution to widespread problems of poorly coordinated and ineffective services, but it is fraught with challenges. First, it is complicated by differing professional responsibilities, within and between the different groups – for example, social workers have to balance responsibilities to each particular service user, to members of the service user's family and to all the other service users on their case-loads; teachers have responsibilities to individual pupils, to that child's parents, to all the other pupils in their class and all the parents; doctors to individual patients and all their patients. Each professional has to reconcile their own potentially competing responsibilities, even before they start trying to reach agreements with other professionals.

These problems are compounded by organisational requirements, to comply with agency procedures and national policies, and to work within budgets. Financial constraints can have a major impact on inter-professional working, even within the same organisation. For example, relationships between child protection social workers and lawyers in local authorities are affected by internal funding systems (Dickens, 2006b). Purchaser–provider arrangements can limit the nature and amount of inter-professional dialogue, and may contribute to misunderstandings and mistrust. Finally, inter-professional working is also complicated by issues of status and power. Members of less powerful occupations can find it very hard to question or challenge members of higher-status groups – and the higher groups may ignore or devalue what the others say. The relationships between social workers and medical professionals such as GPs and hospital consultants are often vulnerable to this (Lymbery, 1998). An example from children's social work is the Victoria Climbié case, where social workers did not feel able to question the opinion of the hospital doctor that the marks on Victoria's body were scabies rather than injuries (Laming, 2003: paras 5.133–8).

Multi-professional teams

Social workers are increasingly working as members of multi-professional teams. Firmly established examples are youth offending teams (YOTs) and community mental health teams (CMHTs), but they are becoming ever more common for all service user groups. The GSCC statement of social work's role and tasks notes that multidisciplinary teams have increased 'as a means of giving people access to a range of expertise, improving coordination and making the best use of scarce professional skills' (GSCC, 2008: paras 40–1). As we saw earlier (Box 1.3), it argues that these work settings require social work

Box 1.3

to be flexible, 'not sticking rigidly to agency or professional boundaries', but (para. 41) 'clear and confident about the expertise it has developed', and with a responsibility 'to feed its knowledge, values and approaches into the work of joint teams to inform their culture and widen their frame of reference'.

This level of flexibility can be stimulating and beneficial for all, but it can also be uncomfortable and threatening. Frost et al. (2005: 188) note that 'professional knowledge boundaries can become blurred and professional identity can be challenged as roles and responsibilities change. Such changes can generate discomfort, anxiety, and anger in team members'. They conclude that the best way of dealing with these risks is for conflicts to be debated openly, but not forced into a uniform view: 'Joined-up working does not necessarily mean doing away with difference' (p. 190). In the teams they studied, there were differences in professional values and cultures, issues of power and status, and organisational thresholds for accepting referrals. Despite the difficulties, they found a strong commitment to multi-professional working, and see a valuable role for social work in such teams.

Another challenge is that professional differences can continue, and even be exacerbated, within multidisciplinary settings. White and Featherstone (2005) show that this can happen because the workers get a closer view of how the other group does things differently to them, and may be critical or dismissive of it. They conclude that co-location 'does not straightforwardly lead to more or better communication' (2005: 215), and argue that the challenge is to help staff reflect on and analyse their own professional language and routine practices.

Professionals, policy and practice

However many policies there are about partnership working, whatever legislation and however many reorganisations, the reality hangs on individuals – their attitudes, behaviour and commitment to inter-professional working. It is back to the street-level bureaucracy idea, although here 'team-level professionals' – but the point is the same, that individuals matter and practice matters. Reder and Duncan (2003) write about the importance of a 'communication mindset' for inter-professional working. This is an approach that is committed to inter-professional dialogue but recognises its complexities, and is able to live and work with the uncertainty *and* potential of flexible and permeable boundaries. This is a challenging and truly professional task. As Harris and Timms (1993: 68) put it: 'Social professionals act in situations which are ambiguous precisely because it is in such situations that they are needed: one does not need an expert to do simple things.'

Schön (1983) expresses a similar notion in his concept of the 'reflective practitioner', arguing that professionals need to move beyond a narrow faith in technical expertise (their professional knowledge and skills, their specialist roles and tasks), towards a more critical and reflective position. The answers to the complex problems they have to face are not to be found just in greater textbook knowledge, better techniques (e.g. of interviewing, assessing, recording), clearer forms, more procedures. Certainly these can help, but not if they become ends in themselves. Sticking rigidly to them can create gulfs between professionals and service users, and between different professionals. Rather, professionals should open themselves up to the complexity and instability of the situations they deal with, engage in what Schön calls a 'reflective conversation' with the situation.

The difficulty is that social policy does not like instability and uncertainty. It likes clear objectives, defined roles and tasks, measurable goals. Policy cannot bring total certainty, but it likes to bring *confidence* (Smith, 2001, 2005), through methods such as national standards, targets, inspections and league tables (although the proliferation of these mechanisms can undermine confidence as well – who knows what to believe? Harris, 2003). Social workers and other social professionals, however, have to work with risk, uncertainty and competing responsibilities (Parton, 1998; Parton and O'Byrne, 2000). Under these pressures, a vital requirement for inter-professional working is *trust*, and the top-down commands for better inter-professional working cannot guarantee this because it takes time and commitment. However, the top-down commands get ever more strident as inquiries find shortcomings in inter-professional working (e.g. Laming, 2009: 7, shouting 'now just do it'). The regularity of these findings suggests that one ought not to be naïve about how difficult it is.

Effective inter-professional working can be desperately hard to achieve in situations of few resources, high-risk decisions, and multiple, sometimes incompatible responsibilities, including complex rules about information sharing and confidentiality (Richardson and Asthana, 2006). On top of all that, as noted earlier, there is the impact of long-standing differences of power, culture and status between different professions.

At times the comments of other professionals can seem like a criticism of one's own professionalism, or a bid to gain control of one's own limited resources. As Woodhouse and Pengelly (1991: 27) put it, it is especially difficult to think about collaboration 'when you are defending the last ditch of your professional identity'. They also warn that 'Communication and co-operation prove most difficult to achieve when they are most needed' (p. 3). Effective inter-professional working depends on the willingness and ability of managers and practitioners to reflect on and analyse the complexities of their own jobs, and to recognise that other professionals face similar dilemmas. It also depends on a policy framework that is honest about the difficulties of the task.

Conclusion

All the developments we have been discussing in this chapter bring opportunities and threats for social work, and for service users and their families. Writing in 2009, there is great pressure for rapid change in social work. In children's services in England this is provoked by the latest child protection scandal, and in adult services by the personalisation agenda. These pressures may bring new support and resources, but could also lead to tighter control of social work policy and practice. The calls for better joined-up working are, in one sense, obvious, if they help avoid unnecessary duplication (different workers asking service users the same questions), or prevent service users falling through the gaps (which is where Seebohm came in – see Chapter 1). In another sense, paradoxically, the need for better joined-up working is an inevitable consequence of the increasing fragmentation of professional roles and regular reorganisations. Whatever the organisational structures, there will be some boundaries somewhere, and reorganising to remove some will inevitably create others; equally, breaking up the tasks that social workers do may free them to spend more time on some, but it will create new gaps as well. Policies to solve one problem always create others. Inter-professional working and multi-professional teams can bring greater flexibility, but they can also be stressful and conflictual. And joined-up working has another side, not so explicit – more closely integrated services

can be more tightly controlling. Information about people is transmitted from one agency to another, one worker to another, noted, saved and transmitted again. So, on the surface we have a better way of helping people, but in the shadows a better technology of surveillance.

The themes of this chapter, the professional status of social work and inter-professional working, shed further light on the discussion in Chapter 1 about the quest for a statement of social work's roles and tasks. The difficulties of coming up with an agreed statement reflect the ambiguous nature of social work's professional identity and status. Social work is shaped by very different notions about the benefits and costs of professionalisation, the opportunities and challenges of working with other professionals, the positives and perils of bureaucracy. At the heart of these tensions are social work's multiple responsibilities to service users, organisational requirements, professional standards and statutory functions.

Questions for reflection

- The chapter has discussed a number of reasons why social work's professional status is so uncertain. What do you think, and can you think of any others?

- What is distinctive about social work as a profession?

- Do you think social workers are more like professionals or bureaucrats? What are your reasons?

- Think about a place where you have worked or been on placement. What sort of inter-professional or multi-professional working went on there? What factors helped or hindered it?

- Is flexibility about professional roles and tasks a sign of professional strength or weakness? What factors make the difference?

Useful websites and further reading

For professionalism, professionalisation and social work, the websites and books mentioned in Chapter 1 are useful again for this chapter. Look out for the report of the Social Work Task Force, due in October 2009.

On the relationship between professionalism and bureaucracy, there is a helpful chapter by Gray and Jenkins in Baldock *et al.* (2007) *Social Policy*, 3rd edn.

On the inter-professional aspects and partnership working:

Glasby (2007) *Understanding Health and Social Care.*

Glasby and Dickinson (2008) *Partnership Working in Health and Social Care.*

Morris (2008) *Social Work and Multi-Agency Working: Making a Difference.*

Douglas (2009) *Partnership Working.*

8 Organisation and regulation

This chapter looks at the organisational and regulatory context of social work, showing the range of different agencies involved in prescribing, delivering and monitoring it, and identifying the major principles that lie behind these arrangements. The chapter gets us back to the old debates about the control of social work, who does run it and who should run it – politicians, professionals, managers, service users? Or, more likely, what are the balances between these different groups, and what methods can each of them use to shape social work policy and practice?

The term 'regulation' is being used here in its broadest sense, to cover any method of setting and maintaining standards, and coordinating activities. This involves a variety of organisations and approaches, and is no longer just the responsibility of national or local government – hence the rise of the term 'governance', which is meant to capture the multi-agency nature of an enterprise that now involves voluntary organisations, businesses, community groups, service users and local residents.

The first part of the chapter describes the main organisations and structures for social work in England, as at April 2009, and identifies the main similarities and differences with the other UK countries. Later

Chapters 4, 6 and 7

sections explore the concepts and principles that lie behind them, which should be relevant to other countries even if the specific structures are not. Previous chapters have discussed rights and service user approaches (Chapters 4 and 6), professionalism and bureaucracy, and inter-professional working (Chapter 7). This chapter adds managerialism, markets, the mixed economy of welfare, law and politics. All the approaches overlap and interweave, sometimes supporting one another and sometimes contradicting. It is through this interaction that policies are formulated, put into practice, challenged and evaluated.

The welfare jigsaw puzzle

Welfare policies and services are not just the responsibility of national government, but are shaped by a jigsaw puzzle of different organisations – international, national and local, statutory, voluntary and private, with a web of vertical and horizontal links between them. Some of the connections are formal and 'strong', enabling one organisation to direct and evaluate the work of another, while others are weaker, relying more on negotiation and inter-professional relationships.

In terms of vertical links, social policy in the four countries of the UK is shaped from above, by international treaties and organisations. At the highest level, the United Nations influences policy through its human rights treaties, discussed in Chapter 4.

Two European intergovernmental organisations have a significant impact: the European Union (EU) and the Council of Europe. The EU approach to social policy tends to focus on employment-related matters such as equal treatment for women and older workers, parental leave, fair working hours. It has extensive policies on tackling discrimination, and on freedom of movement within the EU while maintaining its external borders and controlling immigration. It is also a major funder of social

regeneration projects, through its structural funds. The Council of Europe is a different body to the EU, and has more member countries (for example, it includes Turkey and Russia). All states that belong to the Council have to comply with the European Convention on Human Rights (ECHR), discussed in Chapter 4.

For Deacon (2007), the EU is a prime example of the 'globalisation of social policy', where issues of regulation, redistribution and rights, previously the concern of national governments, now take on an increasingly international dimension. That is, policies to ensure good working conditions and fair welfare provision (regulation) are now framed by an international body; wealthier countries give money to the EU that is spent in the poorer parts of other nations (redistribution); and questions of rights and entitlements now go beyond national citizenship (EU citizens are, generally, entitled to equal treatment in other EU countries, but there are tighter restrictions on the rights of non-EU citizens). Having said that, we are still a long way from a homogeneous 'European welfare state', and different nations within the EU still have very different approaches to social policy issues, reflecting the underlying approaches discussed in Chapter 3. EU law is usually issued in the form of regulations or

directives. Member states have to comply but have some discretion in how they translate directives into national legislation. The European Court of Justice in Luxembourg decides disputes about EU law, and its decisions are binding on UK courts (note that this is a different body from the European Court of Human Rights in Strasbourg).

The national level

In the different countries of the UK, different central government departments have different responsibilities for social welfare and social work. Departmental names and functions change from time to time, but Box 8.1 gives a summary of the major departments in England in April 2009. Box 8.2 gives details of some of the main regulatory and advisory bodies, using the term 'regulatory' to capture any method of setting standards and ensuring high-quality services. Wales, Scotland and Northern Ireland have their own government structures and regulatory bodies, and the principal organisations for those countries are shown in Box 8.3. The commentary in this section focuses on England.

Social work in England currently comes mainly under two departments: the Department of Health (DH), which is responsible for adult social care; and the Department for Children, Schools and Families (DCSF), which takes children's services. In the other countries, social work is still under one central government department. The DCSF was formed in 2007, replacing the Department for Education and Skills (DfES), which was itself formed only in 2003. Responsibility for children's social services moved to the DfES in 2003, but before that children's and adults' social services were together, under the DH.

Box 8.1 Major government departments for social welfare and social work in England, April 2009

- **Department of Health (DH)** National Health Service, adult social care, public health. www.dh.gov.uk

- **Department for Children, Schools and Families (DCSF)** Early years, schools, children's social care. www.dcsf.gov.uk

- **Department for Communities and Local Government (CLG)** Local government, housing, neighbourhood renewal, social cohesion. www.communities.gov.uk

- **Department for Work and Pensions (DWP)** Welfare to work, welfare benefits, disability allowances, pensions. www.dwp.gov.uk

- **Home Office** Policing, immigration, crime reduction, antisocial behaviour. www.homeoffice.gov.uk

- **Ministry of Justice (MoJ)** Courts and legal services, including child care proceedings; probation, youth offending teams, prisons. www.justice.gov.uk

- **Cabinet Office** Coordination of government policy, Office of the Third Sector, Social Exclusion Task Force. www.cabinetoffice.gov.uk

- **The Treasury** Taxation, public expenditure. www.hm-treasury.gov.uk

Social work is a relatively small concern for national government, and the English policy of splitting it across two major government departments may have weakened its position and influence even further. An effective way of incapacitating a group is to split it into smaller bodies and then drop them into much larger and more diverse ones (the old 'divide and rule' idea). The DH also has responsibility for the National Health Service and public health (e.g. vaccinations, safe sex and anti-smoking campaigns), while the DCSF covers early years provision (nurseries, childminding) and schools. The NHS and the

Chapter 9

state education system both have far larger budgets and much higher public profiles than social work (see Chapter 9 for the financial comparisons). It is hard for social work to compete for equal attention with such large, socially popular and politically important public services.

In the UK, social work is mainly delivered through local government, although there have always been voluntary sector agencies, and nowadays there are growing numbers of private agencies. (It is worth noting that private sector involvement in public services is much more widespread in England compared to Wales, Scotland and Northern Ireland: Stewart, 2004; C. Alcock *et al.*, 2008: 108–29). Local authorities carry overall responsibilities for coordinating local activity to promote economic and social wellbeing in their communities (Local Government Act 2000; CLG, 2006; Local Government and Public Involvement in Health Act 2007). This means that the central government department responsible for overseeing local government has a significant role. In England, this is currently called the Department for Communities and Local Government (CLG, created in 2006, replacing the Office of the Deputy Prime Minister, ODPM). It is also responsible for housing and neighbourhood policies.

The Department for Work and Pensions is responsible for welfare benefits and welfare to work programmes in England, Wales and Scotland (Northern Ireland has its own social security agency, but benefits are the same). Benefits include jobseeker's allowance, employment and support allowance, the state pension, and disability payments such as attendance allowance. The DWP is also responsible for the network of Jobcentre Plus offices, although these are run as 'arm's-length' agencies (discussed further below).

Other relevant departments, as shown in Box 8.1, are the Home Office, the Ministry of Justice, and the Cabinet Office, which has an overseeing and coordinating role for government policy. Finally, there is the Treasury, which is responsible for raising public funds through taxation and deciding how much money each department should receive.

Other national regulatory and advisory bodies

In addition to the major government departments, there are other organisations that have an important role in shaping and controlling social work – regulating it, in the widest sense of the term. Some aim to achieve this through target setting or inspection, others by a more educational and advisory approach, others by a combination of methods. This section comments on some of the major bodies in England, but see Box 8.3 for details of parallel organisations in Wales, Scotland and Northern Ireland.

**Box 8.2 A selection of other regulatory and advisory bodies in England,
April 2009**

- **General Social Care Council (GSCC)** Social work register, social care codes of practice, social work education. www.gscc.org.uk

- **Social Care Institute for Excellence (SCIE)** Promotes evidence-based practice via dissemination of research. www.scie.org.uk

- **Care Quality Commission (CQC)** Regulates and inspects health care services and adult social care. www.cqc.org.uk

- **Office for Standards in Education (Ofsted)** Inspects schools, also regulates and inspects children's social care services. www.ofsted.org.uk

- **Sector Skills Council – 'Skills for Care' (SfC)** and **'Children's Workforce Development Council' (CWDC)** National occupational standards; recruitment and training. www.skillsfor care.org.uk; www.cwdc.org.uk

- **Audit Commission** Inspects NHS, local authorities and criminal justice services. Comprehensive area assessments. www.audit-commission.gov.uk

- **Equality and Human Rights Commission (EHRC)** Concerned with inequalities of gender, race, disability, sexuality, age, religion. www.ehrc.org.uk

- **Association of Directors of Children's Services (ADCS)** and **Association of Directors of Adult Social Services (ADASS)** Promote role and views of local authority social care services in policy-making with central government. www.adcs.org.uk; www.adass.org.uk

- **British Association of Social Workers (BASW)** A professional body, not a trade union, that claims to represent the views and interests of social workers in the UK. Has its own code of ethics. www.basw.org.uk

- **Local Government Association (LGA)** Representative body for all local authorities in England and Wales, seeking to influence policy, explain their role and views. www.lga.org.uk

- **Improvement and Development Agency (IDeA)** Funded by the LGA and CLG (see Box 8.1). Helps local authorities to improve their services by sharing ideas about good practice. www.idea.gov.uk

Box 8.3 Major government departments and regulatory bodies for social work in Wales, Scotland and Northern Ireland, April 2009

Wales

- Welsh Assembly Government (WAG) http://wales.gov.uk

- Department of Health and Social Services http://wales.gov.uk/about/departments/dhss/?lang=en

- Care and Social Services Inspectorate Wales (CSSIW) http://wales.gov.uk/cssiwsubsite/cssiw/?lang=en

- Wales Audit Office www.wao.gov.uk

- Social Services Improvement Agency (SSIA) http://www.ssiacymru.org.uk

- Association of Directors of Social Services (Wales) (ADSS Cymru) www.adsscymru.org.uk

Scotland

- Scottish government www.scotland.gov.uk

- Scottish Social Services Council www.sssc.uk.com

- Scottish Commission for the Regulation of Care (Care Commission) Regulates health services, care homes for older people, adoption and fostering. www.carecommission.com

- Social Work Inspection Agency (SWIA) Inspects social work services provided by or on behalf of local authorities, but child protection services currently inspected by Her Majesty's Inspectorate of Education. www.swia.gov.uk/swia

Note: The Scottish Care Commission and SWIA are being reorganised. From April 2011 there will be one organisation for health care and another for social care and social work.

- Institute for Research and Innovation in Social Services www.iriss.ac.uk

- Scottish Human Rights Commission www.scottishhumanrights.com

- Association of Directors of Social Work (ADSW) www.adsw.org.uk

---

Northern Ireland

- **Northern Ireland Executive** www.northernireland.gov.uk

- **Department of Health, Social Services and Public Safety** Health and Social Care Board and five Health and Social Care Trusts. www.dhsspsni.gov.uk

- **Northern Ireland Social Care Council** www.niscc.info

- **Regulation and Quality Improvement Authority** www.rqia.org.uk

- **Northern Ireland Human Rights Commission** www.nihrc.org

Each of the countries has its own social care/services council, which regulates social work by maintaining a register of qualified social workers, and promoting the codes of practice for social care workers and employers (the four countries share the same code). The GSCC has not yet started to register other care workers, although the other countries do. The councils also approve and monitor social work degree programmes, and only holders of approved degrees can register as qualified social workers. Registration entails a commitment to practise and conduct one's private life in accordance with the code, and to keep one's professional knowledge up to date by undertaking at least fifteen days of training or studying every three years. Social workers who break the code may be struck off the register. The councils were created in 2001, replacing a UK-wide body known as the Central Council for Education and Training in Social Work (CCETSW). SCIE was also formed in 2001, replacing the National Institute for Social Work.

In England, adult social care services are inspected by the Care Quality Commission (CQC). Children's social care services are inspected by the Office for Standards in Education (Ofsted). Both bodies inspect local authority services, and register and inspect private and voluntary sector agencies.

The CQC is the most recent regulatory body in England, starting work on 1 April 2009. Like the others, it is not entirely new, rather the result of a rearrangement of responsibilities and structures. The CQC replaced the Commission for Social Care Inspection (CSCI), which was formed in 2004. CSCI itself had replaced the short-lived National Care Standards Commission (2002–4) and the longer-lived Social Services Inspectorate (SSI, 1985–2002). Before the SSI there had been a body called the Department of Health Social Work Service.

The CQC brought together CSCI, the Healthcare Commission and the Mental Health Act Commission, to form a new super-inspectorate for health and adult social care. There was much anxiety about the merger – that it would cause long-lasting disruption, more expense, and undermine the specialist focus held by each of the different bodies (Carvel, 2007). CSCI did a good job of bringing resource shortages

Chapter 4

to the attention of politicians and the public, notably in its annual reports and its analysis of the FACS criteria (see Chapter 4). It is to be hoped that the CQC continues this independent tradition. It will be important to follow its progress over the coming years.

Across the UK, there is a 'sector skills council' for social care, known as Skills for Care and Development. Sector skills councils are employer-led bodies that specify the skills required of the workforce, and work with other agencies to establish strategies to meet them, notably through recruitment and training. The predecessor of Skills for Care and Development was known as the Training Organisation for the Personal Social Services (TOPSS). This produced the National Occupational Standards for social work, a list of six key roles that are used to identify students' learning requirements on social work degrees (TOPSS, 2002; now available via Skills for Care).

The social care/services councils for Scotland, Wales and Northern Ireland act as the sector skills councils in their countries. In England, the role is taken by two bodies, the Children's Workforce Development Council (CWDC), and Skills for Care (SfC) for the adult care workforce. Both of these bodies deal with far larger workforces than just social work: for example, the CWDC also covers early years workers and childminders, and SfC also covers domiciliary care workers and residential care assistants.

Another important regulatory body is the Audit Commission. It inspects services provided by local government, the NHS and the criminal justice system. Founded in 1983, its primary concern is sound financial management and efficient use of resources in the public sector – it is especially concerned with the 'three Es' of economy, efficiency and effectiveness. The Audit Commission makes an annual assessment of the overall performance of each local authority. The results of inspections by the CQC and Ofsted feed into this evaluation, which used to be known as the comprehensive performance assessment, but from 2009 will be called the comprehensive area assessment.

The Equality and Human Rights Commission (EHRC) was formed in 2007 from the merger of the Equal Opportunities Commission (concerned with equality between the sexes), the Commission for Racial Equality and the Disability Rights Commission. It added sexuality, age, religion and belief, and human rights generally to its remit. The EHRC does not regulate social work directly, but the principles and legislation it supports are certainly relevant to every aspect of social work, the practices of local authorities, voluntary organisations, private agencies and individual workers.

There are numerous other organisations that have a say – or hope that they might achieve some sort of say – in shaping social work policy. Four are shown in Box 8.2, but there are many voluntary organisations, campaign groups, representative bodies, research organisations, think-tanks and lobby groups that have an interest in social care, and which might issue publications and run campaigns to change policy. Many have been referenced throughout the book, including the 'Useful websites and further reading' section at the end of each chapter.

The local level

However much social policies are planned at national level, delivery is at local level – for example, through health centres, schools, job centres, local authorities, the local offices of voluntary organisations and welfare businesses. Here the themes are about effective inter-agency working, 'horizontal integration'. Social work in the UK is mainly provided through local authorities (Northern Ireland has a different organisational structure, but it is still local delivery).

Recent reorganisations mean that in England, in 2009, there are now over 150 councils with responsibilities for children's services and adult social care. These are either 'higher-tier' authorities or unitary authorities. That is, in areas where there are two levels of local government, county councils and district councils, it is the county council that has responsibility for social work, along with education, roads, libraries and museums, and economic development, while the district council carries responsibility for housing, parks and leisure facilities, and environmental health (including rubbish collection). In parts of the country where there is only one tier of local government, the council carries all these responsibilities. These include the London boroughs, the metropolitan boroughs (large industrial cities, typically in the Midlands and the north of the country), and a number of newer unitary authorities that serve smaller towns or areas, mostly formed as a result of local government reorganisation in the 1990s (see Craig and Manthorpe, 1999). All local authorities in Wales and Scotland are unitary – 22 in Wales and 32 in Scotland.

Arm's-length agencies and 'quangos'

The technique of delivering and regulating public services via arm's-length agencies, or 'non-departmental public bodies' (NDPBs), is an important feature of policy implementation in the UK. There is a variety of types. There are 'executive agencies', which deliver services for national government, but are run as business units, outside the government department responsible for that area of policy. Examples are the Criminal Records Bureau and Jobcentre Plus. There are also bodies with regulatory roles, sometimes known as 'quangos' (quasi-autonomous non-governmental organisations) – the GSCC and the EHRC are examples. The idea is that separation from direct government control gives the organisations a degree of operational freedom, but they are still bound by national policy and are ultimately answerable to central government.

There are profound questions about the nature and purposes of this semi-independence – or, one might say, this illusion of independence. Supporters see it as a way of achieving greater effectiveness, cutting down government bureaucracy and untoward interference, and bringing businesslike efficiencies. Critics see it as a way of disguising the real extent of government control and the impact of resource limitations (Hoggett, 1996). The use of these semi-independent agencies started under the 1979–97 Conservative government, and has continued since 1997. For example, the approach lies behind the creation of foundation hospitals and city academies, which are separate from the NHS and local authorities, respectively, with their own management arrangements. This breaking-up of large public sector organisations reflects the political mistrust of the old 'welfare bureaucracies'. It is part of the wider approach to modernising public services by introducing a new style of public management, markets and competition.

Managerialism and markets

New Labour's programme to reform the public services hinges on the vision that they should be run more like private businesses, lean and responsive, rather than (what they stereotype as) monolithic one-size-fits-all welfare bureaucracies (PMSU, 2007). The new approaches to organisation, delivery and regulation are intended to achieve this objective. At the heart of these methods are notions of managerialism, markets and (discussed in the next section) the mixed economy of welfare.

The roles and responsibilities of managers are crucially important parts of any organisation, but the concept of 'managerialism', or the 'new public management', is more than just what managers do. It may be considered a set of assumptions and related techniques (Pollitt, 1990) that have been central in the reform of welfare services in the UK since the early 1980s (Clarke and Newman, 1997; Harris, 1998, 2003; Burden *et al.*, 2000; Clarke *et al.*, 2000; Scourfield, 2006; Harris and White, 2009).

The core assumptions are that:

- public services can be managed more effectively, efficiently and economically through the introduction of private sector management techniques and marketplace principles;
- public spending must be tightly restricted, controlled and monitored;
- the practice of front line workers should be tightly specified and closely monitored;
- public services should be more responsive to users' views and choices.

(Dickens, 2008: 49)

Some of the techniques associated with managerialism are traditional bureaucratic methods (procedures, rules), but there is a new intensity of regulation that has transformed the old bureau-professional regimes. These include the use of performance indicators and league tables, audit and inspection (Humphrey, 2003; Munro, 2004; Tilbury, 2004). More than that, there is a greater focus on 'the bottom line', budgets, and the need to demonstrate efficient and effective use of resources ('best value'). Even *within* public sector organisations, marketplace principles prevail and services are structured into purchaser and provider arms, and business units, in the quest for more efficient use of resources (Harris, 2003; Carey, 2008). There is an emphasis on cutting out waste and unnecessary

Chapter 6

expenditure, targeting and eligibility criteria, and greater accountability to service users (as we saw in Chapter 6, service user rhetoric can be a tool for managerial control). Organisational restructuring, new procedures and top-down directives are widely used strategies to achieve these goals.

Managers have a key part to play in implementing this new approach to public services, but the goal is that the values become common sense, so that all staff adopt them, and become self-managing. In

Chapter 1

this sense it echoes the wider objective of social work and social policy that we discussed in Chapter 1, that all citizens adopt the ideas about responsibility and self-sufficiency and become 'self-regulating'. The current drive to personalisation may be seen as a way of extending the principles of self-management to service users themselves (Scourfield, 2007).

Certainly the assumptions and techniques of managerialism and markets have become widespread and are powerfully enforced, but there are contradictions and tensions. There is resistance from the radicals, but even without this there are always gaps between the objectives and the reality. One of the main tensions is between markets and managerialism. The market approach values customer choice and individualised services, but the managerial approach has to consider the volume of demand and budgetary limits. The supporters of personalised services, such as In Control on individual budgets (see Chapter 6), argue that they need not add to the overall cost because they are much more efficient. The

Chapter 6

danger is that this efficiency is achieved at a cost to service users and their families, by shifting burdensome responsibilities to them. One also has to consider the impact of resource shortages on those who do not qualify for a service because of high eligibility criteria (CSCI, 2008a).

Another of the gaps between theory and reality, as Harris points out (2003: 146), is that the rhetoric of markets and consumer choice hangs on middle-class images of shopping in good-quality department stores. There are other sides to markets: poor-quality products, limited choice, overpricing, high-pressure sales and con tricks, poor wages and poor working conditions. CSCI inspections show that private services perform less well than council and voluntary sector services (CSCI, 2009: 146, 164–5). The majority of agencies are good, but there are some very poor-quality services in the private sector, as shown by two editions of the BBC investigative programme *Panorama*, in 2003 and 2009. Although they were over five years apart, they uncovered similar problems of poor care in private home care agencies (BBC, 2003, 2009). And as the banking scandals of 2007–9 have shown, incompetence, greed and dishonesty exist at the highest levels of business. The private sector is not by any means a straightforward role model for the public sector.

There are two prime paradoxes to do with regulation and autonomy. One is that the more services are put out to market, the more need there is for contracts, monitoring, reviews and inspections. So the break-up of the old bureaucratic structures leads to an increase in bureaucracy. The second paradox is that discretion is an unavoidable part of implementing rules, procedures and targets; and the more rules there are, the more individual judgment is required to make sense of them and prioritise them. The good news is that there is still room for creativity and skilled practice that makes a difference to people's lives.

The mixed economy of welfare

The phrase 'the mixed economy of welfare' refers to the combination of four welfare sectors:

- statutory, public sector agencies (e.g. local authorities, the NHS, state schools);

- the private sector (e.g. private hospitals, private pensions, private care homes);

- the voluntary and community sector ('third sector', or 'not-for-profit' sector, including major charities, such as Age Concern and Help the Aged (which merged in 2009), MIND, the NSPCC, the Salvation Army; housing associations; smaller charities and local groups; community and self-help groups; and social enterprises);

- the informal sector (family, friends, neighbours).

These different sectors have always been involved in the provision of welfare, but the patterns of involvement are changing and increasingly complex. Powell (2007) makes the point that we need to think about the interrelationships between the four sectors on three dimensions: *delivery*, *regulation* and *finance*.

The private sector is now widely involved in the delivery of personal social services, notably domiciliary care (home care) for older and disabled people, residential and nursing homes for adults, foster and residential care for children. These services are often paid for and regulated by statutory agencies, although service users may pay themselves, in full or in part. 'Public–private partnerships' have been used for private companies to build and run public services (e.g. schools, hospitals, prisons), in return

for annual fees on long contracts with central or local government. In theory, the private sector can give more choice to service users, and competition raises standards. In reality, choice is often limited and the need to make a profit can undermine standards (see above, the discussion about markets, and Chapter 6 on choice).

The third sector has traditionally been involved through the work of charities and religious organisations, but it is a hugely diverse category (Alcock and Scott, 2007; NCVO, 2009). At one end are high-profile, national (and international) voluntary organisations that employ professional staff to deliver their services and are as bureaucratic (or as managerial and businesslike) as any public sector body. These organisations may still raise money through voluntary donations and charity shops, but are likely to get the bulk of their funding from contracts and grants from central or local government. As service delivery agencies, they can become almost like an arm of the state. There are fears that these close links with the statutory sector, especially the reliance on funding, can create challenges for the independence of voluntary organisations (discussed by Blackmore, 2008).

At the other end, the third sector includes smaller charities, local groups such as clubs and societies, play schemes and older people's visiting schemes, where it blurs with the informal sector; and there is a third point where it blurs with the private sector, for example through different types of social enterprise. These are businesses run for social or environmental purposes, where profits are mostly reinvested in the business or the community for those purposes (so there is a profit, but it is not primarily for personal gain). The breadth of the third sector is shown on the websites of the government's Office of the Third Sector (via the Cabinet Office website) and the National Council of Voluntary Organisations, NCVO (www.ncvo-vol.org.uk).

The government wishes to develop the role and capacity of the voluntary and community sector, not just to deliver services but in a broader sense, typical of an integrationist approach, to promote civil renewal, social inclusion and active citizenship (see Chapter 6 on participation). There are concerns that this is an instrumentalist approach, trying to use the sector for the government's own purposes (see Jochum *et al.*, 2005; Blackmore, 2008). Policy to expand the sector has to be analysed with caution,

asking how much it is about people's welfare and wellbeing, how much about shifting responsibility away from the state, how much about reducing welfare costs (the social policy triangle again). These dilemmas are also clear in the government's policies towards the informal sector.

Chapter 6

The informal sector usually means the family, despite much talk about community involvement, and the family usually means women in their roles as mothers, wives, daughters and partners. There can be personal satisfaction in providing care, but there can also be great physical, emotional and financial costs (HM Government, 2008a; Carers UK website, www.carersuk.org). New Labour has made support for carers a policy priority since the launch of the National Carers' Strategy in 1999 (DH, 1999a). This has since been reviewed and a new strategy was published in 2008, *Carers at the Heart of 21st Century Families and Communities* (HM Government, 2008a).

The revised strategy has to address the new policy context of personalisation and the issues this raises for meeting and balancing the needs and aspirations of carers and the people they care for. It acknowledges that questions about informal care and support for carers are 'one of the key issues facing society today – how to establish the parameters and responsibilities for providing care for the growing number of people who need support, while taking account of an individual's needs and being realistic about what is appropriate for statutory services to provide' (HM Government, 2008a: 31).

The challenges of the social policy triangle run throughout the report – of reconciling wellbeing (of carers and the cared-for), responsibility (of governments, families and society at large) and the economy (the cost of services and the possibilities for working-age carers to combine caring and employment). The government is at pains to emphasise that its role is limited. Rather than seeing government as the primary provider of services, the report argues that the role of central government is to provide leadership, set overall objectives, monitor implementation and promote joined-up services (pp. 37–8). It expects to work in partnership with carers and the people they care for. Carers are expected to accept that caring for someone is one of the responsibilities of family life (p. 39) – that responsibility idea again.

The challenges of the social work diamond are also apparent in the report – balancing the interests of the state, service users and carers, organisational structures and capacities, and the roles of professionals. The report says that carers are to be regarded as experts and partners in providing care, but there is always the potential for conflict between the different viewpoints and priorities. An example is that carers' views may be overruled by professional judgments about what is in the interests of the cared-for person.

Policy about carers is a touchstone for attitudes and suppositions about the informal sector, and indeed, more than that, for the whole notion of a mixed economy of welfare. How much is it being promoted because it is what people want, because it is what is best for them (and who judges that?), or because it is cheap? Do the different sectors have the capacity to deliver everything that is expected of them, and what are the implications and limits of the relationships between them? These questions take us back to the different views about the role of the state. Different political perspectives will look for different relationships between the sectors and will emphasise different benefits of the mixed economy.

The mixed economy comes up again in the next chapter, with reference to the funding of social care. A point to note now is that the integration of the four sectors in planning and coordinating local services is a prominent goal of current social policy. Local authorities are required to establish local strategic partnerships with key public, private and voluntary agencies and produce local area agreements about the goals of their services and partnership working. It is a different role for local authorities, to steer rather than to row, and to share the steering with other organisations – but the overall direction and speed of travel is closely controlled by central government, which sets national

Chapter 9

policy, distributes the money (see Chapter 9) and assesses local performance against a set of national indicators. For more details about local area agreements, see the 'About local government' pages on the CLG website, and see the Audit Commission website on comprehensive area assessments.

Box 8.4 Social work practices

A recent development in children's services in England is the piloting of 'social work practices' for children who are looked after by local authorities (in care). These exemplify the arguments about privatisation, managerialism, markets and the mixed economy of welfare. They are a good example of the tendency to see new organisations as solutions to complex problems.

In 2006 the government published a green paper on children looked after by local authorities in England: *Care Matters: Transforming the Lives of Children and Young People in Care* (DfES, 2006). One of the suggestions was for independent social care practices to undertake the work with the young people on behalf of the authority. The idea was that these new organisations would give greater autonomy and flexibility to social workers to work directly with the young people. The proposal was developed by a working party led by Julian Le Grand (see Box 7.1), and the terminology changed to social work practices. The working party report suggested that the scheme be piloted (Le Grand, 2007). This was taken up in the white paper *Care Matters: Time for Change* (DfES, 2007). The government issued a prospectus (DCSF, 2008c) and the Children and Young Persons Act 2008 made provision for pilot schemes to go ahead. In late 2008, the government announced that six local authorities had been selected to run the pilots, to start in 2009.

The working party report identified a number of well-known problems in local authority social work: the lack of continuity and stability; diminished professional autonomy and responsibility; social workers spending too much time on paperwork and bureaucracy, and too little on working directly with the children; and a lack of incentives for innovation and responsiveness (Le Grand, 2007: 22)

Social work practices were proposed as a solution to these problems. They will be run by voluntary or private sector organisations, or groups of partners, rather like a GP practice. They will take on all the work with the young person, although the local authority will retain legal responsibility and any significant changes to the care plan will have to be agreed in a formal review. The practice will be paid a standard fee for each child, and then extra amounts if they help him/her achieve specified outcomes. By the fourth year of the contract, 60 per cent of the funding for each child will be outcome-related.

The working party report and the DCSF prospectus mention a number of possible attractions for social workers. They refer to research that workers who have a stake in an organisation are more loyal and less likely to leave. They suggest this may be because they feel they can improve their pay and conditions within the organisation, rather than having to move. They say that social workers will not be at the bottom of the hierarchy in social work practices, but will have more control over their work. This could lead to higher morale and status, 'and more commitment to and personal involvement in their work' (DCSF, 2008c: 4). They also consider that the small size of the practices could help social workers be more responsive and build closer relationships with children and families.

Exactly how the practices are going to achieve these goals is not clear. Nor is it clear why it is necessary to set up completely new organisations, rather than enable local authority social workers to exercise more professional judgment, have better support, less paperwork, improved pay, more time with young people and so on. The House of Commons Children, Schools and Families Committee has expressed concern that the practices might lead to greater fragmentation of roles and responsibilities, rather than improving continuity for the children. It has asked the government to evaluate the schemes with care, and to ensure that the views of children and young people are given prominence (House of Commons CSFC, 2009: paras 51–7).

The other important question is what impact the practices will have on the 'other children', those who are not transferred. Will they end up with a poorer service, as funding and staff are drawn to the gleaming new agency? The DCSF prospectus does say that the evaluation will address this wider question. It asserts that the scheme will be rolled-out more widely only 'if the evaluation shows that it does improve outcomes for children in care and does *not* have a negative impact on other social care services' (DCSF, 2008c: 4).

Law and politics

We now look at two further approaches (sets of principles and techniques) that are prominent in organising and regulating social work – law and politics. Thinking back to the social work diamond, these are methods that relate especially to the state. They are closely interlinked (politicians debate and pass laws), but they can also be in conflict (courts can overturn political decisions). As always there are overlaps and tensions, and opportunities for different groups to influence and use the processes – for example, for service users to lobby politicians or take local authority decisions to court for judicial review.

The legal approach

Legislation and the courts are powerful mechanisms for regulating social services. Legislation includes Acts of Parliament ('primary legislation') and regulations, also known as statutory instruments or 'secondary legislation' – as examples, there are regulations about standards and procedures for fostering services and care homes. A third level is 'statutory guidance', which is issued by the relevant central government department. It does not carry the full force of law but local authorities are strongly expected to comply – an example is the *Framework for the Assessment of Children in Need and their Families* (DH *et al.*, 2000), which specifies the areas to be covered in assessments and the timescales for completing them. Courts will normally uphold statutory guidance and authorities may deviate from it only in exceptional circumstances, so it is an important means for government to direct social work practice.

In theory, law should be clear, fair and rational, creating, reflecting and enforcing national polices and priorities. The usual process is that the government publishes a green paper (a discussion document), a white paper (further refined, more concrete proposals), then a bill. This political process gives opportunities for service user groups and professionals to lobby for changes. A bill is debated and amended before becoming an act. There is then often a period of delay while preparations are made for the implementation of the new law, which may include drafting the secondary legislation and government guidance, training professionals, and publicising the changes. But legislation is not always created along such a smooth path. There can be knee-jerk legislation, in response to a public scandal or a media campaign (Butler and Drakeford, 2005); legislation may be unclear, and an astute lawyer can often find loopholes or challenge the way it has been interpreted and applied; and there may well be people who feel hard-done by it. So, law is not always rational, clear or fair. Also, just like bureaucracy, laws do not implement themselves, but rely on professionals to interpret and apply them.

The courts offer opportunities for the state to impose its requirements (for example, to prosecute offenders, to enforce planning laws, to take children into care), but importantly they also give individuals the opportunity to resist, and a means to seek redress for those who feel they have been unfairly treated. Courts are important as independent, objective tribunals that will weigh the different sides of an argument. They are part of the state but can be a check on its powers, as well as a way of enforcing social control. Having said that, courts are intimidating places, and proceedings are often slow and expensive. Those who are most familiar with the system, and who have the greatest resources (money, but also knowledge and experience), are most likely to 'come out ahead' (Galanter, 1974).

There are also questions of whether law is always the right mechanism to resolve welfare problems and disagreements. Law works by reducing disputes to terms it can decide – guilty or not guilty, evidence that is acceptable or unacceptable, actions that are permitted or not permitted. Many of the issues that social workers deal with are not easily amenable to this sort of binary categorisation – for example, a young person may be an offender, but he/she may also be the victim of ill treatment (King and Piper, 1990; King and Trowell, 1992).

The political approach

Political parties and politicians play crucial roles in designing and monitoring social policies. Political decisions determine what policies are adopted and what the budget shall be. Politicians have a crucial role in asking hard questions to managers and professional staff about how they are implementing policies and spending funds. Strong-minded politicians can certainly do this, but once again there are complex interactions and ambiguities in practice. Most politicians are not professionally qualified or experienced in the matters for which they carry political responsibility – e.g. the Secretary of State for Health is not usually a medic, or at a local level the lead councillor for children is not usually a child welfare professional. Politicians therefore need to take advice from professionals and managers, and give support and sufficient resources to enable them to fulfil their tasks; but they are also required to be independent of the professionals and the departments, to hold them to account when necessary.

As for the links between political and service user approaches to social policy, service users can lobby politicians about the proposals they would like to see adopted. However, in a context of limited budgets and conflicting demands, one group's success may well be another's disappointment. Further, groups that use social care services are often poor or socially excluded, with less political power than other interest groups. Indeed, it could be said that if one has to campaign openly, one is already in a weak position: the truly powerful exercise influence much more subtly. The prevailing ways of doing things, beliefs that 'that's the way things are', work quietly but compellingly in their favour (Lukes, 1974).

In theory, the democratic political process weighs up the competing interests of different groups through open debate and decision-making; in reality, it can be very hard for minority issues to secure a prominent place on the political agenda. Political decision-making is also influenced by electoral timescales. Politicians might be reluctant to make an unpopular decision close to an election, even if it might be the one that all the evidence suggests is right. Equally, they might be keen to make a popular decision, even if the experts and advisers argue that it is incorrect. Behind those dilemmas are fundamental questions about politicians' roles and loyalties, which echo questions about the role of social professionals – how far do they follow the wishes of the electorate (service users), or when and how do they take a more active role in trying to *change* attitudes and behaviour? How do they weigh up the wishes and interests of different groups? How do they reconcile compliance with party (organisational) policy, with their own assessment of what is needed?

Conclusion

This chapter has reviewed the organisational and regulatory structures of social work in England in 2009. Recent years have seen huge organisational changes, new regulatory agencies, new legislation, high levels of political intervention in social policy, and the increasing role of the non-statutory sectors in delivering welfare services. Underneath all the activity we can see a number of key approaches, reflecting different views about the proper roles of the state, professionals, organisations and service users.

New Labour's approach to raising standards has been characterised by organisational restructuring and tight top-down control though legislation, targets and inspections. Yet, at field level, reorganisations can be disruptive and expensive, and shift attention away from service users to service structures. Equally, targets can have perverse effects, focusing attention on one aspect of a service to the detriment of other aspects, and absorbing lots of time, energy and money to demonstrate that they have been met. Further, if government policy, procedures and targets are too prescriptive, this can limit the freedom for agencies to respond creatively to new or local needs. Finally, however many reorganisations there might be, and however many targets, the ability of local agencies to deliver effective services is constrained by budgets and resources.

It is important to be wary of one-dimensional solutions to the perceived shortcomings of social work and other public services. Problems are often portrayed as failures of communication, procedural compliance, management, or organisational structure, and therefore amenable to technical fixes such as restructuring and tighter regulation. The lessons of history suggest that things are not as easy as that, and that restructuring and tighter regulation do not eradicate the problems. Indeed, all the regulation can become part of the problem, as procedural compliance and 'looking good on paper' become ever more demanding and remote from the reality.

The issues are too deep-rooted to be solved by organisational structures and inspection regimes. That is not to say that these things do not matter – effective structures can enable people to do better work, and effective regulation can help ensure high-quality services. But we need to be realistic about what they can achieve and their drawbacks, and sensitive to the complexity of the underlying issues. This takes us back to the key principles, responsibilities and priorities of social work and other welfare services, the fundamental questions 'What is welfare for?' and 'What is social work for?' The answers are that they have many purposes that are not always compatible. This complexity makes change and regulation much more difficult than they are often portrayed by inquiries, political comment and media accounts.

Questions for reflection

- Think of a place where you have worked or been on placement. How was the work there regulated? Think of the rules and procedures you had to follow. Where did they come from? Who enforced them, and how? How much room was there for discretion?

- List as many strengths and weaknesses as you can for the four sectors of the mixed economy of welfare. Think about positives and drawbacks from different points of view (e.g. service users, staff, government). Try to be as specific as you can – think of examples from your own experience or knowledge. It works well to do this in a group, to compare ideas and experiences.

Useful websites and further reading

Boxes 8.1, 8.2 and 8.3

Explore the websites of the various organisations listed in Boxes 8.1, 8.2 and 8.3. Also, look for websites of other organisations that research and campaign about social policy or represent the interests of service user groups.

A good way of keeping up-to-date with current developments is a website called Info4local, the government's 'information gateway for people working in local public services'. You can register for a daily e-mail at www.info4local.gov.uk.

The following books are recommended on the themes covered in this chapter:

Harris (2003) *The Social Work Business*.

Harris and White (eds) (2009) *Modernising Social Work*.

Hudson and Lowe (2009) *Understanding the Policy Process*, 2nd edn.

Powell (ed.) (2007) *Understanding the Mixed Economy of Welfare*.

9 Social work and money

This chapter investigates some of the financial aspects of social care. This is a crucial dimension because the sums of money involved are substantial, there are controversial questions about who pays, who should pay and how much should they pay, disagreements about the proper roles of the statutory, private, voluntary and informal sectors, and powerful impacts on the roles and tasks of social workers. Looking at social work through the lens of money brings into sharp focus all the themes that have been discussed throughout the book.

Local authority social services are big business, with a total expenditure in the UK of about £26 billion in 2007–8 (HM Treasury, 2007: 13). By far the largest part of that was spent in England, and later in the chapter we shall analyse the income and expenditure for England in detail. For the moment, it is worth noting that even though £26 billion is a large amount of money, it is far smaller than the amounts spent on education (around £80 billion for the UK in 2007–8), the NHS (£100 billion) and welfare benefits (about £160 billion) (HM Treasury, 2007: 13). The figure also misses out the value of the informal care that families and friends provide, care which is purchased privately, and services which are funded by charitable giving. A study for Carers UK in 2007 put the cash value of informal care to adults at £87 billion per year (Buckner and Yeandle, 2007). The cost of privately purchased residential and home care for older people in England in 2006–7, including charges for local authority services, was estimated at almost £5.9 billion (CSCI, 2008a: 115). Voluntary giving to charities amounted to £13.6 billion in the UK in 2006–7 (NCVO, 2009), although this would not all have gone to projects related to social care.

Also, however large £26 billion may sound, there are many complaints from local authorities and service users that it is not enough, meaning that services have to be tightly rationed. Writing in April 2009, it is clear that the global recession is having a drastic effect on the national budget, and funds for public services will be very tightly restricted over the next few years. Rationing is going to become even more a staple part of social work in the UK.

As well as looking in detail at the way that the personal social services budget is spent, this chapter looks at where the money comes from (central and local taxation, and charges), and considers current debates about social care funding. The government held a public consultation on this in 2007-8, and after considerable delays a green paper was published in July 2009 (HM Government, 2009b).

In summary, the questions that guide this chapter are 'Who pays and who should pay?' and 'Who spends and who should spend?' These questions link with the three core models that run through the book:

- First, in terms of the social work diamond, the questions reflect the tensions between the organisational contexts of social work (local authorities, other providers, restricted budgets, tight systems of financial control), the state context (taxation, government spending, national policy), service user perspectives (discontent over charges, moves to give greater control to service users to purchase services themselves), and professional viewpoints (assessing needs and abilities, working in a context of limited resources).

- Second, in terms of the social policy triangle, the questions reflect the challenges of delivering high-quality welfare services, encouraging and supporting individual and family responsibility, and not undermining the workings of the market economy.

- Third, in terms of the roles of the state, the different answers that people give to these questions reflect the differences but also the overlaps and ambiguities of the minimalist, integrationist, social democratic and radical positions – attitudes towards individual responsibility and choice, to diversifying the range of welfare suppliers, to changing the role of the state.

Where the money comes from

Expenditure on local authority personal social services in England in 2007-8 came to £20.7 billion (NHS Information Centre, 2009b). The cost was £3.2 billion in Scotland and £1.3 billion in Wales (Scottish Government, 2009; LGDU Wales, 2009). Personal social services in Northern Ireland cost £816 million in 2006-7 (DHSSPS, 2008).

We shall look in detail at the figures for England, drawing out four main points:

- The tensions between local authority 'freedoms' and central government control;

- Over half the money is spent on services provided by the private and voluntary sectors;

- Charges to service users make up a significant proportion of the income;
- Social work is a relatively small part of the expenditure.

There are three main sources of funding for local authority social care in England: central government taxes, local government taxes, and charges to service users. Central government taxation includes income tax, value added tax (VAT), extra taxes on alcohol, tobacco and petrol, and taxes on businesses. The government also raises money by borrowing, although this has to be paid back later, by raising taxes or cutting expenditure. Central government funding for local authorities also includes money raised from the 'national non-domestic rates', which are rates on business premises, such as factories, shops and offices. They are collected by local authorities but handed over to central government, which then redistributes simply according to the population size of each authority. The money that comes from central government makes up about 70 per cent of local authorities' budgets.

Local authorities raise their own money via the council tax, which is paid on the value of residential property, and by charging service users. Overall, council tax makes up about 20 per cent of the income, and charges about 10 per cent, but as we shall see, charges for older people's services come to far more than this, about 20 per cent.

The money from central government is given out under three main headings: formula grant, area based grant, and specific grants. Formula grant is the largest part of the budget, a general grant intended to fund the mainstream expenditure of the council. The amount that each authority gets in formula grant depends on its population size and characteristics, and general levels of prosperity. It is calculated according to a system known as the 'relative needs formula' (RNF), described further below.

Area based grant is made up of funding for specific policy initiatives. These tend to change over time, as new priorities are promoted and then become part of the mainstream budget. Recent examples include grants for services for carers, to tackle teenage pregnancy, to improve services for children in care, to implement reforms to the social care workforce. Even though the money is given under specific headings, local authorities are not required to spend it in those ways. They are technically free to decide different priorities, but they will be held to account against relevant national performance targets, and other local agencies and special interest groups may well press them to spend the money on the intended services.

The third funding stream from central government is made up of specific grants which do not fall easily into the area based grant. A current example is the social care reform grant, to assist councils with the personalisation of services. Unless it is specified that these grants are 'ring fenced', it is still technically possible for local authorities to spend the money on other programmes (CLG, 2008b).

Different areas have different levels of need and different levels of prosperity. Some councils, with high levels of need and relatively poorer populations, will have to provide more services and will not be able to raise as much money as others from council tax or user charges. They will therefore need extra funding from central government if they are to provide a level of services comparable to other authorities. The government uses the RNF to decide these allocations.

The RNF uses key social, economic, demographic and geographical indicators to calculate how much each area will get (CLG, 2008a). The total RNF for each authority is made up of a number of component RNFs. These include children's services, adult personal social services, police, fire, roads, and 'environmental, protective and cultural services' (including libraries, museums, housing benefit, flood defence). As an example, the RNF for children's services starts with the number of children in the area, and then takes account of a range of factors, including the proportion living in families dependent on means-tested benefits, the proportion in poor health and the proportion from minority ethnic groups.

The government then takes account of the resources available to each authority – the amount it will get from the national pool of business rates, and the amount it should raise if it sets council tax within the government's approved levels and collects it efficiently. The result of these calculations and some further adjustments gives the amount that the authority will get in formula grant. Area based grant and specific grants come on top of that.

The RNF should be understood as a way of slicing up the cake, rather than deciding how big the whole cake should be. The government says that it is 'not intended to measure the actual amount needed by any authority to provide local services, but simply to recognise the various factors which affect local authorities' costs locally' (CLG, 2008a: 7). The RNF does not determine the overall amount of money that is available for public services, which is decided by central government's comprehensive spending review, every three years (HM Treasury, 2007). Rather, it is a way of comparing levels of need between authorities and deciding how much each gets from the amount available. Inevitably, many authorities complain that it is unfair and fails to recognise the particular challenges and expenses that they face.

Despite central government assertions that local authorities are able to determine their own spending priorities, in some ways there is relatively little freedom for councils to raise their own money and fix their own priorities. As noted in Chapter 8, they work with other local agencies in local strategic partnerships, so they do not have a free hand in decision-making. While they are formally allowed to shift expenditure from one heading to another, they are likely to face resistance if they do so – for example, they could decide to close a library to save money and use it for another service, but this

Chapter 8

would no doubt generate protests from library users and staff. They can raise council tax, but only within set parameters, and they are likely to face complaints from local people if they try to raise it too high. If they want more money for a particular service, it is likely that they will have to charge service users – and that may also prove unpopular.

The system creates an effect known as 'gearing', where the costs of any new, local initiative fall disproportionately on council tax and charges. For example, say a local authority wanted to increase its spending on a particular service from £100 million to £101 million. That is a relatively small increase, only 1 per cent, but unless the authority can make savings elsewhere, that £1 million has to be funded from the council tax and user charges, because they are the only parts it can increase itself. Together, these make up only about a third of the council's budget, so the call for extra money will have a disproportionate impact on this much smaller, and politically sensitive, pot. This makes it very hard for local authorities to increase spending on social services without extra funding from central government.

How the money is spent

This section looks at the way that the local authority social services budget is spent. It draws principally on a report entitled *Personal Social Services Expenditure and Unit Costs, England, 2007-08* (NHS Information Centre, 2009b), but this is an annual report, published every February, and readers are advised to consult the most recent version. It also draws on other reports published by the NHS Information Centre for Health and Social Care. There are a number of annual reports on local authority services for adults (NHS Information Centre 2008a, 2008b, 2009a) and an annual report on local authority personal social services staff (NHS Information Centre 2009c).

The government's headline figure for local authority personal social services expenditure in 2007–8 was £20.7 billion. This sum is called 'gross current expenditure', and excludes money that the authorities recoup through 'client contributions' (sales, charges and fees). The annual report also shows 'net current expenditure', which does take account of client contributions. These came to almost £2.2 billion in 2007–8, so net current expenditure was £18.5 billion. Table 9.1 gives the figures for each of the main service user groups, showing net current expenditure.

The largest category of expenditure is services for older people, which came to over £9 billion (40 per cent of total spending). This funded services for about 1.2 million people aged over sixty-fve in 2007–8 (there were 1.8 million adult service users in total – NHS Information Centre, 2008a: 5). Over the year, just over a million older people received one or more community-based services, and 266,000 received residential or nursing care (permanent or temporary), funded in full or in part by the local authority (NHS Information Centre, 2008a: 6). As Table 9.1 shows, the income from user charges for older people was £1.76 billion, and when this is taken into account, along with sums from other sources (mainly inter-agency arrangements), the net expenditure declines to slightly over £7 billion. User charges repay just under a fifth of the expenditure on older people's services. How these charges are levied and the debates they reflect and provoke are discussed further below.

About a quarter of total expenditure is on services for children and families, but this is for a much smaller number of service users. On a sample day in January 2008, there were an estimated 335,600 'children in need' cases open to local authorities, of whom just under 60,000 were looked after (Mahon, 2008; DCSF, 2008b). (This snapshot figure is less than the total number receiving services over the year, because of cases opening and closing. Also, it is the number of children and does not include parents or other relatives.) User charges are much less important as an income stream, because many families are on income support and/or compelled to use the services.

Another significant feature of the spending is the difference between 'own provision' and 'provision by others'. Overall, £12.69 billion, well over half the budget, is spent on provision by others – that is, services provided by the private and voluntary sectors. As the table shows, this is especially significant for older people's services, at almost £6 billion, two-thirds of the total expenditure on older people. So, local authority social services are big business, but part of this is that they are very big purchasers of services from the independent sector.

Table 9.1

Expenditure and income on selected aspects of local authority personal social services, England 2007–8, £ millions

	Children and families[1]	Older people	Physically disabled adults	Learning disabled adults	Adults with mental health needs	Other adult services[2]	Total[3]
Expenditure							
a) own provision	3,930	3,090	550	1,420	530	170	9,970
b) provision by others	1,580	5,990	1,020	2,990	750	290	12,690
Total expenditure	5,510	9,080	1,570	4,410	1,280	470	22,660
Income							
a) from client contributions[4]	50	1,760	90	230	60	10	2,190
b) from other sources[5]	290	310	100	960	160	120	1,970
Total income	370	2,070	180	1,190	220	130	4,160
Net current expenditure[6]	5,170	7,010	1,390	3,220	1,060	340	18,500

Notes: [1] 'Children and families' does not include services for child asylum seekers, £120 million in 2007–8.

[2] 'Other adult services' does not include services for adult asylum seekers, £20 million in 2007–8.

[3] 'Total' includes services for asylum seekers and general service strategy costs (other administrative costs and overheads not already included under particular service user groups).

[4] 'Client contributions' includes sales, fees and charges.

[5] 'Other sources' includes joint funding arrangements, e.g. with health services.

[6] 'Net current expenditure' is total expenditure less total income.

Figures may not add up due to rounding.

Adapted from NHS Information Centre (2009b: 6)

Other NHS Information Centre reports give more details about the role of the independent sector in residential and domiciliary services for adults. On 31 March 2008, local authorities were funding, in full or in part, 236,100 adults in care and nursing homes (N.B. all adults, and the snapshot figure rather than the flow over the whole year). Over 90 per cent were in the independent sector, up from just 20 per cent in 1993 (NHS Information Centre, 2008b: 4–5). For services in people's own homes, local authorities arranged 4.1 million contact hours to around 328,600 households in a sample week in September 2008, but over 80 per cent of these were supplied by the independent sector, up from 51 per cent in 1999 and just 2 per cent in 1992 (NHS Information Centre, 2009a: 4, 7; Scourfield, 2006: 9).

The shift away from local authority provision is reflected in the staffing figures for local authority social care services. The numbers of residential staff, day care workers and domiciliary staff have fallen over the last ten years as these jobs have moved to the independent sector. Meanwhile, the numbers of senior managers, professional support staff and planning staff have increased, as more work is required to manage the contracts with the independent agencies (NHS Information Centre, 2009c).

There are differences in the patterns of expenditure between adult services and children and families services. Over half the expenditure on older people is on residential provision, whereas for children and families, this is only 20 per cent (NHS Information Centre, 2009b: 9). Over half the expenditure for children and families comes under the heading 'day and domiciliary provision'. This includes foster care, family centres, youth offending teams and leaving care services. The largest item in the category, costing £1.1 billion, is foster care (NHS Information Centre, 2009b: 15).

The annual expenditure report also shows how much is spent on 'assessment and care management', which includes field social work tasks such as receiving referrals, assessing need, defining eligibility, arranging and reviewing packages of care (NHS Information Centre, 2009b: 8–9). Overall, this comes to 16 per cent of the gross expenditure – about a sixth of the money. Breaking this down shows that it takes slightly over a quarter of the gross expenditure on children's services, whereas for older people (a much larger group) it is just 11 per cent.

So, the finances suggest that in some ways social work is a relatively small part of the local authority picture. This is further shown in the numbers of social workers (NHS Information Centre, 2009c). The total number of employees of local authority children's and adult services departments on 30 September 2008 was 267,000 – over a quarter of a million people – but taking account of part-time working this was 202,200 'whole time equivalents' (WTEs). Of them, fewer than a quarter were social workers (45,300 WTE social workers – although they are the largest single group). The number of local authority employees has to be set in an even bigger context, the social care sector as a whole, including private and voluntary agencies, giving a total workforce of about 1.7 million, as noted in Chapter 7.

Chapter 7

The 'unit costs' of services are also of interest – that is, the average cost of the services per head (NHS Information Centre, 2009b: 19–20). For older people cared for in local authority residential homes, the average price per week in 2007–8 was £716. The average price in an independent home was far lower, at £420. Home care was also much cheaper in the independent sector – £12.30 per hour, compared to £22.30. But for children in foster care, the pattern was the other way round, with placements via independent sector agencies being much more expensive (£864 compared to £383).

Paying for social care

As we have seen, charges to service users make up a significant part of the budget for local authorities, but they are highly controversial, and are one of the most important differences between health and social care. Health care is provided free at the point of need, apart from some prescription charges (although many social work service users are likely to be exempt – children, older people, people on welfare benefits). (Wales has recently abolished prescription charges; Northern Ireland will do so by 2010 and Scotland by 2011.) Social care, however, is means-tested and users may be charged – and the charges can be very heavy. They raise three particular problems, shown in Box 9.1.

Such matters have long been causes of concern, and led to the appointment of a Royal Commission on Long-Term Care in late 1997. Its report (1999) broke down long-term care costs into three components: personal care, housing costs and living costs. It defined personal care as care which involves touching the person – e.g. help with bathing, dressing, eating, going to the toilet (Royal Commission, 1999: paras. 6.43–4). It proposed that personal care should be provided free at the point of need (funded from general taxation), although people would still be responsible for their own living and housing costs (but could be eligible for assistance after means-testing). Not everyone on the Commission agreed with this, and there was a 'note of dissent' (Joffe and Lipsey, 1999). This argued that the costs would be too high, and the main beneficiaries would be the middle classes (poor people got it free anyway). The government rejected the proposal of free personal care for all in England (DH, 2000), but Scotland did accept it (see below).

The outcome failed to satisfy many people, and the debate did not go away. The growing number of older people, especially the 'older old', brings an increasing demand for long-term care. The growing number of older people with private pensions and savings, and who own their own property, means that more are liable to pay for aspects of their care. There were two independent reviews of long-term care costs and the funding system, by the Joseph Rowntree Foundation (2003–6) and the King's Fund (2005–6). The government undertook to review the system, particularly in light of the new emphasis on personalisation and independent budgets, and launched a public consultation in spring 2008 (HM Government, 2008b).

Criticisms of the current system and suggestions for change are discussed further below, but the main features of the funding system are outlined first (and see Poole, 2009).

> ### Box 9.1 Three dilemmas in paying for social care
>
> - **Means-testing.** The danger of means tests is that they punish the people 'in the middle'. The rich can afford to pay anyway, and may use their money to purchase private services without even asking for state help. The poor qualify for the service without having to pay. So, the charges fall heaviest on people who see themselves as having been responsible, done what was expected, worked hard, paid taxes and saved their money – and now, when they need some help, the system is unfair and punishes them. But resources are limited and need to be targeted towards those in greatest need. Without some sort of financial assessment, this would be hard to do.
>
> - **Health and social care needs.** Another dilemma arises because of the muddy boundary between a health care need and a social care need. The most striking example is Alzheimer's Disease, with some hotly-contested disagreements about whether a person's needs qualify for health care or 'just' social care. Behind these boundary disputes are questions of fairness. After all, no-one asks to get dementia, any more than they ask to get cancer (although some might say that people who behave in certain ways – smoking for example – bring ill health on themselves). Yet the person with dementia is likely to be charged for their care, while the person with cancer will not be.
>
> - **Local variation.** There is considerable variation between eligibility levels and charging policies in different local authorities, meaning that people with similar conditions may qualify for local authority services in some areas while they do not in others, and they might pay very different amounts for similar services. This 'postcode lottery' is another source of great discontent and controversy. But local authorities are required to work with their partners to assess the needs of their area and make locally agreed plans on how to meet them. The challenge is to balance local flexibility and national fairness.

The situation in April 2009

If a person is assessed as needing 'continuing NHS health care', they will not have to pay for any of their care costs. The test for this is that their 'primary need' is a health need (DH, 2007b). So, for a person with a complex medical condition requiring ongoing, regular and specialist care, all care will be paid for by the NHS – nursing care, personal care and, if residential care is required to meet their health needs, their care or nursing home fees (although continuing care can be supplied in a person's own home).

If the person's health needs are at a lower level, the *nursing* care component will be 'free', whether the person is at home or in a care home. This is defined as the sort of care that requires a registered nurse to deliver or supervise it. But other care needs are not covered, including personal care, and the person is responsible for paying, subject to means-testing (in England and Wales; Scotland does cover all personal care costs, and in Northern Ireland people aged over seventy-five are not charged for home care if they meet the eligibility criteria). The distinction between nursing care and personal care is crucial.

If the person is in a care home (a residential or nursing home), the assessed nursing component of their care will be free (paid for by the NHS, from taxation), but they will have to meet the costs of personal care and the 'board and lodging' element. They may receive help with these costs from the local authority if they have been assessed as needing to be in a care home, and subject to means-testing. Even if the social care assessment is that they need to be in a care home, they will have to pay the full cost (except for nursing care) if they have assets above a certain limit (revised annually, but £23,000 in 2009: DH, 2009a). If they are below that but above the prescribed minimum (£14,000 in 2009), they will have to pay a proportion of the costs on a sliding scale, with the local authority paying the balance. They will not have to pay if they fall below the lower level, when the local authority meets the fees. There are detailed rules about what counts as assets and how charges are calculated (DH, 2009a). The major feature is that if the person owns their house, it will count as part of their assets (unless their partner or another 'qualifying person' lives there).

If the person requires community care services from a local authority (domestic help, personal care, meals at home, equipment and adaptations, day care), they will be needs-tested and almost certainly means-tested. Any nursing care they require will be free, but they will probably have to pay towards any personal and social care. Local authorities are not required to charge, but if they do, their charges must be reasonable. There is government guidance about charging policies, but within that there is a degree of freedom for local authorities to assess and set charges in their own way (DH, 2003a). As an example, the majority of authorities set a maximum weekly charge, but in 2007-8 this varied from £60 to £450 (Counsel and Care, 2008: 11; see also Coalition on Charging, 2008). The value of a person's house is not included in their assets for home care, but the costs can quickly eat up a person's savings.

As noted earlier, charges for older people came to £1.76 billion in 2007-8, but restrictions on funding mean that there is also a significant number of council-funded service users who pay *top-ups*. Over a third of council-supported residents in care homes have third-party payments (e.g. relatives topping up the council payment to the care home's fees), and about a quarter of community care recipients pay for extra services (CSCI, 2008a: 114-15; 2009: 19). There are others who pay entirely privately for residential or home care.

Scotland

In 2002, Scotland introduced free personal care for people aged over sixty-five. This was seen as an important flagship policy for devolution (Bowes and Bell, 2007). For people in residential care, the policy means a fixed payment to cover the cost, and for people in their own homes, the provision of services or direct payments (although very few people have taken up the latter: Vestri, 2007). Some people living at home would have received free personal care before the policy came into force, because of means-testing. The new policy does away with means-testing, although there is still an assessment of eligibility (needs-testing). There has been considerable research into the impact of free personal care, and this section highlights the main findings (see Dickinson and Glasby, 2006; McNamee, 2006; Bowes and Bell, 2007; Bell et al., 2007, Vestri, 2007; Sutherland, 2008).

The policy does seem to have contributed to an increase in the number of people using home care services, although it is hard to unravel the specific impact of free personal care from wider trends towards greater use of intensive home care (Bell et al., 2007). What is clear is that there has been a shift within the group of people receiving home care, so that there is now a higher proportion receiving personal care and fewer receiving non-personal care, such as cleaning and shopping. Local authorities still have to manage within budgets, as in England, and so they have to prioritise – and the priority has shifted to personal care. In some local authorities non-personal services are not given now unless they are part of a package involving personal care (Vestri, 2007: 65–6). In other words, the lower-level, preventive services are at risk, as they are in England, because of financial restrictions.

Another key finding is that free personal care has not reduced the amount of informal care that relatives provide, but rather has allowed some to change the sort of care and support they offer. It has taken away some of the tasks they may find difficult and time-consuming, freeing them up to do other things, and enabling them to continue as carers (Bell et al., 2007; Vestri, 2007).

There is strong public support for free personal care, but a lack of understanding about the details – for example, the limits on what counts as personal care, and that non-personal care still has to be paid for, subject to means-testing. However, it is not only the public who are confused – there has been considerable dispute about some of the grey areas, notably food preparation. There is also variation between local authorities about eligibility levels, the amounts that they spend on personal care and the services they provide (Vestri, 2007).

Funding has proved to be the big issue, examined in depth by Sutherland (2008). He found that the policy was adequately funded for the first few years, but as take-up increased, a shortfall built up. Sutherland (who chaired the 1999 Royal Commission) calculated this to be £40 million in 2007–8 (2008: 32). This needs to be seen in the context of total spending on long-term care, which he estimated at £2.3 billion in Scotland that year (£1.2 billion by local authorities, £0.5 billion by the DWP, £343 million by the NHS and £374 million by individuals themselves: 2008: 78). The Scottish government allocated the extra £40 million for personal care in its 2009–10 budget, but Sutherland's report notes that the financial pressures are likely to increase as more people reach greater ages, and argues that the whole system will need reform to cope with the challenge of demographic change.

Overall, free personal care is 'a relatively small component of a complex system of care and the total costs of care' (Sutherland, 2008: 46). The importance of this broader context is crucial for all countries. Social care for older people, as for all service users, needs to be seen in the context of the full range of public services, notably housing, social care, health services, transport, pensions and welfare benefits, together with the practical and financial contributions of families and individuals.

A new care and support system?

There has been long-standing discontent with the current system and concerns about the future costs of long-term care, yet the government barely mentioned funding in the 2005 green paper *Independence, Well-being and Choice*, saying that its proposals about greater personalisation would have to be met within existing resources (DH, 2005: 40–2). The reviews by the King's Fund and the Joseph Rowntree Foundation made proposals for change, and the government responded with a public consultation in 2008.

The JRF review (2006) judged that long-term care costs were likely to quadruple between 2000 and 2051, from £12.9 billion to £53.9 billion. This looks like a huge increase, but assuming steady economic growth it would be a relatively small rise as a proportion of the country's total economy. However, as the last two years have shown us, we cannot count on consistent growth. Also, under present policies much of the rising cost would fall on individuals (JRF, 2006: 4). It made three main criticisms of the current system:

- overall funding levels are inadequate;

- the system is complex, incoherent and arbitrary (e.g. the different support for health and social care needs, the postcode lottery);

- the system is unfair in the heavy burdens in places on individuals, especially because of means-testing.

The JRF review found that public opinion supports a greater role for the state, even if that does mean higher taxes, but also that people are generally prepared to pay something towards their costs, if this payment is perceived as fair and reasonable. Research by Caring Choices (2008) also found popular support for the idea that the state should provide something for everyone, but contribute more to the costs of those who cannot afford it ('progressive universalism'). For those who can afford it there should be a system of shared payments, but fairer and more transparent than the current one.

The King's Fund review reported its findings in *Securing Good Care for Older People* (Wanless, 2006; and see the background papers on the King's Fund website). It proposed a 'partnership model' for funding long-term care. The idea is for a national framework of entitlements, clearly linked to levels of impairment. Once assessed as having certain needs, the person would be entitled to a set level of support free of charge, without any means-test. Wanless suggested that this level should be two-thirds of the full amount they are assessed as needing. After that, the person would have to contribute, but for every pound they paid, the government would pay another pound, up to the benchmark level. People who wish to buy additional services beyond that could do so, but the state would not contribute. People might choose not to pay their full portion, but for those who cannot afford to pay, there would be means-tested help from welfare benefits.

Wanless argued for this co-payment method on a number of grounds. One is that it would help keep costs down (although it would still be much more expensive than the current system), but he also considered it would deter unnecessary use of services, encourage people to save, and empower them by giving them a sense of entitlement to the services they are receiving (2006: xxxiii).

As usual in social work, behind the technical suggestions, the procedures and rules are fundamental questions about fairness and the sort of society we would like to live in. How much do we expect individuals to pay, what do we expect from families, and what are we prepared to pay ourselves – from our own savings when we need care, or as carers, or as taxpayers?

These questions are clearly reflected in the government's 2008 consultation paper, as shown in Box 9.2. The opening extract emphasises the ethical aspects, about what is right in a civilised society; and the issues of equity, what is fair. It also reflects the three points of the social policy triangle. There are the elements of welfare and wellbeing ('care and support', 'protection and dignity'), the economy ('changing demographics' and 'sustainable in the future') and responsibility ('individuals, families and the government').

Box 9.2 Key questions in *The Case for Change: Why England Needs a New Care and Support System* (HM Government, 2008b)

The consultation document opens by saying:

> In a civilised society, we have a moral obligation to ensure that people in need are not left without any care or support. The existing care and support system is not sustainable, because of the impact of changing demographics and expectations in our society ... The long-term challenge is to create a new settlement between individuals, families and the government that will be sustainable in the future, that offers us all protection and dignity, and that is fair.
>
> (HM Government, 2008b: 7)

It goes on to identify three main questions for the consultation (p. 10):

• What more is needed to make the vision of independence, choice and control a reality?

• What should be the balance of responsibility between the family, the individual and the government?

• Should the system be the same for everybody or should there be different ways of allocating government funding? As examples, should there be different systems for different types of need (health needs or social care, older people or younger people); how to reconcile local flexibility and national consistency; how to target resources towards those least able to pay but also support people who plan and save?

The government's question about how to balance the responsibilities of the individual, the family and the government gives us a new triangle for thinking about the funding and delivery of social care – and it is worth remembering that 'government' means us, as taxpayers. If we think about this new triangle in terms of the different perspectives on the role of the state, we can see the complexities and challenges. From a minimalist point of view, the state promotes individual and family responsibility by not interfering. Integrationists look for the state to support voluntary and private provision, such as private insurance schemes, policies to balance care and employment, and independent sector services. Social democrats and radicals will look for a greater direct role for the state, through progressive taxation policies, generous funding and service provision, but the radical perspective will add a more critical look at the issues – for example, highlighting the assumptions about the roles of women. As the discussion document concludes: 'There are pros and cons to each side of every trade-off' (HM Government, 2008b: 51).

Weighing up the issues

This section summarises a number of issues and principles that need to be taken into account when weighing up those pros and cons. The main sources are the various reviews mentioned in the discussion so far, and a JRF discussion paper by Glendinning and Bell (2008).

- *Fairness*: the central requirement is for the system to be fair, but there are different aspects of fairness to be considered (Glendinning and Bell, 2008: 4–7). First, how the system raises money. For a system to be fair it should raise money progressively – i.e. the better-off pay more. But how much more and in what ways (charges, taxes, social insurance, private insurance, co-payments) are devilish political questions, and the different political perspectives give different answers to them. Two other aspects of fairness are 'diagnostic equity', so that people with similar levels of impairment receive similar levels of resources, and 'spatial equity' – that is, that people with similar conditions in different areas are treated the same and receive the same level of resources. There is also a question of inter-generational equity, meaning that one generation should not have to bear an unfair burden. This is a risk if the older population grows rapidly, leaving a smaller working population to pay, and may have to be counteracted by extra payments from the older group themselves.

- *Prevention and integrated support*: the social care system must be integrated with other social services, notably housing, welfare benefits and health, to ensure that sufficient support is available, at the right time, to help people maintain independence and wellbeing. Policy goals of prevention and personalisation are undermined by funding restrictions that mean social care services are not available until people are high up the pyramid of need.

- *Sustainability*: the system must be sustainable, not only in an economic sense, but in terms of public support and acceptability. People are prepared to pay towards their long-term care, but the system must be clear and not punish those who have saved.

- *Family care*: there should be proper support for family members but no assumptions that they will provide care. The challenge is to balance support, independence and choice for both carers and the

  person who is cared for. England has extensive legislation and policy about carers (see Chapter 8), but this must be properly put into effect, otherwise 'heavy reliance on informal care is likely to lead to excessive burdens, stress and longer term impoverishment' (Glendinning and Bell, 2008: 10).

- *Choice*: the current emphasis is on the greater control that cash payments can give to service users, but Glendinning and Bell sound a note of caution (2008: 8–9). Cash payments can be an added burden, and paying family members for care can bind them into caring roles. The provision of services may be more effective to ensure they get respite and freedom to do other things. Lessons from other countries are that services are more effective in helping women to take paid work outside the home (see also Moullin, 2008: 33–5). In Scotland, as discussed above, personal care services have freed carers to do other tasks. The point is to have flexibility rather than one option only.

- *Standards*: it is important to ensure that people receive safe and high-quality services that respect

  their rights and dignity. The safeguards that come from consumer-type behaviour, shopping around and choosing between providers, are not always available if people need care urgently, when they are alone, housebound, or in areas where there are few services. There are risks in market sector provision, as discussed in Chapter 8.

All this suggests that there is a vital role for the state, and one it must not shirk by divesting responsibility to individuals and families. There are particular implications for the relationship between central and local government. Local authorities have the major role in social care, but this leads to unfair variation. They resent having extra responsibilities and high levels of regulation without adequate funding (and, as noted above, they have very little power to raise their own funds). Therefore, there is a need for central government to play a full part in raising sufficient funds and ensuring fairness across the country (Glendinning and Bell, 2008: 7–8; and see Glendinning, 2007). Central government has the responsibility for taxation and national budgets, and has the power to bring together the different funding streams (social care, NHS, housing, DWP payments). It can ensure consistency with tax, national insurance and pensions policies. Greater powers for central government might be mistrusted by local authorities, but Glendinning and Bell hold that 'enlightened central control need not be inimical to flexibility and innovation' (2008: 8).

Conclusion

The chapter has highlighted the substantial costs of social care, and the complexities of the financial issues – who pays, who spends, how much on what, and who decides. There is a great deal of money involved, but it has to be said that the sums involved are small compared to the whole public sector budget, and tiny compared to the whole size of the economy. Also, as we are reminded by the massive amounts of money that were produced to rescue ailing banks in the credit crunch of 2007–9, money can always be found for anything that has a sufficiently high political priority.

An important message is that spending decisions are not just about the three Es of economy, efficiency and effectiveness, but that there are two others – ethics and equity (Balogh *et al.*, 1989, in Hugman, 1998: 187). Questions of what is right and what is fair are fundamental, but as discussed throughout the book, there are no straightforward answers because these depend on one's views about the proper role of the state and the proper balances between welfare, the economy and responsibility.

These debates have a special resonance for social workers. Our job often involves working with people who are poor, and we do so within limited and tightly controlled budgets. We assess people's needs and often their financial circumstances. We have to make tough decisions about who qualifies for a service. The social work diamond sets out the dilemmas. We have professional knowledge about need and support, and service users have their requests, their demands and their unspoken needs; but the state sets the overall priorities and budget, and the organisation we work for will have its own policies and procedures about decision-making and spending. Financial assessments and budget-based decisions can be some of the most uncomfortable, personally and professionally challenging parts of the job.

Questions for reflection

Pages
164–5

- Consider the possible reasons for the differences in unit costs. Make a list of factors that you would want to take into account to draw fair comparisons of costs between the independent sector and local authorities.

- Should service users pay charges for social care? What are your reasons?

- It can be very distressing for people to see their savings shrink as they pay for care, when they had hoped to leave the money to their family. Others feel that the money is there to be spent when it is needed, and the complaints come mainly from middle-class families who are anxious to keep their inheritance. What do you think, and what are your reasons?

- If you have done a financial assessment of a service user in your work or on placement, how did it make you feel? If not yet, how do you think it might?

Useful websites and further reading

Read the green paper *Shaping the Future of Care Together*, published in July 2009 (HM Government, 2009b). It outlines a number of options for funding long-term care, and proposes the creation of a National Care Service. The government launched a consultation about the proposals, which it called 'The Big Care Debate' (see the English government website on long-term care, http://careandsupport.direct.gov.uk/). The consultation ran until November 2009, and the plan is for a white paper to be published in 2010 – but with a general election due before the end of spring 2010, it is far from certain what will happen next. One thing is certain, though: the issues will not go away, so it will be crucial to follow the debates and keep up-to-date with developments.

The NHS Information Centre website is an important source of data about social care services and budgets: www.ic.nhs.uk/statistics-and-data-collections/social-care.

The Personal Social Services Research Unit (PSSRU) has detailed information and research about social care costs: www.pssru.ac.uk.

Also see the DH social care reform website: www.dh.gov.uk/en/SocialCare/Socialcarereform.

The Scottish government has a website on free personal and nursing care in Scotland: www.scotland.gov.uk/Topics/Health/care/17655.

The paper by Glendinning and Bell (2008) *Rethinking Social Care and Support*, is available on the JRF website: www.jrf.org.uk.

The leading text book on the financial aspects of social policy is Glennerster (2009) *Understanding the Finance of Welfare*, 2nd edn.

Conclusion
Between the middle and the margins

This book has shown how social work is a profession 'in the middle'. It is in the middle of powerful sets of demands – from state, organisation, profession and service users. It is at the heart of wider social policy balances between welfare, responsibility and the economy – what sort of help, and how much help, should governments offer, to whom, under what conditions? It is at the centre of some of society's most testing dilemmas – the tensions of balancing needs and resources, participation and protection, choices and budgets, fairness for individuals and fairness for society. Furthermore, it is often in the middle of all the other services that come under the banner 'social policy', because social work involves working with other professionals and organisations, to obtain and coordinate services and support for individuals and families.

Given all this, why is it that social work sometimes seems so marginal in the wider social policy picture? As we have discussed, current social policy initiatives and programmes often seem to miss out social work, not giving it the chance to make the contribution it could. Politicians often seem to be equivocal when they speak about social work and social workers – 'They do some wonderful work, they are undervalued by society, but . . ', and there's the rub. 'But there are too many mistakes, they spend too much time on paperwork, they need to get better at responding to service users', or whatever the most recent complaint happens to be. Few professions face the vitriol that social workers receive when things go wrong, and the criticisms of social work tend to go further than just 'a few bad apples in the barrel', maintaining that the whole enterprise is flawed.

A social policy and social values perspective helps to shed some light on this ambivalence about social work, the paradox of why it is so firmly in the middle and yet on the margins. The discomfort about social work is not so much about social work itself, as about the difficult issues it tackles and the fundamental, contradictory social principles that stand behind it. These are captured in the tensions and similarities, overlaps and ambiguities, between minimalist, integrationist, social democratic and radical approaches to social policy and social work.

Conclusion

Social workers are criticised for refusing services to needy people *and* for spending too much time and money on 'undeserving' cases; they are criticised for failing to take action in time to protect vulnerable people *and* for being 'too quick to break up loving family homes' (as the popular press might put it). Behind the criticisms are fundamental tensions about the role of the state and the privacy of the family, about the deserving and undeserving, about the responsibilities of taxpayers and individuals, about social attitudes to people who are poor, disabled, elderly or mentally unwell. Whether the criticisms are fair in any particular case is not entirely the point; rather, when things seem to go wrong in social work, all society's discomfort and anxiety about these difficult questions suddenly gets a focal point, a scapegoat. It is important to get away from this, and look at the broader policy picture. Just as it is important to understand the needs of service users in a broader context, so it is important to understand social work in its wider context of social values, social policies and other social services. If there are individual shortcomings, these have to be addressed, but it is not just a matter of a few bad apples, or even a few unlucky apples. We have to look at the barrel itself – the wider expectations on social work, its many functions, its many responsibilities. To pursue the analogy, the problem is that the barrel is made up of different types of wood, some strips wedged together tightly, some very loose, some cracked, some straining apart – all those different social values, their overlaps and tensions, the ambiguities and the contradictions between them.

How can social work respond to the public and political criticisms and ambivalence? Three current ways of doing so are to emphasise the evidence base, the interpersonal elements, and the values of social work. Each of these is important, but not enough.

The idea behind the evidence-based approach is that if we have better knowledge about what works in social work policy and practice, through scientific-style research, we will be able to help people better and so overcome the ambivalence about social work. Research is important, but not enough by itself. Social work is not a pure science but a human science, and we have to apply the messages of research to tricky and unpredictable situations. Furthermore, rights and values come into play – it is not just a matter of applying the relevant formula and the correct answer will pop out; we have to consider questions of justice and fairness.

The interpersonal side is crucial too, and good social work builds relationships with people that support them, and challenge them, and help them to achieve their goals. Reliable, caring, consistent and persistent relationships are vital, but again not enough by themselves. Social work is shaped by law and policy, social values about individual freedom, safety and fairness, responsibilities for the best use of public money, organisational priorities. The therapeutic and counselling side is important, but social work is more than interpersonal helping relationships.

The third approach emphasises the importance of social work values. Again, this is crucial but not enough. Social work's values are not so different from those of any social profession: to respect service users' dignity and rights, to treat people fairly, to meet people's needs and help them develop their potential, to act with integrity, to develop one's knowledge and skills (BASW, 2002). At one level they sound rather banal. At another, they are very demanding indeed. Some of the situations and people that social workers encounter test these values to the limit – for example, how much allowance one makes for disadvantage or difference in ways of bringing up children. Fair to whom, in what ways?

So, we need to keep the evidence-based, interpersonal and values-based approaches, but all of them, not just one. More than that, though, we have to accept the paradox of always being in the middle and on the margins. The roles and tasks that social work has in society mean that it will always be caught in this conundrum. We cannot escape it, but we can try to understand it and explain it. To do this, we need to add three dimensions: the intellectual, the political and the ethical. Social work involves these every day – they are not additional tasks or optional extras, but fundamental aspects of the job. It is intellectual, political and ethical because it involves hard questions about the duties and powers of the state, the freedoms and obligations of individuals, needs and rights, rights and responsibility, the meaning and implications of inequality, participation, choice, the nature of professionalism.

Emphasising the intellectual dimension is not to avoid the painful or interpersonal aspects of the job, but it is to go a step beyond a simplistic 'research says . . .' approach. To emphasise the political is not to say that we have to get involved in party politics or radical campaigning. Some might want to, but the point is to appreciate that we 'do' politics every day, in our decisions about resources, rights, intervention, participation. Also, it is to encourage a wider view on the policies and decisions that shape our jobs, about budgets, priorities, organisational structures – to see these in the bigger political context, about the role of the state and the duties of citizens. And emphasising the ethical aspects is to add an extra dimension to values – to go beyond the important but rather basic 'respect the rights of service users' approach, to draw out the challenges and dilemmas of working with uncertain and contradictory social values.

In relation to the questions at the start of the book, then, what and who is social work for? It is for different things, for different people. It is for service users, certainly, but different service users have different needs and strengths, and so social workers will perform different roles in different circumstances. It is for society more widely, in that it deals with some of its most troubling problems, and is part of a range of services and professions that try to prevent those problems arising in the first place. But society expects different and contradictory things – to help families stay together and to rescue children, to provide support to people but not to spend very much money – and no profession can meet all of these all of the time.

Finally, social work is 'for' social workers, but not just because it provides careers and salaries. For a start, there are few riches on offer, although the growth of private sector involvement in social care suggests that there are good profits to be made for those minded to look for them. But more than that, it is 'for' social workers because it is a practically and intellectually rewarding occupation. It gives the opportunity of helping people, but it is much more difficult, ambiguous and interesting than just that.

Bibliography

Abbott, P. and Meerabeau, L. (1998) 'Professionals, professionalization and the caring professions', in Abbott, P. and Meerabeau, L. (eds) *The Sociology of the Caring Professions*, 2nd edn, London: UCL Press.

Abriuox, E. (1998) 'Degrees of participation: a spherical model – the possibilities for girls in Kabul, Afghanistan', in Johnson, V., Ivan-Smith, E., Gordon, G., Pridmore, P. and Scott, P. (eds) *Stepping Forward: Children and Young People's Involvement in the Development Process*, London: Intermediate Technology Publications.

Acheson, D. (1998) *Independent Inquiry into Inequalities in Health*, London: TSO. Online. Available: <http://www.archive.official-documents.co.uk/document/doh/ih/ih.htm> (accessed 25 May 2009).

Adams, R. (2008) *Empowerment, Participation and Social Work*, 4th edn, Basingstoke: Palgrave Macmillan.

ADSS (Cymru) (Association of Directors of Social Services, Wales) (2005) *Social Work in Wales: A Profession to Value*. Online. Available: <http://www.ssiacymru.org.uk/media/pdf/m/e/Social_Work_in_Wales_-_A_Profession_to_Value.pdf> (accessed 22 May 2009).

ADSS and LGA (Association of Directors of Social Services and Local Government Association) (2003) *All Our Tomorrows: Inverting the Triangle of Care*, London: ADSS and LGA. Online. Available: <http://www.lga.gov.uk/lga/publications/publication-display.do?id=21169> (accessed 22 May 2009).

Alcock, C., Daly, G. and Griggs, E. (2008) *Introducing Social Policy*, 2nd edn, Harlow: Pearson.

Alcock, P. (2006) *Understanding Poverty*, 3rd edn, Basingstoke: Palgrave Macmillan.

Alcock, P., Erskine, A. and May, M. (2008) *The Student's Companion to Social Policy*, 3rd edn, Oxford: Blackwell.

Alcock, P. and Scott, D. (2007) 'Voluntary and community sector welfare', in Powell, M. (ed.) *Understanding the Mixed Economy of Welfare*, Bristol: Policy Press.

Arnstein, S. (1969) 'A ladder of citizen participation', *Journal of the American Institute of Planners*, 35 (4): 216–24.

Ashforth, B. and Kreiner, G. (1999) 'How can you do it? Dirty work and the challenge of constructing a positive identity', *Academy of Management Review*, 24 (3): 413–34.

Asquith, S., Clark, C. and Waterhouse, L. (2005) *The Role of the Social Worker in the 21st Century: A Literature Review*, Edinburgh: Scottish Executive. Online. Available: <http://www.scotland.gov.uk/Publications/2005/12/1994633/46334> (accessed 22 May 2009).

Audit Commission (2003) *Human Rights: Improving Public Service Delivery*, London: Audit Commission. Online. Available: <http://www.audit-commission.gov.uk/SiteCollectionDocuments/AuditCommissionReports/National Studies/HumanRights-report.pdf> (accessed 22 May 2009).

Bailey, R. and Brake, M. (eds) (1975) *Radical Social Work*, London: Edward Arnold.

Baldock, J., Manning N. and Vickerstaff, S. (2007) *Social Policy*, 3rd edn, Oxford: Oxford University Press.

Balloch, S., Fisher, M. and McLean, J. (1999a) 'Conclusions and policy issues', in Balloch, S., McLean, J. and Fisher, M. (eds) *Social Services: Working under Pressure*, Bristol: Policy Press.

Balloch, S., McLean, J. and Fisher, M. (eds) (1999b) *Social Services: Working under Pressure*, Bristol: Policy Press.

Balls, E. and Johnson, A. (2009) *Joint Letter to Social Workers in England*, London: DCSF and DH. Online. Available: <http://www.dcsf.gov.uk/swtf/downloads/DCSF-DH-SoS-Joint-Letter-to-Social-Workers-In-England.pdf> (accessed 22 May 2009).

Banks, S. (1999) 'The social professions and social policy: proactive or reactive?', *European Journal of Social Work*, 2: 327–39.

Barclay, P. (1982) *Social Workers: Their Roles and Tasks*, London: Bedford Square Press.

Barnes, C., Mercer, G. and Din, I. (2003) *Research Review on User Involvement in Promoting Change and Enhancing the Quality of Social Care Services for Disabled People*, Leeds: Centre for Disability Studies, University of Leeds. Online. Available: <http://www.leeds.ac.uk/disability-studies/archiveuk/Barnes/SCIE%20user%20involvement%202.pdf> (accessed 22 May 2009).

BASW (British Association of Social Workers) (2002) *Code of Ethics*. Online. Available: <http://www.basw.co.uk/Default.aspx?tabid=64> (accessed 22 May 2009).

BBC (2003) 'A carer's story', *Panorama*, 16 November. Online. Available: <http://news.bbc.co.uk/1/hi/programmes/panorama/current_archive/3216461.stm> (accessed 14 May 2009).

BBC (2009) 'Britain's home care scandal', *Panorama*, 9 April. Online. Available: <http://news.bbc.co.uk/panorama/hi/front_page/newsid_7990000/7990682.stm> (accessed 14 May 2009).

Begum, N. (2006) *Doing It for Themselves: Participation and Black and Minority Ethnic Service Users*, London: SCIE. Online. Available: <www.scie.org.uk/publications/reports/report14.pdf> (accessed 22 May 2009).

Bell, D., Bowes, A. and Dawson, A. (2007) *Free Personal Care in Scotland: Recent Developments*, York: JRF. Online. Available: <http://www.jrf.org.uk/node/2634> (accessed 22 May 2009).

Beresford, P. (2007a) *The Changing Roles and Tasks of Social Workers from Service Users' Perspectives: A Literature Informed Discussion Paper*, London: Shaping Our Lives. Online. Available: <http://www.gscc.org.uk/NR/rdonlyres/072DD7D6-B915-4F41-B54B-79C62FDB9D95/0/SoLSUliteraturereviewreportMarch07.pdf> (accessed 22 May 2009).

Beresford, P. (2007b) 'Give the users and practitioners a voice', *Guardian Society*, 24 October, p. 4. Online. Available: <http://www.guardian.co.uk/society/2007/oct/24/comment.guardiansocietysupplement> (accessed 22 May 2009).

Beresford, P. and Croft, S. (2004) 'Service users and practitioners reunited: the key component for social work reform', *British Journal of Social Work*, 34: 53–68.

Beveridge, W. (1942) *Report of the Inter-Departmental Committee on Social Insurance and Allied Services*, Cm. 6404, London: HMSO.

BIHR (British Institute for Human Rights) (2008) *The Human Rights Act: Changing Lives*, 2nd edn, London: BIHR. Online. Available: <http://www.bihr.org.uk/documents/policy/changing-lives-second-edition> (accessed 22 May 2009).

Blackmore, A. (2008) *Standing Apart, Working Together: A Study of the Myths and Realities of Voluntary and Community Sector Independence*, 2nd edn, London: NCVO. Online. Available: <http://www.ncvo-vol.org.uk/policy/index.asp?id=1393> (accessed 12 May 2009).

Blakemore, K. and Griggs, E. (2007) *Social Policy: An Introduction*, 3rd edn, Maidenhead: Open University Press/McGraw Hill.

Blewett, J., Lewis, J. and Tunstill, J. (2007) *The Changing Roles and Tasks of Social Work: A Literature Informed Discussion Paper*, London: GSCC. Online. Available: <http://www.gscc.org.uk/NR/rdonlyres/8BE06845-9895-465B-98C2-31CF227D7422/0/SWrolestasks.pdf> (accessed 22 May 2009).

Bochel, H., Bochel, C., Page, R. and Sykes, R. (2009) *Social Policy: Issues and Developments*, 2nd edn, Harlow: Pearson Education.

Bogues, S. (2008) *People Work Not Just Paperwork: What People Told Us during the Consultation Conducted for the NISCC Roles and Tasks of Social Work Project*, Belfast: NISCC. Online. Available: <http://www.niscc.info/roles_and_tasks_of_social_work-115.aspx> (accessed 22 May 2009).

Bowes, A. and Bell, D. (2007) 'Free personal care for older people in Scotland: issues and implications', *Social Policy and Society*, 6 (3): 435–45.

Bradshaw, J. (1972) 'The concept of social need', *New Society*, 19: 640–3.

Brent, London Borough of (1985) *A Child in Trust: The Report of the Panel of Inquiry Investigating the Circumstances Surrounding the Death of Jasmine Beckford*, London: London Borough of Brent.

Brindle, D. (2008) 'Low-key plans for social work futures', *Guardian Society*, 8 April, p. 2. Online. Available: <http://www.guardian.co.uk/society/2008/apr/02/socialcare.publicsectorcareers> (accessed 22 May 2009).

Brodie, I., Nottingham, C. and Plunkett, S. (2008) 'A tale of two reports: social work in Scotland from *Social Work and the Community* (1966) to *Changing Lives* (2006)', *British Journal of Social Work*, 38: 697–715.

Brown, P., Hadley, R. and White, K. (1982) 'A case for neighbourhood-based social work and social services', appendix in Barclay, P., *Social Workers: Their Roles and Tasks*, London: Bedford Square Press.

Buckner, L. and Yeandle, S. (2007) *Valuing Carers: Calculating the Value of Unpaid Care*, London: Carers UK. Online. Available: <http://www.carersuk.org/Policyandpractice/Research/Profileofcaring/1201108437> (accessed 22 May 2009).

Burden, T., Cooper, C. and Petrie, S. (2000) *'Modernising' Social Policy: Unravelling New Labour's Welfare Reforms*, Aldershot: Ashgate.

Butler, I. and Drakeford, M. (2001) 'Which Blair project? Communitarianism, social authoritarianism, and social work', *Journal of Social Work*, 1 (1): 1–19.

Butler, I. and Drakeford, M. (2005) *Social Policy, Social Welfare and Scandal: How British Public Policy is Made*, 2nd edn, Basingstoke: Palgrave Macmillan.

Carey, M. (2008) 'Everything must go? The privatization of state social work', *British Journal of Social Work*, 38: 918–35.

Carey, M. (2009) 'Happy shopper? The problem with service user and carer participation', *British Journal of Social Work*, 39: 179–88.

Caring Choices (2008) *The Future of Care Funding: Time for a Change*, London: Caring Choices, c/o The King's Fund. Online. Available: <http://www.caringchoices.org.uk/wp-content/uploads/the-future-of-care-funding-final-report-jan08.pdf> (accessed 22 May 2009).

Carr, S. (2004) *Has Service User Participation Made a Difference to Social Care Services?*, SCIE Position Paper 3, London: SCIE. Online. Available: <http://www.scie.org.uk/publications/positionpapers/pp03.pdf> (accessed 22 May 2009).

Carr, S. and Dittrich, R. (2008) *Personalisation: A Rough Guide*, Adults' Services Report 20, London: SCIE. Online. Available: <http://www.scie.org.uk/publications/reports/report20.asp> (accessed 22 May 2009).

Carr, S. and Robbins, D. (2009) *The Implementation of Individual Budget Schemes in Adult Social Care*, SCIE Research Briefing 20, London: SCIE (update of *Choice, Control and Individual Budgets*, 2007). Online. Available: <http://www.scie.org.uk/publications/briefings/briefing20/index.asp> (accessed 22 May 2009).

Carvel, J. (2007) 'Sleepwalking into an unhealthy alliance', *Guardian Society*, 14 November, p. 4. Online. Available: <http://www.guardian.co.uk/society/2007/nov/14/guardiansocietysupplement.comment> (accessed 22 May 2009).

Clarke, J., Gewirtz, S. and McLaughlin, E. (eds) (2000) *New Managerialism, New Welfare?* London: Sage.

Clarke, J. and Newman, J. (1997) *The Managerial State: Power, Politics and Ideology in the Remaking of Social Welfare*, London: Sage.

CLG (Department for Communities and Local Government) (2006) *Strong and Prosperous Communities: The Local Government White Paper*, London: CLG. Online. Available: <http://www.communities.gov.uk/documents/localgovernment/pdf/152456.pdf > (accessed 22 May 2009).

CLG (2007) *Independence and Opportunity: Our Strategy for Supporting People*, London: CLG. Online. Available: <http://www.spkweb.org.uk/About_Supporting_People/> (accessed 22 May 2009).

CLG (2008a) *A Guide to the Local Government Finance Settlement*, London: CLG. Online. Available: <http://www.local.communities.gov.uk/finance/0910/simpguid.pdf> (accessed 22 May 2009).

CLG (2008b) *Area Based Grant: General Guidance 2008*, London: CLG. Online. Available: <http://www.communities.gov.uk/publications/localgovernment/areabasedgrantguidance> (accessed 22 May 2009).

CLG (2008c) *Creating Strong, Safe and Prosperous Communities: Statutory Guidance*, London: CLG. Online. Available: <http://www.communities.gov.uk/publications/localgovernment/strongsafeprosperous> (accessed 22 May 2009).

CLG (2008d) *Lifetime Homes, Lifetime Neighbourhoods: A National Strategy for Housing in an Ageing Society*, London: CLG. Online. Available: <http://www.communities.gov.uk/publications/housing/lifetimehomesneighbourhoods> (accessed 22 May 2009).

CLG (2009a) *Improving Opportunity, Strengthening Society: A Third Progress Report*, London: CLG. Online. Available: <http://www.communities.gov.uk/publications/communities/raceequalitythirdreport> (accessed 22 May 2009).

CLG (2009b) *Improving Opportunity, Strengthening Society: A Third Progress Report on the Government's Strategy for Race Equality and Community Cohesion, Volume 2: Race Equality in Public Services: Statistical Report*, London: CLG. Online. Available: <http://www.communities.gov.uk/publications/communities/raceequalitythirdreport> (accessed 22 May 2009).

CLG (2009c) *Tackling Race Inequalities: A Discussion Document*, London: CLG. Online. Available: <http://www.communities.gov.uk/publications/communities/tacklingraceinequalities> (accessed 22 May 2009).

Coalition on Charging (2008) *Charging into Poverty? Charges for Care Services at Home and the National Debate on Adult Care Reform in England*, London: Coalition on Charging, c/o National Centre for Independent Living. Online. Available: <http://www.ncil.org.uk/uploads/pdf/830684841_835674465_Charging_Into_Poverty_FINAL.pdf> (accessed 22 May).

Collins, S. (2009) 'Some critical perspectives on social work and collectives', *British Journal of Social Work*, 9: 334–52.

Compass (2007) *Closer to Equality: Assessing New Labour's Record on Equality after 10 Years in Government*, London: Compass. Online. Available: <http://clients.squareeye.com/uploads/compass/documents/closertoequality.pdf> (accessed 22 May 2009)

Conservative Party (2007) *No More Blame Game: The Future for Children's Social Workers*, Report of the Conservative Party Commission on Social Workers, London: The Conservative Party. Online. Available: <http://www.conservatives.com/~/media/Files/Downloadable%20Files/No%20More%20Blame%20Game.ashx?dl=true-2008-09-12> (accessed 25 May 2009).

Conservative Party (2009) *Conservative Party Commission on Social Workers, Response to Lord Laming's Inquiry*, London: The Conservative Party. Online. Available: <http://www.conservatives.com/News/~/media/Files/Downloadable%20Files/SWC_Submission_to_Lord_Laming.ashx> (accessed 22 May 2009).

Corby, B., Doig, A. and Roberts, V. (2001) *Public Inquiries into Residential Abuse of Children*, London: Jessica Kingsley.

Counsel and Care (2008) *Care Contradictions: Putting People First? The Harsh Reality for Older People, Their Families and Carers of Increasing Charges and Tightening Criteria*, London: Counsel and Care. Online. Available: <http://www.counselandcare.org.uk/assets/library/documents/Care_Contradictions_2008.pdf> (accessed 22 May 2009).

Cowden, S. and Singh, G. (2007) 'The "user": friend, foe or fetish? A critical exploration of user involvement in health and social care', *Critical Social Policy*, 27 (1): 5–23.

CPAG (Child Poverty Action Group) (2008) *Child Poverty: The Stats: Analysis of the Latest Poverty Statistics*, London: CPAG. Online. Available: <http://www.cpag.org.uk/info/briefings_policy/CPAG_poverty_the_stats_1008.pdf> (accessed 22 May 2009).

CPAG (2009) *Ending Child Poverty: A Manifesto for Success*, London: CPAG. Online. Available: <http://www.cpag. org.uk/info/Povertystats.htm> (accessed 22 May 2009).

Craig, G. and Manthorpe, J. (1999) *Unfinished Business? Local Government Reorganisation and Social Services*, Bristol: Policy Press.

Cree, V. and Davis, A. (2007) *Social Work: Voices from the Inside*, London: Routledge.

Cree, V. and Myers, S. (2008) *Social Work: Making a Difference*, Bristol: Policy Press

CSCI (Commission for Social Care Inspection) (2008a) *The State of Social Care in England, 2006–07*, London, CSCI. Executive summary online. Available: <http://image.guardian.co.uk/sys-files/Society/documents/2008/01/29/ csci.pdf> (accessed 22 May 2009).

CSCI (2008b) *Cutting the Cake Fairly: CSCI Review of Eligibility Criteria for Social Care*, London: CSCI. Online. Available: <http://www.cqc.org.uk/_db/_documents/FACS_2008_03.pdf> (accessed 22 May 2009).

CSCI (2009) *The State of Social Care in England, 2007–08*, London, CSCI. Online. Available: <http://www.cqc.org. uk/_db/_documents/SOSC08%20Report%2008_Web.pdf> (accessed 22 May 2009).

CWDC (Children's Workforce Development Council) (2009) *The State of the Children's Social Care Workforce 2008, Summary Report*, Leeds: CWDC. Online. Available: <http://www.cwdcouncil.org.uk/assets/0000/1348/State _of_the_children_s_care_workforce_summary_report.pdf> (accessed 22 May 2009).

DCA (Department for Constitutional Affairs) (2006a) *Human Rights, Human Lives: A Handbook for Public Authorities*, London: DCA. Online. Available: <http://www.justice.gov.uk/docs/hr-handbook-public-authorities. pdf> (accessed 22 May 2009).

DCA (2006b) *Review of the Implementation of the Human Rights Act*, London: DCA. Online. Available: <http:// www.justice.gov.uk/guidance/docs/full_review.pdf > (accessed 22 May 2009).

DCSF (Department for Children, Schools and Families) (2007) *The Children's Plan: Building Brighter Futures*, Norwich: TSO. Online. Available: <http://www.dcsf.gov.uk/childrensplan> (accessed 22 May 2009).

DCSF (2008a) *Better Outcomes for Children and Young People: From Talk to Action*, London: DCSF. Online. Available: <http://www.everychildmatters.gov.uk/resources-and-practice/IG00327> (accessed 25 May 2009).

DCSF (2008b) *Children Looked After in England (Including Adoption and Care Leavers) Year Ending 31 March 2008*, London: DCSF. Online. Available: <http://www.dcsf.gov.uk/rsgateway/DB/SFR/s000810/index.shtml> (accessed 22 May 2009).

DCSF (2008c) *Piloting the Social Work Practice Model: A Prospectus*, Nottingham: DCSF. Online. Available: <http:// www.everychildmatters.gov.uk/socialcare/childrenincare/swppilots> (accessed 22 May 2009).

DCSF (2009) *The Protection of Children in England: Action Plan. The Government's Response to Lord Laming*, Norwich: TSO. Online. Available: <http://www.everychildmatters.gov.uk/socialcare/safeguarding> (accessed 22 May 2009).

Deacon, B. (2007) *Global Social Policy and Governance*, London: Sage.

DfES (Department for Education and Skills) (2006) *Care Matters: Transforming the Lives of Children and Young People in Care*, Cm. 6932, Norwich: TSO. Online. Available: <http://www.everychildmatters.gov.uk/_files/ Green%20Paper.pdf> (accessed 22 May 2009).

DfES (2007) *Care Matters: Time for Change*, Cm. 7137, Norwich: TSO. Online. Available: <http://www.every childmatters.gov.uk/_files/timeforchange.pdf> (accessed 22 May 2009).

DfES and DH (Department of Health) (2006) *Options for Excellence: Building the Social Care Workforce of the Future*, London: TSO. Online. Available: <http://www.dh.gov.uk/en/Publicationsandstatistics/Publications/ PublicationsPolicyAndGuidance/DH_4139958> (accessed 22 May 2009).

DH (Department of Health) (1991a) *Child Abuse: A Study of Inquiry Reports 1980–1989*, London: HMSO.

DH (1991b) *Children Act Guidance and Regulations: Volume 2, Family Support, Day Care and Educational Provision for Young Children*, London: HMSO.

DH (1998) *Modernising Social Services: Promoting Independence, Improving Protection, Raising Standards*, Cm. 4169, London: TSO. Online. Available: <http://www.dh.gov.uk/en/Publicationsandstatistics/Publications/ PublicationsPolicyAndGuidance/DH_4009575> (accessed 22 May 2009).

DH (1999a) *Caring about Carers: A National Strategy for Carers*, London: DH. Online. Available: <http://www.dh. gov.uk/en/Publicationsandstatistics/Publications/PublicationsPolicyAndGuidance/DH_4006522> (accessed 22 May 2009).

DH (1999b) *Saving Lives: Our Healthier Nation*, London: TSO. Online. Available: <http://www.archive.official-documents.co.uk/document/cm43/4386/4386.htm> (accessed 22 May 2009).

DH (2000) *The NHS Plan: The Government's Response to the Royal Commission on Long-Term Care*, Cm. 4818-II, London: DH. Online. Available: <http://www.dh.gov.uk/en/Publicationsandstatistics/Publications/Publications PolicyandGuidance/DH_4002674> (accessed 22 May 2009).

DH (2002) *Fair Access to Care Services: Guidance on Eligibility Criteria for Adult Social Care*, London: DH. Online. Available: <http://www.dh.gov.uk/en/Publicationsandstatistics/Publications/PublicationsPolicyAndGuidance/ DH_4009653> (accessed 22 May 2009).

DH (2003a) *Fairer Charging Policies for Home Care and Other Non-Residential Social Services: Guidance for Councils with Social Services Responsibilities*, London: TSO. Online. Available: <http://www.dh.gov.uk/en/Publications andstatistics/Publications/PublicationsPolicyAndGuidance/DH_4117930> (accessed 22 May 2009).

DH (2003b) *Tackling Health Inequalities: A Programme for Action*, London: DH. Online. Available: <http://www. dh.gov.uk/en/Publicationsandstatistics/Publications/PublicationsPolicyAndGuidance/DH_4008268> (accessed 22 May 2009).

DH (2005) *Independence, Well-Being and Choice: Our Vision for the Future of Social Care for Adults in England*, Cm. 6499, Norwich: TSO. Online. Available: <http://www.dh.gov.uk/en/publicationsandstatistics/publications/ publicationspolicyandguidance/dh_4106477> (accessed 22 May 2009).

DH (2006) *Our Health, Our Care, Our Say: A New Direction for Community Services*, Cm. 6737, Norwich: TSO. Online. Available: <http://www.dh.gov.uk/en/Healthcare/Ourhealthourcareoursay/DH_065882> (accessed 22 May 2009).

DH (2007a) *Independence, Choice and Risk: A Guide to Best Practice in Supported Decision-Making*, London: DH. Online. Available: <http://www.dh.gov.uk/en/Publicationsandstatistics/Publications/PublicationsPolicyAnd Guidance/DH_074773> (accessed 22 May 2009).

DH (2007b) *The National Framework for NHS Continuing Health Care and NHS-Funded Nursing Care*, London: DH. Online. Available: <http://www.dh.gov.uk/en/Publicationsandstatistics/Publications/PublicationsPolicyAnd Guidance/DH_076288> (accessed 22 May 2009).

DH (2008a) *High Quality Care for All: NHS Next Stage Review Final Report*, Cm. 7432 (Darzi Review), Norwich: TSO. Online. Available: <http://www.dh.gov.uk/en/Publicationsandstatistics/Publications/PublicationsPolicyAnd Guidance/DH_085825> (accessed 22 May 2009).

DH (2008b) *Human Rights in Health Care: A Short Introduction*, London: DH. Online. Available: <http://www. dh.gov.uk/en/Publicationsandstatistics/Publications/PublicationsPolicyAndGuidance/DH_088970> (accessed 25 May 2009).

DH (2008c) *Putting People First: Transforming Adult Social Care: The Whole Story*, London: DH. Online. Available: <http://www.dh.gov.uk/en/Publicationsandstatistics/Publications/PublicationsPolicyAndGuidance/DH_ 089665> (accessed 22 May 2009).

DH (2008d) *Tackling Health Inequalities: Progress and Next Steps*, London: DH. Online. Available: <http://www. dh.gov.uk/en/Publicationsandstatistics/Publications/PublicationsPolicyAndGuidance/DH_085307> (accessed 25 May 2009).

DH (2009a) *Charging for Residential Accommodation Guide (CRAG)*, London: DH. Online. Available: <http:// www. dh.gov.uk/en/Publicationsandstatistics/Publications/PublicationsPolicyAndGuidance/DH_097578> (accessed 22 May 2009).

DH (2009b) *Personal Health Budgets: First Steps*, London: DH. Online. Available: <http://www.dh.gov.uk/en/ Publicationsandstatistics/Publications/PublicationsPolicyAndGuidance/DH_093842> (accessed 22 May 2009).

DH and Home Office (2000) *No Secrets: Guidance on Developing and Implementing Multi-Agency Policies and*

Procedures to Protect Vulnerable Adults from Abuse, London: DH. Online. Available: <http://www.dh.gov.uk/en/Publicationsandstatistics/Publications/PublicationsPolicyAndGuidance/DH_4008486> (accessed 22 May 2009).

DH and OPG (Office of the Public Guardian) (2009) *Deprivation of Liberty Safeguards: A Guide for Primary Care Trusts and Local Authorities*, London: DH. Online. Available: <http://www.dh.gov.uk/en/Publicationsand statistics/ Publications/PublicationsPolicyAndGuidance/DH_094347> (accessed 22 May 2009).

DH, Department for Education and Employment and Home Office (2000) *Framework for the Assessment of Children in Need and Their Families*, London: TSO. Online. Available: <http://www.dh.gov.uk/en/Publications andstatistics/Publications/PublicationsPolicyAndGuidance/DH_4003256> (accessed 25 May 2009).

DH, Ministry of Justice and Home Office (2008) *Safeguarding Adults: A Consultation on the Review of the 'No Secrets' Guidance*, London: DH. Online. Available: <http://www.dh.gov.uk/en/Consultations/Liveconsultations/DH_089098> (accessed 22 May 2009).

DHSS (Department of Health and Social Security) (1974) *Report of the Committee of Inquiry into the Care and Supervision Provided in Relation to Maria Colwell*, London: HMSO.

DHSS (1982) *Child Abuse: A Study of Inquiry Reports 1973–1981*, London: HMSO.

DHSS (1988) *Report of the Inquiry into Child Abuse in Cleveland 1987*, Cm. 412, London: HMSO.

DHSSPS (Department of Health, Social Services and Public Safety) (2008) *Summary of HPSS Expenditure in Northern Ireland, 1 April 2006–31 March 2007*, Belfast: DHSSPS. Online. Available: <http://www.dhsspsni. gov.uk/summary_of_expenditure_2006-07.pdf> (accessed 22 May 2009).

Dickens, J. (2006a) 'Care, control and change in child care proceedings: dilemmas for social workers, managers and lawyers', *Child and Family Social Work*, 11 (1): 23–32.

Dickens, J. (2006b) 'Social work, law, money and trust: paying for lawyers in child protection work', *Journal of Social Welfare and Family Law*, 28 (3–4): 283–95.

Dickens, J. (2008) 'Welfare, law and managerialism: inter-discursivity and inter-professional practice in child care social work', *Journal of Social Work*, 8 (1): 45–64.

Dickinson, H. and Glasby, J. (2006) *Free Personal Care in Scotland*, Background Paper for the Wanless Social Care Review, London: King's Fund. Online. Available: <http://www.kingsfund.org.uk/research/publications/appendices_to.html> (accessed 25 May 2009).

Dingwall, R., Eekelaar, J. and Murray, T. (1995) *The Protection of Children: State Intervention and Family Life*, 2nd edn, Aldershot: Avebury (1st edn: Oxford: Basil Blackwell, 1983).

Doel, M., Carroll, C., Chambers, E., Cooke, J., Hollows, A., Laurie, L., Maskrey, L. and Nancarrow, S. (2007) *Participation: Finding out What Difference it Makes*, SCIE Guide 20, London: SCIE. Online. Available: <http://www.scie.org.uk/publications/guides/guide20/files/guide20.pdf> (accessed 22 May 2009).

Donzelot, J. (1980) *The Policing of Families: Welfare versus the State*, London: Hutchinson.

Douglas, A. (2009) *Partnership Working*, London: Routledge.

DSS (Department of Social Security) (1999) *Opportunity for All: Tackling Poverty and Social Exclusion*, Cm. 4445, London: TSO.

Duffy, S. (1996) *Unlocking the Imagination: Strategies for Purchasing Services for People with Learning Difficulties*, London: Choice Press. Online. Available: <http://www.in-control.org.uk/site/INCO/Templates/General.aspx?pageid=522&cc=GB> (accessed 22 May 2009).

Duffy, S. and Waters, J. (2008) *Fairness Requires Transparency: Submission on the Reform of Social Care Funding*, London: In Control. Online. Available: <http://www.in-control.org.uk/site/INCO/Templates/General.aspx?pageid=844&cc=GB> (accessed 25 May 2009).

Dustin, D. (2007) *The McDonaldization of Social Work*, Aldershot: Ashgate.

DWP (Department of Work and Pensions) (2003) *Measuring Child Poverty*, London: DWP. Online. Available: <http://www.dwp.gov.uk/ofa/related/final_conclusions.pdf> (accessed 25 May 2009).

DWP (2008) *Raising Expectations and Increasing Support: Reforming Welfare for the Future*, London: DWP. Online. Available: <http://www.dwp.gov.uk/welfarereform/raisingexpectations/> (accessed 22 May 2009).

DWP (2009) *Households Below Average Income: An Analysis of the Income Distribution 1994/95 – 2007/08*, London: DWP. Online. Available: <http://www.dwp.gov.uk/asd/hbai/hbai2008/contents.asp> (accessed 22 May 2009).

EHRC (Equality and Human Rights Commission) (2008) *Ours to Own: Understanding Human Rights*, London: EHRC. Online. Available: <http://www.equalityhumanrights.com/en/publicationsandresources/Pages/Oursto own.aspx> (accessed 22 May 2009).

Ellis, K. (2007) 'Direct payments and social work practice: the significance of "street-level bureaucracy" in determining eligibility', *British Journal of Social Work*, 37: 405–22.

Equalities Review (2007) *Fairness and Freedom: The Final Report of the Equalities Review*, Wetherby: CLG. Online. Available: <http://archive.cabinetoffice.gov.uk/equalitiesreview/publications.html> (accessed 22 May 2009).

Ermisch, J., Francesconi, M. and Pevalin, D. (2001) *The Outcomes for Children of Poverty*, DWP Research Report 158, London: DWP. Summary online. Available: <http://www.dwp.gov.uk/asd/asd5/158summ.asp> (accessed 22 May 2009).

Esping-Andersen, G. (1990) *The Three Worlds of Welfare Capitalism*, Oxford: Polity Press.

Evans, T. (2009) 'Managing to be professional: team managers and practitioners in modernized social work', in Harris, J. and White, V. (eds) *Modernising Social Work: Critical Considerations*, Bristol: Policy Press.

Evans, T. and Harris, J. (2004) 'Street-level bureaucracy, social work and the (exaggerated) death of discretion', *British Journal of Social Work*, 34: 871–95.

Ferguson, H. (2004) *Protecting Children in Time: Child Abuse, Child Protection and the Consequences of Modernity*, Basingstoke: Palgrave Macmillan.

Ferguson, I. (2007) 'Increasing user choice or privatizing risk? The antinomies of personalization', *British Journal of Social Work*, 37: 387–403.

Ferguson, I. (2008) *Reclaiming Social Work: Challenging Neo-Liberalism and Promoting Social Justice*, London: Sage.

Ferguson, I. and Woodward, R. (2009) *Radical Social Work in Practice*, Bristol: Policy Press.

Foster, P. and Wilding, P. (2000) 'Whither welfare professionalism?', *Social Policy and Administration*, 34 (2): 143–59.

Foucault, M. (1977) *Discipline and Punish: The Birth of the Prison*, Harmondsworth: Penguin.

Fraser, D. (2003) *The Evolution of the British Welfare State*, 3rd edn, Basingstoke: Palgrave Macmillan.

Fraser, N. (1989) 'Talking about needs: interpretive contests as political conflicts in welfare sate societies', *Ethics*, 99: 291–313.

Frost, N., Robinson, M. and Anning, A. (2005) 'Social workers in multi-disciplinary teams: issues and dilemmas for professional practice', *Child and Family Social Work*, 10: 187–96.

Galanter, M. (1974) 'Why the "haves" come out ahead: speculations on the limits of legal change', *Law and Society*, 9: 95–160.

GEO (2009) *A Fairer Future: The Equality Bill and Other Action to Make Equality a Reality*, London: GEO. Online. Available: <http://www.equalities.gov.uk/equality_bill.aspx> (accessed 25 May 2009).

Gibb, M. (2009) *First Report of the Social Work Task Force*, Letter to Secretaries of State, London: SWTF. Online. Available: <http://www.everychildmatters.gov.uk/socialcare/safeguarding> (accessed 25 May 2009).

Giddens, A. (1998) *The Third Way: The Renewal of Social Democracy*, Cambridge: Polity Press.

Glasby, J. (2007) *Understanding Health and Social Care*, Bristol: Policy Press.

Glasby, J. and Dickinson, H. (2008) *Partnership Working in Health and Social Care*, Bristol: Policy Press.

Glasby, J. and Littlechild, R. (2009) *Direct Payments and Personal Budgets*, Bristol: Policy Press.

Glendinning, C. (2007) 'Improving equity and sustainability in UK funding for long-term care: lessons from Germany', *Social Policy and Society*, 6 (3): 411–22.

Glendinning, C. and Bell, D. (2008) *Rethinking Social Care and Support*, York: JRF. Online. Available: <http://www.jrf.org.uk/publications/rethinking-social-care-and-support-identifying-principles-reform-england> (accessed 26 May 2009).

Bibliography

Glendinning, C., Challis, D., Fernandez, J., Jacobs, S., Jones, K., Knapp, M., Manthorpe, J., Moran, N., Netten, A., Stevens, M. and Wilberforce, M. (2008a) *Evaluation of the Individual Budgets Pilot Programme: Final Report*, York: Social Policy Research Unit, University of York. Online. Available: <http://php.york.ac.uk/inst/spru/research/summs/ibsen.php> (accessed 25 May 2009).

Glendinning, C., Challis, D., Fernandez, J., Jacobs, S., Jones, K., Knapp, M., Manthorpe, J., Moran, N., Netten, A., Stevens, M. and Wilberforce, M. (2008b) *Evaluation of the Individual Budgets Pilot Programme: Summary Report*, York: Social Policy Research Unit, University of York. Online. Available: <http://php.york.ac.uk/inst/spru/research/summs/ibsen.php> (accessed 25 May 2009).

Glennerster, H. (2009) *Understanding the Finance of Welfare: What Welfare Costs and How to Pay for It*, 2nd edn, Bristol: Policy Press.

Graham, H. (2007) *Unequal Lives: Health and Socioeconomic Inequalities*, Maidenhead: Open University Press.

Gray, A. and Jenkins, B. (2007) 'Professions and bureaucracy', in Baldock, J., Manning, N. and Vickerstaff, S. (eds) *Social Policy*, 3rd edn, Oxford: Oxford University Press.

Gray, M. and McDonald, C. (2006) 'Pursuing good practice? The limits of evidence-based practice', *Journal of Social Work*, 6 (1): 7–20.

Greenwich, London Borough of (1987) *A Child in Trust: Protection of Children in a Responsible Society. Report of the Commission of Inquiry into the Circumstances Surrounding the Death of Kimberley Carlile*, London: London Borough of Greenwich.

GSCC (General Social Care Council) (2007a) *Roles and Tasks of Social Work in England, Consultation Paper*, London: GSCC. Executive summary online. Available: <http://www.gscc.org.uk/Policy/Consultations/Roles+and+Tasks+of+social+work> (accessed 25 May 2009).

GSCC (2007b) *Statement of Social Work Roles and Tasks, Final Draft*, London: GSCC. Online. Available: <http://www.communitycare.co.uk/Assets/GetAsset.aspx?ItemID=5947> (accessed 25 May 2009).

GSCC (2008) *Social Work at its Best: A Statement of Social Work Roles and Tasks for the 21st Century*, London: GSCC. Online. Available: <http://www.gscc.org.uk/Policy/Consultations/Roles+and+Tasks+of+social+work> (accessed 25 May 2009).

Hardiker, P. (2002) 'A framework for conceptualising need and its application to planning and providing services', in Ward, H. and Rose, W. (eds) *Approaches to Needs Assessment in Children's Services*, London: Jessica Kingsley.

Hardiker, P., Exton, K. and Barker, M. (1991) 'The social policy contexts of prevention in child care', *British Journal of Social Work*, 21: 341–59.

Harker, L. (2006) *Delivering on Child Poverty: What Would it Take? A Report for the Department of Work and Pensions*, Cm. 6951, Norwich: TSO. Online. Available: <http://www.dwp.gov.uk/publications/dwp/2006/harker> (accessed 25 May 2009).

Harris, B. (2004) *The Origins of the British Welfare State: Society, State and Social Welfare in England and Wales, 1800–1945*, Basingstoke: Palgrave Macmillan.

Harris, J. (1998) 'Scientific management, bureau-professionalism, new managerialism: the labour process of state social work', *British Journal of Social Work*, 28: 839–62.

Harris, J. (2003) *The Social Work Business*, London: Routledge.

Harris, J. (2008) 'State social work: constructing the present from moments in the past', *British Journal of Social Work*, 38: 662–79.

Harris, J. and White, V. (eds) (2009) *Modernising Social Work: Critical Considerations*, Bristol: Policy Press.

Harris, R. and Timms, N. (1993) *Secure Accommodation in Child Care: Between Hospital and Prison or Thereabouts*, London: Routledge.

Hart, R. (1992) *Children's Participation: From Tokenism to Citizenship*, Florence: UNICEF. Online. Available: <http://www.unicef-irc.org/cgi-bin/unicef/Lunga.sql?ProductID=100> (accessed 26 May 2009).

Hart, R. (1997) *Children's Participation: The Theory and Practice of Involving Young Citizens in Community Development and Environmental Care*, London: Earthscan.

Hatton, C. and Waters, J. (2008) 'Evaluation Report: Phase 2 on In Control's work, 2005–2007', in Poll, C. and

Duffy, S. (eds) *A Report on In Control's Second Phase: Evaluation and Learning 2005–2007*. London: In Control. Online. Available: <http://www.in-control.org.uk/site/INCO/Templates/General.aspx?pageid=522&cc=GB> (accessed 25 May 2009).

Healy, K. and Meagher, G. (2004) 'The reprofessionalization of social work: collaborative approaches for achieving professional recognition', *British Journal of Social Work*, 34: 243–60.

Henwood, M. and Hudson, B. (2008) *Keeping it Personal: Supporting People with Multiple and Complex Needs: A Report to the Commission for Social Care*, London: CSCI. Online. Available: <http://www.cqc.org.uk/_db/_documents/SOSC08%20Background%20study%20complex%20needs%2011-12-08amended-dom3.pdf> (accessed 22 May 2009).

Hill, M. and Irving, Z. (2009) *Understanding Social Policy*, 8th edn, Oxford: Wiley-Blackwell.

Hills, J., Sefton, T. and Stewart, K. (2009a) 'Conclusions: climbing every mountain or retreating from the foothills?', in Hills, J., Sefton, T. and Stewart, K. (eds) *Towards a More Equal Society? Poverty, Inequality and Policy since 1997*, Bristol: Policy Press.

Hills, J., Sefton, T. and Stewart, K. (eds) (2009b) *Towards a More Equal Society? Poverty, Inequality and Policy since 1997*, Bristol: Policy Press. Summary on the Joseph Rowntree Foundation website. Available: <http://www.jrf.org.uk/publications/poverty-inequality-and-policy-1997> (accessed 25 May 2009).

Hirsch, D. (2008) *What is Needed to End Child Poverty by 2020?*, York: JRF. Online. Available: <http://www.jrf.org.uk/publications/what-needed-end-child-poverty-2020> (accessed 25 May 2009).

HM Government (2004) *Every Child Matters: Change for Children*, London: TSO. Online. Available: <http://www.everychildmatters.gov.uk/_files/F9E3F941DC8D4580539EE4C743E9371D.pdf> (accessed 25 May 2009).

HM Government (2006) *Reaching Out: An Action Plan on Social Exclusion*, London: Cabinet Office. Online. Available: <http://www.cabinetoffice.gov.uk/social_exclusion_task_force/publications/reaching_out.aspx> (accessed 25 May 2009).

HM Government (2007) *Putting People First: A Shared Vision for the Transformation of Adult Social Care*, London: DH. Online. Available: <http://www.dh.gov.uk/en/Publicationsandstatistics/Publications/PublicationsPolicyAndguidance/DH_081118> (accessed 25 May 2009).

HM Government (2008a) *Carers at the Heart of 21st Century Families and Communities: A Caring System by Your Side, a Life of Your Own*, London: DH. Online. Available: <http://www.dh.gov.uk/en/Publicationsandstatistics/Publications/PublicationsPolicyAndGuidance/DH_085345> (accessed 25 May 2009).

HM Government (2008b) *The Case for Change: Why England Needs a New Care and Support System*, London: DH. Online. Available: <http://www.dh.gov.uk/en/Publicationsandstatistics/Publications/PublicationsPolicyAndGuidance/DH_084725> (accessed 25 May 2009).

HM Government (2009a) *New Opportunities: Fair Chances for the Future*, Cm. 7533, Norwich: TSO. Online. Available: <http://www.hmg.gov.uk/media/9102/NewOpportunities.pdf> (accessed 25 May 2009).

HM Government (2009b) *Shaping the Future of Care Together*, Cm. 7673, Norwich: TSO. Online. Available: <http://www.dh.gov.uk/en/Publicationsandstatistics/Publications/PublicationsPolicyAndGuidance/DH_102338> (accessed 7 September 2009).

HM Treasury (2003) *Every Child Matters*, Cm. 5860, Norwich: TSO. Online. Available: <http://www.everychildmatters.gov.uk/_files/EBE7EEAC90382663E0D5BBF24C99A7AC.pdf> (accessed 25 May 2009).

HM Treasury (2007) *Meeting the Aspirations of the British People: 2007 Pre-Budget Report and Comprehensive Spending Review*, London: HM Treasury. Online. Available: <http://www.hm-treasury.gov.uk/pbr_csr07_index.htm> (accessed 25 May 2009).

HM Treasury, DWP and DCSF (2008) *Ending Child Poverty: Everybody's Business*, London: HM Treasury. Online. Available: <http://www.hm-treasury.gov.uk/d/bud08_childpoverty_1310.pdf> (accessed 25 May 2009).

Hoggett, P. (1996) 'New modes of control in the public service', *Public Administration*, 74: 9–32.

Hope, P. (2008) *Government Response to 'Cutting the Cake Fairly, CSCI Review of Eligibility Criteria for Social Care'*, London: DH. Online. Available: <http://www.dh.gov.uk/en/Publicationsandstatistics/Publications/PublicationsPolicyAndGuidance/DH_089618> (accessed 25 May 2009).

Horner, N. (2009) *What is Social Work? Context and Perspectives*, 3rd edn, Exeter: Learning Matters.

House of Commons CSFC (Children, Schools and Families Committee) (2009) *Looked After Children, Third Report of Session 2008–09*, Volume 1, HC 111-I, London: TSO. Online. Available: <http://www.publications.parliament.uk/pa/cm/cmchilsch.htm> (accessed 25 May 2009).

House of Commons PASC (Public Administration Select Committee) (2005) *Choice, Voice and Public Services, Fourth Report of Session 2004–05*, Volume 1, HC 49-I, London: TSO. Online. Available: <http://www.publications.parliament.uk/pa/cm200405/cmselect/cmpubadm/49/49i.pdf> (accessed 25 May 2009).

Howe, D. (1986) *Social Workers and Their Practice in Welfare Bureaucracies*, Aldershot: Gower.

Howe, D. (1992) 'Child abuse and the bureaucratisation of social work', *Sociological Review*, 40: 491–508.

Hudson, B. and Henwood, M. (2008) *Prevention, Personalisation and Prioritisation in Social Care: Squaring the Circle?*, London: CSCI. Online. Available: <http://www.cqc.org.uk/_db/_documents/SOSC08%20Background%20study%20complex%20needs%2011-12-08amended-dom3.pdf> (accessed 22 May 2009).

Hudson, J. and Lowe, S. (2009) *Understanding the Policy Process*, 2nd edn, Bristol: Policy Press.

Hughes, E. (1958) *Men and Their Work*, Glencoe, IL: Free Press.

Hugman, R. (1998) 'Social work and de-professionalization', in Abbott, P. and Meerabeau, L. (eds) *The Sociology of the Caring Professions*, 2nd edn, London: UCL Press.

Humphrey, J. (2003) 'New Labour and the regulatory reform of social care', *Critical Social Policy*, 23: 5–24.

Humphries, B. (2004) 'An unacceptable role for social work: implementing immigration policy', *British Journal of Social Work*, 34: 93–107.

Ife, J. (2001) *Human Rights and Social Work: Towards Rights-Based Practice*, Cambridge: Cambridge University Press.

IFSW/IASSW (International Federation of Social Workers and International Association of Schools of Social Work) (2001) *Ethics in Social Work: Statement of Principles*. Online. Available: <http://www.ifsw.org/f38000032.html> (accessed 25 May 2009).

Illich, I. (1977) 'Disabling professions', in Illich, I., Zola, I., McKnight, J., Caplan, J. and Shaiken, H., *Disabling Professions*, London: Marion Boyars.

JCHR (Joint Committee on Human Rights) (2008) *A Bill of Rights for the UK? Twenty-ninth Report of Session 2007–08*, HL Paper 165-I, HC 150-I, Norwich: TSO. Online. Available: <http://www.publications.parliament.uk/pa/jt200708/jtselect/jtrights/165/16502.htm> (accessed 25 May 2009).

Jochum, V., Pratten, B. and Wilding, K. (2005) *Civil Renewal and Active Citizenship: A Guide to the Debate*, London: NCVO. Online. Available: <http://www.ncvo-vol.org.uk/publications/publication.asp?id=1512> (accessed 25 May 2009).

Joffe, J. and Lipsey, D. (1999) 'Note of Dissent', in Royal Commission on Long-Term Care, *With Respect to Old Age: Long-Term Care – Rights and Responsibilities*, Cm. 4192, Norwich: TSO. Online. Available: <http://www.royal-commission-elderly.gov.uk> (accessed 25 May 2009).

Johnson, T. (1972) *Professions and Power*, Basingstoke: Macmillan.

Jones, C., Ferguson, I., Lavalette, M. and Penketh, L. (2004) *Social Work and Social Justice: A Manifesto for a New Engaged Practice* ('The Social Work Manifesto'). Online. Available: <http://www.socialworkfuture.org/?page_id=50> (accessed 25 May 2009).

Jones, C. and Novak, T. (1993) 'Social work today', *British Journal of Social Work*, 23: 195–212.

Jordan, B. (2004) 'Emancipatory social work? Opportunity or oxymoron', *British Journal of Social Work*, 34: 5–19.

Jordan, B. (2007) *Social Work and Well-Being*, Lyme Regis: Russell House.

Jordan, B. with Jordan, C. (2000) *Social Work and the Third Way: Tough Love as Social Policy*, London: Sage.

JRF (Joseph Rowntree Foundation) (2006) *Paying for Long Term Care*, York: JRF. Online. Available: <http://www.jrf.org.uk/publications/paying-long-term-care-moving-forward> (accessed 25 May 2009).

Kilbrandon, Lord (1964; reprinted 1995) *Report of the Committee on Children and Young Persons, Scotland*, Scottish Home and Health Department and Scottish Education Department, Edinburgh: HMSO. Online. Available: <http://www.scotland.gov.uk/Publications/2003/10/18259/26875> (accessed 26 May 2009).

King, M. and Piper, C. (1990) *How the Law Thinks about Children*, Aldershot: Gower.

King, M. and Trowell, J. (1992) *Children's Welfare and the Law: The Limits of Legal Intervention*, London: Sage.

Lambeth, London Borough of (1987) *Whose Child? The Report of the Public Inquiry into the Death of Tyra Henry*, London: London Borough of Lambeth.

Laming, Lord H. (2003) *The Victoria Climbié Inquiry Report*, Cm. 5370, London: TSO. Online. Available: <http://www.victoria-climbie-inquiry.org.uk> (accessed 25 May 2009).

Laming, Lord H. (2009) *The Protection of Children in England: A Progress Report*, HC 330, London: TSO. Online. Available: <http://publications.everychildmatters.gov.uk/eOrderingDownload/HC-330.pdf> (accessed 25 May 2009).

Le Grand, J. (2003) *Motivation, Agency and Public Policy: Of Knights and Knaves, Pawns and Queens*, Oxford: Oxford University Press.

Le Grand, J. (2007) *Consistent Care Matters: Exploring the Potential of Social Work Practices*, Nottingham: DfES. Online. Available: <http://publications.everychildmatters.gov.uk/default.aspx?PageFunction=productdetails&PageMode=publications&ProductId=DFES-00526-2007&> (accessed 25 May 2009).

Leadbetter, C. (2004) *Personalisation through Participation: A New Script for Public Services*, London: Demos.

Leadbetter, C. and Lownsborough, H. (2005) *Personalisation and Participation: The Future of Social Care in Scotland*, London: Demos. Online. Available: <http://www.socialworkscotland.org.uk/resources/cp-sd/PersonalisationThroughParticipationReport.pdf> (accessed 26 May 2009).

Leece, J. and Bornat, J. (2006) *Developments in Direct Payments*, Bristol: Policy Press.

Leece, D. and Leece, J. (2006) 'Direct payments: creating a two-tiered system in social care?', *British Journal of Social Work*, 36: 1379–93.

Levitas, R. (1998; 2nd edn 2005) *The Inclusive Society? Social Exclusion and New Labour*, Basingstoke: Macmillan.

LGDU (Local Government Data Unit) Wales (2009) *Social Services Statistics Wales, 2007–08*, Cardiff: LGDU Wales. Online. Available: <http://www.dataunitwales.gov.uk/Documents/Publications/lgd01007_sssw_2007_08_web_whole_eng.pdf> (accessed 25 May 2009).

Lipsky, M. (1980) *Street-Level Bureaucracy: Dilemmas of the Individual in Public Services*, New York: Russell Sage Foundation.

Lister, R. (2001) 'New Labour: a study of ambiguity from a position of ambivalence', *Critical Social Policy*, 21 (4): 425–47.

Lister, R. (2003) 'Investing in the citizen: workers of the future', *Social Policy and Administration*, 37 (5): 427–43.

Lister, R. (2004) *Poverty*, Cambridge: Polity Press.

Local Government Ombudsman and Parliamentary and Health Service Ombudsman (2009) *Six Lives: The Provision of Public Services to People with Learning Disabilities*, Part 1: Overview and Summary Investigation Reports, HC 230-I, Norwich: TSO. Online. Available: <http://www.ombudsman.org.uk/pdfs/Six_Lives_Part_1_%200verview.pdf> (accessed 25 May 2009).

Lorenz, W. (1994) *Social Work in a Changing Europe*, London: Routledge.

Lukes, S. (1974; 2nd edn 2005) *Power: A Radical View*, London: Macmillan.

Lymbery, M. (1998) 'Care management and professional autonomy: the impact of community care legislation on social work with older people', *British Journal of Social Work*, 28: 863–78.

Lymbery, M. (2001) 'Social work at the crossroads', *British Journal of Social Work*, 31: 369–84.

Macpherson, W. (1999) *The Stephen Lawrence Inquiry: Report of an Inquiry by Sir William Macpherson of Cluny*, Cm. 4262-I, London: TSO. Online. Available: <http://www.archive.official-documents.co.uk/document/cm42/4262/4262.htm> (accessed 25 May 2009).

Mahon, J. (2008) *Towards the New Children in Need Census*, Research Report by York Consulting for DCSF, DSCF-RW309, London: DCSF. Online. Available: <http://www.dcsf.gov.uk/research/data/uploadfiles/DCSF-RW 039.pdf> (accessed 25 May 2009).

Mandelson, P. (2008) Letter to the *Guardian*, 12 January, p. 41. Online. Available: <http://www.guardian.co.uk/politics/2008/jan/12/tonyblair.labour> (accessed 25 May 2009).

Manthorpe, J. and Stevens, M. (2008) *The Personalisation of Adult Social Care in Rural Areas*, Cheltenham:

Commission for Rural Communities. Online. Available: <http://www.ruralcommunities.gov.uk/files/CRC%2078%20Adult%20Social%20Care.pdf> (accessed 25 May 2009).

McLaughlin, K. (2008) *Social Work, Politics and Society*, Bristol: Policy Press.

McNamee, P. (2006) *The Effects of Free Personal Care Policy in Scotland*, Background Paper for the Wanless Social Care Review, London: King's Fund. Online. Available: <http://www.kingsfund.org.uk/research/publications/appendices_to.html> (accessed 25 May 2009).

Means, R., Richards, S. and Smith, R. (2008) *Community Care: Policy and Practice*, 4th edn, Basingstoke: Palgrave Macmillan.

Mencap (2007) *Death by Indifference*, London: Mencap. Online. Available: <http://www.mencap.org.uk/document.asp?id=284> (accessed 25 May 2009).

Michael, J. (2008) *Healthcare for All, Report of the Independent Inquiry into Access to Healthcare for People with Learning Disabilities*, London: DH. Online. Available: <http://www.iahpld.org.uk/Healthcare_final.pdf> (accessed 25 May 2009).

MoJ (Ministry of Justice) (2007) *The Governance of Britain*, Cm. 7170, Norwich: TSO. Online. Available: <http://www.official-documents.gov.uk/document/cm71/7170/7170.pdf> (accessed 25 May 2009).

MoJ (2009) *Rights and Responsibilities: Developing Our Constitutional Framework*, Cm. 7577, Norwich: TSO. Online. Available: <http://www.justice.gov.uk/publications/rights-responsibilities.htm> (accessed 25 May 2009).

Moriarty, J., Rapaport, P., Beresford, P., Branfield, F., Forrest, V., Manthorpe, J., Martineau, S., Cornes, M., Butt, J., Iliffe, S., Taylor, B. and Keady, J. (2007) *The Participation of Adult Service Users, Including Older People, in Developing Social Care*, SCIE Practice Guide 17 (formerly 11), London: SCIE. Online. Available: <http://www.scie.org.uk/publications/guides/guide17/files/guide17.pdf> (accessed 25 May 2009).

Morris, K. (ed.) (2008) *Social Work and Multi-Agency Working: Making a Difference*, Bristol: Policy Press.

Moullin, S. (2008) *Just Care? A Fresh Approach to Adult Services*, London: IPPR. Online. Available: <http://www.ippr.org/publicationsandreports/publication.asp?id=605> (accessed 25 May 2009).

Mount, F. (2008) *Five Types of Inequality*, York: JRF. Online. Available: <http://www.jrf.org.uk/publications/five-types-inequality> (accessed 25 May 2009).

Munro, E. (2004) 'The impact of audit on social work practice', *British Journal of Social Work*, 34: 1075–95.

Murray, C. (1990) *The Emerging British Underclass*, London: Institute of Economic Affairs.

NCSR (National Centre for Social Research) (2008) *Housing in England 2006/07: A Report Based on the 2006/07 Survey of English Housing*, London: CLG. Online. Available: <http://www.communities.gov.uk/publications/housing/housingengland2006-07> (accessed 25 May 2009).

NCVO (National Council for Voluntary Organisations) (2009) *Civil Society Almanac, Executive Summary*, London: NCVO. Online. Available: <http://www.ncvo-vol.org.uk/publications/publication.asp?id=12516> (accessed 25 May 2009).

NHS Information Centre (2008a) *Community Care Statistics 2007–08: Referrals, Assessments and Packages of Care for Adults, England, National Summary*, Leeds: Information Centre for Health and Social Care. Online. Available: <http://www.ic.nhs.uk/statistics-and-data-collections/social-care/adult-social-care-information> (accessed 25 May 2009).

NHS Information Centre (2008b) *Community Care Statistics 2008: Supported Residents (Adults), England*, Leeds: Information Centre for Health and Social Care. Online. Available: <http://www.ic.nhs.uk/statistics-and-data-collections/social-care/adult-social-care-information> (accessed 25 May 2009).

NHS Information Centre (2009a) *Community Care Statistics 2008: Home Care Services for Adults, England*, Leeds: Information Centre for Health and Social Care. Online. Available: <http://www.ic.nhs.uk/statistics-and-data-collections/social-care/adult-social-care-information> (accessed 25 May 2009).

NHS Information Centre (2009b) *Personal Social Services Expenditure and Unit Costs, England, 2007–08*, Leeds: Information Centre for Health and Social Care. Online. Available: <http://www.ic.nhs.uk/statistics-and-data-collections/social-care/adult-social-care-information> (accessed 25 May 2009).

NHS Information Centre (2009c) *Personal Social Services: Staff of Social Services Departments as at 30 September 2008, England*, Leeds: Information Centre for Health and Social Care. Online. Available: <http://www.ic.nhs.uk/statistics-and-data-collections/social-care/adult-social-care-information> (accessed 25 May 2009).

O'Brien, M. and Penna, S. (1998) *Theorising Welfare: Enlightenment and Modern Society*, London: Sage.

ODI (Office for Disability Issues) (2008) *Independent Living: A Cross-Government Strategy about Independent Living for Disabled People*, London: ODI. Online. Available: <http://www.officefordisability.gov.uk/working/independentlivingstrategy.asp> (accessed 25 May 2009).

ONS (Office for National Statistics) (2004) 'Education: exam results differ by social class', London: ONS. Online. Available: <http://www.statistics.gov.uk/CCI/nugget.asp?ID=1003> (accessed 25 May 2009).

ONS (2005) *National Statistics Socio-Economic Classification User Manual*, London: ONS. Online. Available: <http://www.statistics.gov.uk/methods_quality/ns_sec/downloads/NS-SEC_User_2005.pdf> (accessed 25 May 2009).

ONS (2007) 'Health inequalities: death rates highest for routine workers', London: ONS. Online. Available: <http://www.statistics.gov.uk/CCI/nugget.asp?ID=1899&Pos=2&ColRank=2&Rank=256> (accessed 25 May 2009).

Orme, J. (2001) 'Regulation or fragmentation? Directions for social work under New Labour', *British Journal of Social Work*, 31: 611–24.

Palmer, G., MacInnes, T. and Kenway, P. (2008) *Monitoring Poverty and Social Exclusion 2008*, York: JRF. Online. Available: <http://www.npi.org.uk/publications/poverty.htm> (accessed 25 May 2009).

Parker, H. (ed.) (2002) *Modest but Adequate: A Reasonable Living Standard for Households Aged 65–74 Years*, York: Family Budget Research Unit, University of York. Online. Available: <http://www.york.ac.uk/res/fbu/documents/ageconcernmodad2002.pdf> (accessed 25 May 2009).

Parry, N. and Parry, J. (1979) 'Social work, professionalism and the state', in Parry, N., Rustin, M. and Satyamurti, C. (eds) *Social Work, Welfare and the State*, London: Edward Arnold.

Parton, N. (1991) *Governing the Family: Child Care, Child Protection and the State*, Basingstoke: Macmillan.

Parton, N. (1998) 'Risk, advanced liberalism and child welfare: the need to rediscover uncertainty and ambiguity', *British Journal of Social Work*, 28: 5–27.

Parton, N. (2009) 'From Seebohm to *Think Family*: reflections on 40 years of policy change of statutory children's social work in England', *Child and Family Social Work*, 14 (1): 68–78.

Parton, N. and O'Byrne, P. (2000) *Constructive Social Work: Towards a New Practice*, Basingstoke: Macmillan.

Payne, M. (2006) *What is Professional Social Work?*, 2nd edn, Bristol: BASW/Policy Press.

Pinker, R. (1982) 'An alternative view', appendix in Barclay, P., *Social Workers: Their Roles and Tasks*, London: Bedford Square Press.

Pithouse, A. (1998) *Social Work: The Social Organisation of an Invisible Trade*, 2nd edn, Aldershot: Ashgate.

Platt, L. (2009) *Ethnicity and Child Poverty*, DWP Research Report 576, Norwich: HMSO. Online. Available: <http://www.dwp.gov.uk/asd/asd5/rports2009-2010/rrep576.pdf> (25 May 2009).

PMSU (Prime Minister's Strategy Unit) (2005) *Improving the Life Chances of Disabled People*, London: Cabinet Office. Online. Available: <http://www.cabinetoffice.gov.uk/strategy/work_areas/disability.aspx> (accessed 26 May 2009).

PMSU (2007) *Building on Progress: Public Services*, London: Cabinet Office. Online. Available: <http://www.cabinetoffice.gov.uk/media/cabinetoffice/strategy/assets/building.pdf> (accessed 26 May 2009).

Poll, C. and Duffy, S. (eds) (2008) *A Report on in Control's Second Phase: Evaluation and Learning 2005–2007*, London: In Control. Online. Available: <http://www.in-control.org.uk/site/INCO/Templates/General.aspx?pageid=522&cc=GB> (accessed 25 May 2009).

Poll, C., Duffy, S., Hatton, C., Sanderson, H. and Routledge, M. (2006) *A Report on In Control's First Phase 2003–05*, London: In Control. Online. Available: <http://www.in-control.org.uk/site/INCO/Templates/General.aspx?pageid=522&cc=GB> (accessed 25 May 2009).

Pollitt, C. (1990) *Managerialism and the Public Services: The Anglo-American Experience*, Oxford: Basil Blackwell.

Poole, T. (2009) *Funding Adult Social Care in England*, London: King's Fund. Online. Available: <www.kingsfund.org.uk/document.rm?id=8243> (accessed 25 May 2009).

Powell, F. (2001) *The Politics of Social Work*, London: Sage.

Powell, M. (ed.) (2007) *Understanding the Mixed Economy of Welfare*, Bristol: Policy Press.

Reamer, F. (1993) *The Philosophical Foundations of Social Work*, New York: Columbia University Press.

Reder, P. and Duncan, S. (2003) 'Understanding communication in child protection networks', *Child Abuse Review*, 12: 82–100.

Reder, P., Duncan S. and Gray, M. (1993) *Beyond Blame: Child Abuse Tragedies Revisited*, London: Routledge.

Reichert, E. (2003) *Social Work and Human Rights: A Foundation for Policy and Practice*, New York: Columbia University Press.

Reichert, E. (2006) *Understanding Human Rights: An Exercise Book*, Thousand Oaks, CA: Sage.

Rein, M. (1976) *Social Science and Public Policy*, Harmondsworth: Penguin.

Richardson, S. and Asthana, S. (2006) 'Inter-agency information sharing in health and social care services: the role of professional culture', *British Journal of Social Work*, 36: 657–69.

Roach Anleu, S. (1992) 'The professionalisation of social work: a case study of three organisational settings', *Sociology*, 26 (1): 23–43.

Robson, P., Sampson, A., Dime, N., Hernandez, L. and Litherland, R. (2008) *Seldom Heard: Developing Inclusive Participation in Social Care*, SCIE Position Paper 10, London: SCIE. Online. Available: <http://www.scie.org.uk/publications/positionpapers/pp10.pdf> (accessed 26 May 2009).

Royal Commission on Long-Term Care (1999) *With Respect to Old Age: Long-Term Care – Rights and Responsibilities*, Cm. 4192, Norwich: TSO. Online. Available: <http://www.royal-commission-elderly.gov.uk> (accessed 25 May 2009).

Samuel, M. (2008) 'Social work statement published after 18-month review', *Community Care*, 28 March. Online. Available: <http://www.communitycare.co.uk/Articles/2008/03/28/107744/gscc-publishes-statement-on-roles-and-tasks-of-social-work.html> (accessed 26 May 2009).

Sassi, F. (2009) 'Health inequalities: a persistent problem', in Hills, J., Sefton, T. and Stewart, K. (eds) *Towards a More Equal Society? Poverty, Inequality and Policy since 1997*, Bristol: Policy Press.

Satyamurti, C. (1979) 'Care and control in local authority social work', in Parry, N., Rustin, M. and Satyamurti, C. (eds) *Social Work, Welfare and the State*, London: Edward Arnold.

Schön, D. (1983) *The Reflective Practitioner: How Professionals Think in Action*, New York: Basic Books.

Scottish Executive (2006) *Changing Lives: Report of the 21st Century Social Work Review*, Edinburgh: Scottish Executive. Online. Available: <http://www.socialworkscotland.org.uk/resources/pub/ChangingLivesMainReport.pdf> (accessed 26 May 2009).

Scottish Government (2009) *Scottish Local Government Financial Statistics 2007–08*, Edinburgh: Scottish Government. Online. Available: <http://www.scotland.gov.uk/Publications/2009/03/24121531/3> (accessed 25 May 2009).

Scourfield, P. (2006) '"What matters is what works"? How discourses of modernization have both silenced and limited debate on domiciliary care for older people', *Critical Social Policy*, 26 (1): 5–30.

Scourfield, P. (2007) 'Social care and the modern citizen: client, consumer, service user, manager and entrepreneur', *British Journal of Social Work*, 37: 107–22.

Seebohm, F. (1968) *Report of the Committee on Local Authority and Allied Personal Social Services*, Cm. 3703, London: HMSO.

SETF (Social Exclusion Task Force) (2008) *Think Family: Improving the Life Chances of Families at Risk*, London: Cabinet Office. Online. Available: <http://www.cabinetoffice.gov.uk/social_exclusion_task_force/publications.aspx#t> (accessed 25 May 2009).

SEU (Social Exclusion Unit) (1999) *Teenage Pregnancy*, Cm. 4342, London: SEU. Online. Available: <http://www.cabinetoffice.gov.uk/social_exclusion_task_force/publications.aspx#t> (accessed 25 May 2009).

SEU (2003) *A Better Education for Children in Care*, London: SEU. Online. Available: <http://www.cabinetoffice.gov.uk/social_exclusion_task_force/publications.aspx#t> (accessed 25 May 2009).

SEU (2004) *Mental Health and Social Exclusion*, London: ODPM. Online. Available: <http://www.cabinetoffice.gov.uk/social_exclusion_task_force/publications.aspx#t> (accessed 25 May 2009).

SEU (2006) *A Sure Start to Later Life: Ending Inequalities for Older People*, London: ODPM. Online. Available : <http://www.cabinetoffice.gov.uk/social_exclusion_task_force/publications.aspx#t> (accessed 25 May 2009).

Shropshire, J. and Middleton, S. (1999) *Small Expectations: Learning to be Poor?*, York: JRF. Summary online. Available: <http://www.jrf.org.uk/publications/experiences-and-attitudes-children-low-income-families-towards-money> (accessed 25 May 2009).

Smith, C. (2001) 'Trust and confidence: possibilities for social work in "high modernity"', *British Journal of Social Work*, 31: 287–305.

Smith, C. (2005) 'Understanding trust and confidence: two paradigms and their significance for health and social care', *Journal of Applied Philosophy*, 22 (3): 299–316.

Spandler, H. (2004) 'Friend or foe? Towards a critical assessment of direct payments', *Critical Social Policy*, 24 (2): 187–209.

Statham, J., Cameron, C. and Mooney, A. (2006) *The Tasks and Roles of Social Workers: A Focused Review of Research Evidence*, London: Thomas Coram Research Unit, Institute of Education, University of London. Online. Available: <http://eprints.ioe.ac.uk/59/> (accessed 26 May 2009).

Stewart, J. (2004) *Taking Stock: Scottish Social Welfare after Devolution*, Bristol: Policy Press.

Stewart, K. (2009) '"A scar on the soul of Britain": child poverty and disadvantage under New Labour', in Hills, J., Sefton, T. and Stewart, K. (eds) *Towards a More Equal Society? Poverty, Inequality and Policy since 1997*, Bristol: Policy Press.

Strand, S. (2007) *Minority Ethnic Pupils in the Longitudinal Study of Young People in England*, DCSF Research Report DCSF-RR002, London: DCSF. Online. Available: <http://www.dcsf.gov.uk/research/data/uploadfiles/DCSF-RR002.pdf> (accessed 15 May 2009)

Strand, S. (2008) *Minority Ethnic Pupils in the Longitudinal Study of Young People in England: Extension Report on the Performance in Public Examinations at Age 16*, DCSF Research Report DCSF-RR029, London: DCSF. Online. Available: <http://www.dcsf.gov.uk/research/data/uploadfiles/DCSF-RR029.pdf> (accessed 15 May 2009).

Sutherland, Lord S. (2008) *Independent Review of Free Personal and Nursing Care in Scotland*, Edinburgh: Scottish Government. Online. Available: <http://www.scotland.gov.uk/Publications/2008/04/25105036/16> (accessed 26 May 2009).

Thoburn, J. (2007) *Globalisation and Child Welfare: Some Lessons from a Cross-National Study of Children in Out-of-Home Care*, Social Work Monograph 228, Norwich: University of East Anglia. Online. Available: <https://www.uea.ac.uk/polopoly_fs/1.103398!globalisation%201108.pdf> (accessed 26 May 2009).

Thomas, N. (2000) *Children, Family and the State: Decision-Making and Child Participation*, Bristol: Policy Press.

Thomas, N. (2007) 'Towards a theory of children's participation', *International Journal of Children's Rights*, 15: 199–218.

Tilbury, C. (2004) 'The influence of performance measurement on child welfare policy and practice', *British Journal of Social Work*, 34: 225–41.

Titmuss, R. (1974) *Social Policy: An Introduction*, London: George Allen and Unwin.

TOPSS (Training Organisation for the Personal Social Services) (2002) *National Occupational Standards for Social Work*. Online. Available: <http://www.skillsforcare.org.uk/developing_skills/National_Occupational_Standards/social_work.aspx> (accessed 26 May 2009)

Toren, N. (1977) *Social Work: The Case of a Semi-Profession*, Beverly Hills: Sage.

Townsend, P. (1979) *Poverty in the United Kingdom*, Harmondsworth: Penguin.

Toynbee, P. (2003) *Hard Work: Life in Low-Pay Britain*, London: Bloomsbury.

Trinder, L. (1996) 'Social work research: the state of the art (or science)', *Child and Family Social Work*, 1 (4): 233–42.

UN Committee on the Rights of the Child (2008) *Concluding Observations: United Kingdom of Great Britain and Northern Ireland, 49th Session, Consideration of Reports Submitted by States Parties Under Art. 44 of the*

Convention, CRC/C/GBR/CO/4. Online. Available: <http://www2.ohchr.org/english/bodies/crc/docs/Advance Versions/CRC.C.GBR.CO.4.pdf> (accessed 26 May 2009).

Utting, W. (1997) *People Like Us: The Report of the Review of the Safeguards for Children Living away from Home*, London: TSO.

Vestri, P. (2007) *Evaluation of the Operation and Impact of Free Personal Care*, Hexagon Research and Consulting for the Scottish Executive, Edinburgh: Scottish Executive. Online. Available: <http://www.scotland.gov.uk/Resource/Doc/167844/0046181.pdf> (accessed 26 May 2009).

WAG (Welsh Assembly Government) (2007) *Fulfilled Lives, Supportive Communities: A Strategy for Social Services in Wales over the Next Decade*, Cardiff: WAG. Online. Available: <http://new.wales.gov.uk/topics/health/publications/socialcare/strategies/fulfilledlives?lang=en> (accessed 26 May 2009).

Wanless, D. (2006) *Securing Good Care for Older People: Taking a Long Term View*, London: The King's Fund. Online. Available: <http://www.kingsfund.org.uk/publications/the_kings_fund_publications/securing_good.html> (accessed 26 May 2009).

Warren, J. (2007) *Service User and Carer Participation in Social Work*, Exeter: Learning Matters.

Waterhouse, R. (2000) *Lost in Care: Report of the Tribunal of Inquiry into the Abuse of Children in Care in the Former County Council Areas of Gwynedd and Clwyd since 1974*, London: DH. Online. Available: <http://www.dh.gov.uk/en/Publicationsandstatistics/Publications/PublicationsPolicyAndGuidance/DH_4003097> (accessed 26 May 2009).

Weber, M. (1947) *The Theory of Social and Economic Organisation*, New York: Free Press.

White, S. and Featherstone, B. (2005) 'Communicating misunderstandings: multi-agency work as social practice', *Child and Family Social Work*, 10: 207–16.

White, V. (2009) 'Quiet challenges? Professional practice in modernized social work', in Harris, J. and White, V. (eds) *Modernising Social Work: Critical Considerations*, Bristol: Policy Press.

Wilkinson, R. (2005) *The Impact of Inequality: How to Make Sick Societies Healthier*, London: Routledge.

Wilkinson, R. and Marmot, M. (eds) (2003) *Social Determinants of Health: The Solid Facts*, 2nd edn, Copenhagen: World Health Organisation, Regional Office for Europe. Online. Available: <http://www.euro.who.int/DOCUMENT/E81384.PDF> (accessed 26 May 2009).

Wilkinson, R. and Pickett, K. (2009) *The Spirit Level: Why More Equal Societies Almost Always Do Better*, London: Allen Lane.

Williams, F. (2004) 'What matters is who works: why every child matters to New Labour. Commentary on the DfES Green Paper "Every Child Matters"', *Critical Social Policy*, 24 (3): 406–27.

Willis, P. (1977) *Learning to Labour: How Working Class Kids Get Working Class Jobs*, Farnborough: Saxon House.

Woodhouse, D. and Pengelly, P. (1991) *Anxiety and the Dynamics of Collaboration*, Aberdeen: Aberdeen University Press.

Wright, P., Turner, C., Clay, D. and Mills, H. (2006) *The Participation of Children and Young People in Developing Social Care*, SCIE Practice Guide 11 (formerly 6), London: SCIE. Online. Available: <http://www.scie.org.uk/publications/guides/guide11/files/guide11.pdf> (accessed 26 May 2009).

Index